WOMEN LEADERS IN THE STUDENT CHRISTIAN MOVEMENT

American Society of Missiology Series, No. 55

WOMEN LEADERS IN THE STUDENT CHRISTIAN MOVEMENT

1880–1920

Thomas A. Russell

ORBIS BOOKS
Maryknoll, New York 10545

Fathers and Brothers
MARYKNOLL™

Founded in 1970, Orbis Books endeavors to publish works that enlighten the mind, nourish the spirit, and challenge the conscience. The publishing arm of the Maryknoll Fathers and Brothers, Orbis seeks to explore the global dimensions of the Christian faith and mission, to invite dialogue with diverse cultures and religious traditions, and to serve the cause of reconciliation and peace. The books published reflect the views of their authors and do not represent the official position of the Maryknoll Society. To learn more about Maryknoll and Orbis Books, please visit our website at www.maryknollsociety.org.

Library of Congress Cataloging-in-Publication Data

Names: Russell, Thomas Arthur, 1954– author.
Title: Women leaders in the Student Christian Movement, 1880–1920 / Thomas A. Russell.
Description: Maryknoll : Orbis Books, 2017. | Series: American Society of Missiology series ; No. 55 | Includes bibliographical references and index.
Identifiers: LCCN 2017041287 (print) | LCCN 2017018493 (ebook) | ISBN 9781626982567 (pbk.) | ISBN 9781608337217 (e-book)
Subjects: LCSH: Student Christian Movement (Great Britain)—History. | Student movements. | Missions—Societies, etc. | Women in church work. | Women in missionary work. | Church work with college students. | College students—Religious life.
Classification: LCC BV970.S6 R87 2017 (ebook) | LCC BV970.S6 (print) | DDC 267/.13—dc23
LC record available at https://lccn.loc.gov/2017041287

Dedicated to

Zola R. Cavanaugh

and

Dr. Dale A. Johnson

Contents

Preface to the American Society of Missiology Series

The purpose of the American Society of Missiology Series is to publish—without regard for disciplinary, national, or denominational boundaries—scholarly works of high quality and wide interest on missiological themes from the entire spectrum of scholarly pursuits relevant to Christian mission, which is always the focus of books in the series.

By mission is meant the effort to effect passage over the boundary between faith in Jesus Christ and its absence. In this understanding of mission, the basic functions of Christian proclamation, dialogue, witness, service, worship, liberation, and nurture are of special concern. And in that context questions arise, including how does the transition from one cultural context to another influence the shape and interaction between these dynamic functions, especially in regard to the cultural and religious plurality that constitute the global context of Christian life and mission.

The promotion of scholarly dialogue among missiologists, and among missiologists and scholars in other fields of inquiry, may involve the publication of views that some missiologists cannot accept, and with which members of the Editorial Committee themselves do not agree. Manuscripts published in the series, accordingly, reflect the opinions of their authors and are not understood to represent the position of the American Society of Missiology or of the Editorial Committee. Selection is guided by such criteria as intrinsic worth, readability, coherence, and accessibility to a range of interested persons and not merely to experts or specialists.

The ASM Series, in collaboration with Orbis Books, seeks to publish scholarly works of high merit and wide interest on numerous aspects of missiology—the scholarly study of mission. Able presentations on new and creative approaches to the practice and understanding of mission will receive close attention.

The ASM Series Committee
Jonathan J. Bonk
Angelyn Dries, OSF
Scott W. Sunquist

Introduction

During the 1900–1901 collegiate year, Mary Geraldine Guinness Taylor, then an American Student Volunteer Movement for Foreign Missions Traveling Secretary, gave a public speech to an all-male college audience.[1] Assuming it was a secular lecture, the men sat down to listen with their feet on the backs of the chairs in front of them. From the speaker's perspective the audience was made up of "soles." To any other speaker the scene might have been quite disturbing, but it was reported later that Taylor "rose to the occasion," and addressed herself to their "souls." She was determined to make their "soles disappear." Taylor had been speaking at most fifteen minutes before almost every shoe had vanished and the "whole audience was hanging on her every word."[2]

This speech by Taylor provides just one good example of the ministries that women leaders had with men in the global Student Christian Movement (SCM) in the years 1880–1920. This heretofore relatively unknown group of women had a wide range of leadership opportunities with men and in mixed groups of women and men. What noted historian Adrian Hastings observed about the British SCM, could be applied to every section of the movement at the time: "By 1920, women were taking full part in its leadership. People like Zoe Fairfield, Ruth Rouse, Winifred Sedgwick and Margaret Wrong were able to attain roles of national significance through the SCM which would have been almost unthinkable in other sides of Christian life."[3]

The movement that these women served was called the Student Christian Movement. The SCM began in the mid-nineteenth century. In its heyday between 1880 and 1920, the SCM spread rapidly around the globe with its goal of reaching the student world for Christ and through students, triggering a transformation of the world. The SCM combined a rather dizzying array of local, regional, and national societies into one very large international student movement, which both men and women could join and lead.

---

1. For more information on Geraldine Guinness Taylor, see chapters 6 and 10.

2. Joy Guinness, *Mrs. Howard Taylor: Her Web of Time* (London: SCM Press, 1949), 174.

3. Adrian Hastings, *A History of English Christianity, 1920–1990*, 3rd ed. (London: SCM Press, 1991), 43.

Groups falling under the SCM umbrella included the Young Men's Christian Association (YMCA), the Young Women's Christian Association (YWCA), and the Student Volunteer Movement for Foreign Missions (SVMFM) and their non–North American counterparts, SCMs in different countries and the global World Student Christian Federation (WSCF).

The SCM's descendants exist today in a variety of movements, and its women leaders are even more strongly present. Visit a typical college or university campus throughout the world and a person can discover a wealth of religious societies geared for students. Each campus organization has a leadership structure, and many have women who possess administrative and even spiritual authority with their fellow collegians, both male and female. Inter-Varsity Christian Fellowship, Campus Crusade, and Navigators serve the Evangelical Protestant community. Most denominations have campus ministries, such as Newman Clubs for Roman Catholics and Baptist Student Unions for Baptists. Islamic Student Associations and Jewish Hillels provide community for Muslim and Jewish students. Beyond the local community are a variety of national and international student movements, such as the International Fellowship of Evangelical Students and the World Student Christian Federation.

The story of this notable group of women is important to tell for several reasons. First, the story of the SCM's women leaders is largely unknown. This is true even among those women leaders in today's SCMs who owe part of their leadership with men and in mixed groups of men and women to this interesting original group of women. When I mention these women and their ministries to contemporary women leaders of campus religious groups, I have drawn blank faces followed by a curiosity to learn more. The usual statement is "I did not know these women existed."

Outside of contemporary SCMs, the same lack of knowledge holds true. Late in the summer of 2003, I had the serendipitous privilege of standing in a rather long buffet line with the former archbishop of Canterbury, Lord George Carey. I asked him if he recognized the name of an English woman named Clara Ruth Rouse. Rouse was arguably the most important international SCM women leader between 1890 and 1950 and a woman featured in my book. Carey responded enthusiastically, "Why yes, a great woman, too bad she is unknown today. We should have a day in the Anglican annual calendar just for her for her contributions." When I mentioned some other women from my research (and this book), Carey was intrigued and supportive.

A major reason for the lack of knowledge on these women is that SCM in general and its women in particular have not been the focus of much scholarly interest.[4] Previous projects have provided some interesting and significant information on a few of these women leaders, especially in the role of pioneer.[5] Some of these appear as biographies of a few women leaders with short, if any, sections on their SCM ministries.[6]

---

4. This is true for dated works such as Tissington Tatlow's large volume, *The Story of the Student Christian Movement of Great Britain and Ireland* (London: SCM Press, 1933) and more recently, Charles Howard Hopkins's definitive biography *John R. Mott, 1865–1955* (Grand Rapids, MI: Eerdmans, 1980). Tatlow identifies some of these important women and has some interesting somewhat hagiographical information on one woman, Winifred Sedgwick, and some details on Zoe Fairfield's work as a general secretary for the British movement. It is not surprising that Hopkins says very little about the SCM's women leaders because his focus was on Mott, who appeared at first glance to have a primary focus on men. But there is more to Mott's view of women leaders than has been suggested. And that will be dealt with in this book.

Some past and present contributions have included women in the SCM narrative. In the dated but extremely helpful book *The World's Student Christian Federation: A History of the First Thirty Years* (London: SCM Press, 1948), Ruth Rouse deals with how women joined the leadership team of the pre–World War I WSCF by one particular mode, gradualism. She includes personal stories of her own ministry with the SCM as well.

More recent discussions include my article "Can the Story Be Told without Them? The Role of Women in the Student Volunteer Movement," *Missiology: An International Journal* 17, no. 2 (April 1989): 159–75, which provides a much-needed jump-start on the issue of women's ministries in the SCM.

Also, there has been some good material on a few specific SCM women leaders. One of the first texts to explore the role of one woman, Ruth Rouse, was Wilmina M. Rowland, "The Contribution of Ruth Rouse to the World's Student Christian Federation" (MA thesis, Yale University, 1937). It does an excellent job detailing Rouse's ministry, including some unique personal interviews with her subject and other friends of Rouse. Ruth Franzén's laser focus on Ruth Rouse provides excellent material on her. Two of these include "The Legacy of Ruth Rouse," *International Bulletin of Missionary Research* (October 1993): 154–58, and *Ruth Rouse among Students: Global, Missiological, and Ecumenical Perspectives* (Uppsala: Swedish Institute of Mission Research, 2008).

5. Johanna Selles has two excellent contributions: "Women's Role in the History of the World Student Christian Federation, 1895–1995: An Essay Commissioned to Commemorate the Centennial of the Founding of the WSCF," *Divinity School Library Occasional Bulletin* 6 (New Haven, CT: Yale Divinity School Library, 1995), and *The World Student Christian Federation, 1895–1925: Motives, Methods, and Influential Women* (Eugene, OR: Pickwick, 2011). The last text handily explores the historical development of the WSCF, the interactions between men and women and the ministry of SCM secretaries in areas outside of the United Kingdom and the United States. But it is limited to one major leadership role, the pioneer.

6. For examples, see B. E. Schneller, "Isabella Bird Bishop," in *Dictionary of British Women Writers*, ed. Jan Todd (London: Routledge, 1989), 66; Vera Brittain, *The Rebel Passion: A Short History of Some Pioneer Peacemakers* (Nyack, NY: Fellowship Publishers, 1964); Mary L. Hammack, "Lilian Stevenson Sinclair," in *A Dictionary of Women in Church History* (Chicago: Moody Press, 1984), 138–39; John Ferguson, "Stevenson, Lilian

Second, this narrative has a different focus than most examinations of turn-of-the-century women religious leaders that have typically explored women's leadership with women.[7] Instead, the rather unique emphasis of this book is the leadership of women in groups of men or in mixed groups of men and women. This new focus expands what is known about women's roles in turn-of-the-century Christianity and turns on its head all sorts of unfounded assumptions, such as that women did not possess this kind of spiritual and administrative authority between 1880 and 1920. These women and their contributions to a broadening definition of appropriate roles for Victorian women are at the heart of this book.

Third, this book provides some background for some issues that are hotly debated today, and can contribute to the ongoing debate on appropriate roles for women in religious communities, Christian and otherwise.

- Can and should women have spiritual and administrative authority in religious groups for men only and in mixed groups of men and women?
- Can women be Anglican bishops?
- Can Southern Baptist women be local head pastors?
- Can Roman Catholic women be priests?
- Can women lead groups of men and mixed groups of men and women in Navigators, Campus Crusade for Christ, and Inter-Varsity Christian Fellowship?
- Can women be leaders of Muslim student associations?

To learn about these women and the roles they played in the SCM, this book introduces readers to the SCM, its leadership structure, and why, where, and how women ministered within that structure. It includes biographies of specific women, most of whom are largely unknown. Those included have been chosen from over forty women available from my research.

Sinclair," in *Biographical Dictionary of Modern Peace Leaders,* ed. Harold Josephson (Westport, CT: Greenwood Press, 1985), 902; and Janice P. Nimura, *Daughters of the Samurai: A Journey from East to West and Back* (New York: Norton, 2015).

7. An excellent example of the topic of women's work with women is Ian Welch, "Women's Work for Women: Women Missionaries in 19th-Century China," a paper presented to the Eighth Women in Asia Conference 9/26–9/28/2005. Women's Caucus of the Asian Studies Association of Australia & the University of Technology. Reproduced on Project Canterbury, 2005, 1–30, see http://anglicanhistory.org.

1

Obeying God's Call

Edith May Hazlett Wiley, a traveling secretary for the Student Volunteer Movement for Foreign Missions (SVMFM) from 1917 to 1920, spoke for all women leaders in Student Christian Movement (SCM) circles when she stated why she became a pivotal character in the SCM story.

Since the SCM was a Christian organization, her straightforward and simple answer was that God called her to be one. In a 1916 letter to SVMFM headquarters, Wiley observed, "From the beginning, I have realized that if such an opportunity should come to me it would only be fulfilling 2 Timothy 1:9." This Bible verse says, "Who saved us and called us with a holy calling, not according to our works, but according to his own purposes." And, according to Wiley, "That has been my only explanation for many wonderful experiences that have come into my life."[1] As part of sorting out her call, Wiley went so far as to say there was "no outside influence—but that the realization that my life had been powerless since I had put the question aside."[2]

Wiley's summons came in two stages: the call to a life of missionary work and the call to SVMFM work as one part of that missionary work. Her call to lifetime missionary service was an important part of her life from childhood. Wiley felt that she had always "vaguely wished to do something—but had not definitely faced the question."

---

1. Edith May Hazlett to Fennell P. Turner, November 24, 1916, Archives of the SVMFM, Record Group No. 42 (Box 482, Folder 5722), Special Collections, Yale Divinity School Library.

2. Edith May Hazlett, Volunteer Blank (May 6, 1912), 2, Archives of the SVMFM, Record Group No. 42 (Box 116, Folder 1207), Special Collections, Yale Divinity School Library. Fennell P. Turner (1867–1932), a minister of the Methodist Episcopal Church, South, was a graduate of Vanderbilt University (Bachelor of Arts, 1891). He studied in, but did not graduate from, its School of Theology (1891–1892). In his lengthy SCM career, Turner served as secretary of the North Carolina YMCA (1895–1897), General Secretary of the SVMFM (1897–1919), and WSCF Executive Committee member (1912–1919). He also attended the 1910 World Missionary Conference and was a member of the International Missionary Council (1920–1928).

Her sense of a missionary call evolved as she listened to others: "I have heard so many missionary talks that it is hard to say that any one was the means," and she said she was influenced by "Dr. Coan of Persia, Muriel Smith of Occidental College, Philip A. Swartz and Bertha Condé." Wiley also believed that she felt a call to missions as she read a variety of books that stimulated her thinking in this area. She identified *The Supreme Decision, The Value of Purpose*, but "principally the Bible" as most influential.

The second stage of Wiley's call—the decision to become an SVMFM traveling secretary—came later. In letters dealing with her upcoming ministry, much can be learned about Wiley's understanding of the call to this work.[3] An August 15, 1916, letter noted that she had all the spiritual qualifications needed for the job, which included a testimony of a living Christian faith and a call to missionary work and the position.[4]

On May 21, 1917, Wiley stated that she saw the ministry as "a call from God." Because she had a summons to this job, she understood that it was a "great trust from God." Wiley also wrote that she was not worried about finances: "I know He will make a way. . . . I am looking to my heavenly Father for the strength I need, for there is no power in me, but He is able to do 'above that we can ask or think.'"[5]

EDITH MAY HAZLETT WILEY (1891–1983)

Edith May Hazlett was born in Des Moines, Iowa, in 1891. When she was six, her father died, and her mother moved the family to Los Angeles. Wiley graduated Phi Beta Kappa from Occidental College in 1914. She received her teaching certificate from Los Angeles State Normal (1915) and studied at Yale Divinity School (1923–1924).

After teaching in California public schools for two years, Wiley served as traveling secretary for the SVMFM (1917–1920). From 1920 to 1923, she taught at the American School for Girls in Beirut, Lebanon, under the auspices of the American Presbyterian Board. In 1923, she married Walter

---

3. There are few official references to Hazlett in SVMFM materials. SVMFM Executive Committee Minutes from September 30, 1919, state that she had traveled for the movement for the past two years. *Minutes of the Executive Committee of the SVM* (September 30, 1919), 6, Archives of the SVMFM, Record Group No. 42 (Box 450, Folder 5277), Special Collections, Yale Divinity School Library. Other records of her work include letters of reference and correspondence between Wiley and Turner at SVMFM Headquarters.

4. Gary Seaman to Fennell P. Turner, August 15, 1916, Archives of the SVMFM, Record Group No. 42 (Box 482, Folder 5722), Special Collections, Yale Divinity School Library.

5. Edith May Hazlett to Fennell P. Turner, May 21, 1917, Archives of the SVMFM, Record Group No. 42 (Box 482, Folder 5722), Special Collections, Yale Divinity School Library.

Edith May Hazlett Wiley
(Special Collections, Yale Divinity School)

Wiley, then a Yale Divinity School student, and eventually had one son and two daughters. Wiley later said that the SVMFM had brought them together.

After teaching in Beirut, the Near East Mission of the American Board of Commissioners for Foreign Missions appointed the couple as career missionaries in Turkey (1924–1963) with a few trips back to the United States.

After a year of language school in Istanbul (1924–1925), she and her husband taught at Merzifoun, Marash, and Gazientep (formerly called Aintab), Turkey. Wiley ministered to a wide variety of men and women, including children, farmers, members of interfaith groups, religious seekers, refugees, and United States military personnel and students. Between 1935 and 1946, she was a pastor's wife in Walpole, New Hampshire; Pittsfield, Massachusetts; and for the English-speaking Union Church of Istanbul between 1947 and 1958. From 1961 to 1963, she and her husband were "loaned" to the World Council of Churches.

After completing her overseas missionary work in 1963, Wiley made her residence in Los Angeles. At this time, the United Church Board for World Ministries voted Wiley and her husband "Missionary Emeriti."[6]

---

6. The United Church Board for World Ministries was created in 1961 by a merger

She joined the Claremont United Church of Christ, where she taught Sunday school and led the Women's Fellowship.

Wiley died in Claremont, California, in 1983. A memorial card prepared after her death describes some of her traits: "She always accepted cheerfully the tasks that came her way even though they changed with the many moves that also came to her and her family. She showed great friendliness and neighborliness to people of various nationalities that surrounded her."[7]

THE STUDENT CHRISTIAN MOVEMENT:
A DEFINITION

The movement that Wiley and other women helped lead was called the Student Christian Movement. Ruth Rouse pinpointed the focus of this international ministry when she wrote that "these were student movements, of students, by students, and for students."[8]

The SCM's primary goals were to preach the Gospel to male and female college students and to transform the world through them. In addition to the personal and individual devotional focus of earliest student societies, the nineteenth century's SCMs added evangelism, as they sought "the evangelization of the world in this generation."

Starting in the 1890s, the SCM supplemented devotional and evangelistic concerns with emphases on social change. As a result, campus associations supported outreach programs, such as settlement houses, and dealt with issues of racism, war, and women's rights.

THE STUDENT CHRISTIAN MOVEMENT:
ITS ORIGINS

Even though there were some ministries to students earlier, these student Christian societies blossomed as a direct result of the 1857–1859 revival in England and North America.[9] This awakening began

---

of the American Board of Commissioners for Foreign Missions or the American Board and other missionary societies as an agency of the United Church of Christ.

 7. Amerikan Bord Heyeti (American Board), Istanbul, "Memorial Records for Edith Hazlett Wiley," American Research Institute in Turkey, Istanbul Center Library, online in Digital Library for International Research Archive, Item #17490, http://www.dlir.org.

 8. Ruth Rouse and Stephen Charles Neill, *A History of the Ecumenical Movement, 1517–1948*, 2nd ed. (London: SPCK, 1967), 2:343. For more information about Rouse, see chapter 6.

 9. For more information on student revivals prior to the 1850s, see Clarence Prouty Shedd, *Two Centuries of Student Christian Movements* (New York: Association Press, 1934), and Tissington Tatlow, *The Story of the Student Christian Movement of Great*

in North America in 1857 as a prayer-focused, lay-led phenomenon, and then traveled quickly to Great Britain via Ireland and Scotland. It remained in effect for many years, and crisscrossed the Atlantic between Great Britain and the United States and Canada. A unique "spiritual relationship" between these nations existed throughout this era.

Because of this spiritual awakening, a common set of ideas and practices developed. According to David Bebbington, four traits marked this revival: it was biblicist (the revival emphasized the central authority and importance of the Bible), it was crucicentric (the revival focused on Jesus's death on the cross, not his incarnation), it was conversionist (a person could not be a Christian without a personal experience with Jesus Christ), and finally, the revival was activist. Because of the biblical mandate to preach the Gospel (Christ's death and resurrection on the cross for the forgiveness of sins) and the necessity of conversion, these Christians felt a compelling burden to translate their beliefs into missionary activity at home and abroad. This took many forms, such as social work, educational and medical ministries, and personal evangelism.[10]

James Edwin Orr wrote that the 1857–1859 revivals also caused the formation of Christian associations in state universities in the United States and daily prayer meetings (later to be called Christian associations) in the universities of Great Britain.[11]

Though the judgment that the British and American movements played the most important role in the development of the SCM is accurate, it has masked the fact that other groups, such as those in Germany, Scandinavia, and Japan, also played pivotal roles in early SCM developments. Rouse tempered her belief that the United States and Great Britain were the initiators of the movement by reminding her readers that "the Federation will never forget that twice in those years, the East through Japan supplied a powerful stimulus."[12] Alongside the American

Britain and Ireland (London: SCM, 1933), 3–4. For more information on the 1857–1859 revival, see Kathryn Teresa Long, *The Revival of 1857–1858: Interpreting an American Religious Awakening*, 1st ed. Religion in America Series (New York: Oxford University Press, 1998).

10. Mark Noll, David Bebbington, and George A. Rawlyk, eds., *Evangelicalism: Comparative Studies of Popular Protestantism in North America, the British Isles, and Beyond, 1700–1900* (New York: Oxford University Press, 1994), 6.

11. James Edwin Orr, *The Fervent Prayer: The Worldwide Impact of the Great Awakening of 1858* (Chicago: Moody Press, 1974), 156.

12. Ruth Rouse, *The World's Student Christian Federation: A History of the First Thirty Years* (London: SCM, 1948), 25. In the past twenty years, there have been investigations of SCM's outside the United States and Great Britain. A notable example is Ruth Franzén, *Student Ecumenism and Revivalism: The Student Christian Movement of Finland at the International Crossroads, 1924–1950* (Helsingfors: Finska Kyrkohistoriksa Samfundet, 1987).

and British, movements sprung up in Asia (1889, Japan), Scandinavia (1890, Norway, Denmark, and Sweden) and Germany.

THE STUDENT CHRISTIAN MOVEMENT: ITS MAJOR GROUPS

The SCM combined a dizzying array of autonomous local, regional, national, and international groups. The SCM had movements for men, for women, and for mixed groups of men and women. The same was true for leadership opportunities. There were groups led by men and groups led by women. And there were groups led by men and women together.

As mentioned in the introduction, notable groups falling under the SCM umbrella included the American Intercollegiate Young Men's Christian Association (YMCA) and Young Women's Christian Association (YWCA) and the Student Volunteer Movement for Foreign Missions (SVMFM) and their non–North American counterparts, SCMs in different countries, and the global World Student Christian Federation (WSCF).

THE YOUNG MEN'S CHRISTIAN ASSOCIATION

In 1844, George Williams, a London draper, founded the Young Men's Christian Association (YMCA) as a safe Christian environment for rural young men coming to cities for work in the industrial revolution. His inspiration came from his meetings for prayer and Bible reading for his fellow employees in London businesses. By 1851, there were YMCAs in the United Kingdom, Australia, Belgium, Canada, France, Germany, the Netherlands, Switzerland, and the United States. Today it has one-hundred and twenty-five national associations with a headquarters in Geneva, Switzerland. One of its ministries has been with students.

In the atmosphere of the 1857–1859 revivals, over forty student associations were established in the colleges and universities of the United States. Most of these were linked to the YMCA. Early groups were launched at the University of Virginia (1858) and the University of Michigan (also 1858). In Great Britain, Christian associations were established at Cambridge University (1858), the University of Edinburgh (1865), and Glasgow University (1865).

Clarence Prouty Shedd described these groups as mainly local associations formed by Christians who sought out others on their campuses who had similar conversion experiences. Students were eager to share with each other the life-changing experience each had had with Jesus

Christ. With them, they established campus Christian groups with as few as two members. From the beginning, these groups could be composed of men and women together or men and women separately. In either type of group the routine included fellowship in prayer meetings, Bible study, social betterment work, student evangelism, missionary recruitment, conferences, and conventions.

Many campus administrators went from disapproval to tentative support and then to outspoken endorsement. College presidents, such as Martin Brewster Anderson of the University of Rochester (president, 1853–1888), claimed to have "witnessed the beneficial working of such a college organization."[13] He "most heartily" recommended the establishment of these throughout the United States.

In 1877, fifty student religious societies first joined together to establish the American Intercollegiate YMCA. The initial work was carried out by the Philadelphia Society at Princeton University under the able leadership of Luther Wishard.[14]

Expansion was rapid and widespread. Originally, local YMCA groups were composed of males only or were combined groups of men and women. However, beginning around 1880, the YMCA moved toward sponsoring men's groups only. At the 1880 annual YMCA convention, a resolution was passed that said that only men could hold offices or have voting privileges in YMCA groups. At the 1881 annual convention leaders asked the YMCA to limit its groups to men only.

Because of his opposition to the plan to limit the YMCA to men only, evangelist and YMCA leader D. L. Moody "threatened to 'go on the warpath with his tomahawk' because he was convinced that the movement was 'all wrong . . . in excluding women from our privileges.'"[15] In

---

13. Shedd, *Two Centuries*, 105–6.

14. Luther D. Wishard (1854–1925) earned a BA from Princeton University (1877) and was a Princeton seminary student (1877–1879). He worked for the international YMCA as corresponding secretary of the college department (1877–1888), a traveling secretary (1888–1892), and foreign secretary (1892–1899). From 1899 to 1902, Wishard was the director of the Forward Movement for the American Board of Foreign Missions. He spearheaded the 1877 organization of the American Intercollegiate SCM and also helped organize the American YWCA. From 1902 until his death in 1925, Wishard was a businessman. For more information on Luther Wishard's role in the establishment of the SCM, see Charles K. Ober, *Luther D. Wishard: Projector of World Movements* (New York: Association Press, 1927).

15. Charles Howard Hopkins, *History of the YMCA in North America* (New York: Association Press, 1951), 240. Dwight Lyman Moody (1837–1899), or D. L. Moody, was an American evangelist, publisher, and educator with deep ties to the SCM. At the least he helped create the environment in which the SCM could arise. Even more than that, Moody served as a spiritual and practical inspiration and adviser to SCM members. His Northfield Conference Center became a popular Victorian conference center and was

an 1890 letter, George Hall wrote that he had never seen Moody "so stirred up."[16]

As a result, some mixed YMCAs became independent Christian associations, and others decided to become men's clubs. Many of the latter helped women organize their own campus unions. Most of these later affiliated with the intercollegiate YWCA. Between 1877 and 1885, 181 YMCA college associations were organized. Total members were 10,000 out of the 37,000 students at these universities and colleges.[17]

Student outreach has continued to be a part of YMCA work. As late as 2016, 507 of the 1,349 YMCAs in North America worked with college students.

THE YOUNG WOMAN'S CHRISTIAN ASSOCIATION

Launched in 1855, the Young Women's Christian Association (YWCA) quickly became an international movement focused on improving the lives of women. Student work was part of the American YWCA from its inception. The first student YWCA was organized in 1873 at Illinois State Normal School. Between 1883 and 1886 eighty to ninety YWCAs were established on college campuses. An official national student group was organized in 1886 after the formerly mixed YMCA no longer wanted women members. Campus associations created state councils and then joined together under the auspices of the American Committee of the YWCA. When the YWCA of the United States was established in 1906, the YWCA student community had 469 local associations and 147 city associations, which had a broader focus than work with students. At that time, YWCA student membership was

the site of the birth of the SVMFM. For more information on Moody, see J. F. Findlay, *Dwight L. Moody: American Evangelist, 1837–1899* (Grand Rapids, MI: Baker Books, 1973); Lyle W. Dorsett, *A Passion for Souls: The Life of D. L. Moody* (Chicago: Moody Publishers, 2003); and Kevin Belmonte, *D. L. Moody, A Life: Innovator, Evangelist, World Changer* (Chicago: Moody Publishers, 2014).

16.   Hopkins's footnote reads, "193. Letter, Geo. A. Hall to C. K. Ober, October 23, 1890. Hall reporting 'a long talk with Mr. Moody yesterday at Buffalo.'" Hopkins, *History*, 759.

17.   Rouse, *World's Student Christian Federation*, 29. For a history of the YMCA, see Hopkins, *History*; Richard Clay Morse, *History of the North American YMCAs* (New York: Association Press, 1913); *International Survey of the YMCA and YWCA's: An Independent Study of the Foreign Worker of the Christian Associations of the United States and Canada* (New York: International Survey Committee, 1932); Clarence Prouty Shedd, *A History of the World's Alliance of YMCAs* (London: SPCK, 1955); and Kenneth Scott Latourette, *World Service: A History of the Foreign Work and World Service of the Young Men's Christian Association of the United States and Canada* (New York: Association Press, 1957).

42,000 of 186,000 total YWCA members. As of 1997, the American YWCA had twenty-nine student groups and a national student council of fifteen officers.[18]

THE STUDENT VOLUNTEER MOVEMENT
FOR FOREIGN MISSIONS

Originating in 1886, the Student Volunteer Movement for Foreign Missions (SVMFM) challenged university and college students in the United States to become foreign missionaries. It also publicized and advocated for the missionary movement in general.

The American SVMFM was launched in 1887 after the previous year's student missionary conference called by D. L. Moody at Mt. Hermon, Massachusetts. At that meeting, one hundred men had volunteered for missionary work. During the 1886–1887 school year, more than 2,000 men and women university students across the United States chose missionary careers by signing the movement's Volunteer Pledge. Used in Student Christian Movement circles in the late nineteenth and early twentieth centuries, this pledge stated, "It is my purpose, if God permits, to become a foreign missionary." John R. Mott, then a Cornell University student, was persuaded to lead the fledgling movement. As time passed, he became the "father figure" of the entire SCM. He was considered so significant that one scholar noted that it "complicates the task of isolating and analyzing the merits of the early organization's structure independent of Mott and his influence."[19] He was aided by an executive committee made up of representatives of the YMCA, the YWCA, and the Inter-Seminary Alliance.

Between 1887 and 1920, the SVMFM experienced rapid growth and then went into a period of decline. In 1959, it merged with two other student groups to form the National Student Christian Foundation, which became part of the University Christian Movement in 1966. The movement dissolved in 1969. The SVMFM passion for missions has

---

18.   For a history of the YWCA, see Rebecca Morse, *Young Women: A History of the American Committee of the YWCA* (Chicago: American Committee of the YWCA, 1901); Elizabeth Wilson, *Fifty Years of Association Work amongst Young Women, 1866–1916* (New York: YWCA, 1916); Elizabeth Wilson, *The Story of Fifty Years of the YWCA in India, Burma, and Ceylon* (Calcutta: Association Press, 1923); Anna Rice, *A History of the World's Young Women's Christian Association* (New York: Woman's Press, 1948); and Nancy Boyd, *Emissaries: The Overseas Work of the American YWCA, 1895–1970* (New York: Woman's Press, 1986).

19.   Timothy C. Wallstrom, *The Creation of a Student Movement to Evangelize the World: A History and Analysis of the Early Stages of the SVMFM* (Pasadena, CA: William Carey International University, 1980), 61.

been carried on by different evangelical student groups such as Inter-Varsity Christian Fellowship. During its history, the SVMFM encouraged over 20,000 American collegians to become foreign missionaries.[20] The movement no longer exists.

THE STUDENT VOLUNTEER MISSIONARY UNION

Launched in 1889, the Student Volunteer Missionary Union (SVMU) was the United Kingdom's version of the American Student Volunteer Movement for Foreign Missions. Its establishment was encouraged by the American group and its first leaders. The SVMU sponsored the Cambridge Seven. These seven were famous British cricketers who captured the imagination of the British student population by giving up fame and fortune for a career in foreign missions.[21] These men visited colleges and universities throughout the British Isles to speak about the cause of foreign missions and to seek both male and female recruits for missionary service. SVMU groups were officially established in many institutions.

THE BRITISH SCM

The Christian movement among students quickly spread throughout England, Scotland, Ireland, and Wales and eventually developed into the British SCM in 1892. The United Kingdom's SCM eventually extended its ministry to all undergraduate and graduate students in Great Britain.

---

20. For a history of the SVMFM, see John R. Mott, *Addresses and Papers of John R. Mott: The Student Volunteer Movement for Foreign Missions*, vol. 1 (New York: Association Press, 1946); and *Achievements of the SVMFM during the First Generation of Its History, Report of the Executive Committee, 1920* (New York: SVM, 1920); Robert Wilder, *The Student Volunteer Movement for Foreign Missions: Some Reminiscences of Its Origin and Early History* (New York: SVM, 1935); William M. Beahm, "Factors in the Development of SVMFM" (PhD diss., University of Chicago, 1941); Wallstrom, *Creation*; Ben Harder, "The Student Volunteer Movement for Foreign Missions and Its Contribution to 20th-Century Missions," *Missiology: An International Review* 8, no. 2 (April 1980): 141–54; Thomas Russell, "Can the Story Be Told without Them? The Role of Women in the Student Volunteer Movement," *Missiology: An International Review* 17, no. 2 (April 1989): 159–75; Nathan Showalter, *The End of a Crusade: The Student Volunteer Movement for Foreign Missions and the Great War*, ATLA Monograph Series 44 (Lanham, MD: Scarecrow Press, 1998); and Michael Parker, *The Kingdom of Character: The Student Volunteer Movement for Foreign Missions, 1886–1926* (Lanham, MD: American Society of Missiology and University Press of America, 1998).

21. For more information on the Cambridge Seven, see J. C. Pollock, *The Cambridge Seven* (Basingstoke, Hants: Marshalls, 1985); and Joan Clifford, *The Cambridge Seven: For Christ and China* (London: Marshall Pickering, 1990).

It quickly became the largest student organization there. While the Oxford and Cambridge Christian Associations were particularly influential in the development of this intercollegiate movement, it was the product of several student Christian movements, such as the Oxford and Cambridge Christian Unions, the Student Foreign Missionary Union and the Student Volunteer Missionary Union.

During the 1920s, the British movement split into two groups: Inter-Varsity Christian Fellowship and the SCM.[22] The organizational descendant of the Evangelical wing, the Universities and College Christian Fellowship (UCCF) has more than two hundred unions across the United Kingdom. It is affiliated with the International Fellowship of Evangelical Students. The SCM has groups in approximately sixty universities and other higher educational institutions, and it is a constituent member of the World Student Christian Federation.

THE WORLD STUDENT CHRISTIAN FEDERATION

Founded in 1895, the World Student Christian Federation (WSCF) was established as an international federation of national Student Christian Movements. Early on, it had members and leaders from Eastern, Protestant, and Roman Catholic religious communities. The WSCF was fueled by Mott's imagination, vision, and initiative with the assistance of key student leaders, both male and female, from Great Britain, Germany, Scandinavia, and the student movement in mission lands. It had the enthusiastic support of religious, university, and political leaders. At the time of its founding, the WSCF had 5,000 associations and unions and 35,000 members.

From that time, the WSCF experienced phenomenal growth. The number of associations or unions in the WSCF was 5,000 (1895), 13,500 (1900), 17,000 (1905), 22,000 (1910), and 24,000 (1915). Numbers of WSCF members rose as well. There were 35,000 members

---

22. For a history of the British SCM, see Henry Wingate Oldham, *The Student Christian Movement of Great Britain and Ireland: Its Origin, Development, and Present Position* (London: British College Christian Union, 1899); Tatlow, *Story*; and Eric Fenn, *Learning Together* (London: SCM Press, 1939). For the evangelical branch of the British SCM, see Inter-Varsity Christian Fellowship, *A Brief History of the Inter-Varsity Fellowship* (London: IVFEU, 1929); F. D. Coggan, ed., *Christ and the Colleges: A History of the Inter-Varsity Fellowship of Evangelical Unions* (London: IVFEU, 1934); J. C. Pollock, *The Cambridge Movement* (London: John Murray, 1953); and Douglas Johnson, *Contending for the Faith: A History of the Evangelical Movement in the Universities and Colleges* (London: Inter-Varsity Press, 1979). For the non-evangelical branch of the British SCM, see J. Davis McCaughey, *Christian Obedience in the Universities: Studies in the Life of the SCM of Great Britain and Ireland, 1930–1950* (London: SCM Press, 1958).

in 1895, 62,000 (1900), 112,000 (1905), 150,000 (1910), and 190,000 (1915). By 1920, the WSCF claimed over 190,000 members and 23,000 associations and unions.

Eventually, the WSCF split along fundamentalist and modernist lines. Today, the more conservative movement, the International Fellowship of Evangelical Students, can be found in one hundred and sixty nations. The nonevangelical group, the WSCF, can be found in ninety nations and boasts a membership of 2 million as of 2016.[23]

THE LEADERSHIP STRUCTURE OF THE SCM

The SCM had a similar leadership structure across the spectrum of its movements. It also had a fresh approach to organization with women serving in the highest corridors of power. Depending on the movement, they became leaders of women, men, and in mixed groups of men and women.

Suggested by Charles Kellogg Ober, a YMCA leader, the SCM's leadership structure was based on the organizational style of the newly developed YMCA.[24]

According to Mott, Ober "recognized clearly the possibilities of the movement if properly guarded, developed and extended; and firmly believed that all the dangerous techniques would be checked by the judicious organi-

---

23. For a history of the WSCF, see Philip Potter and Thomas Wieser, *Seeking and Serving the Truth: The First Hundred Years of the World Student Christian Federation* (Geneva: WCC Publications, 1997); and Risto Lehtonen, *Story of a Storm: The Ecumenical Student Movement in the Turmoil of Revolution, 1968–1973* (Grand Rapids, MI: William B. Eerdmans, 1998).

24. Charles Kellogg Ober (1856–1948) attended Williams College from 1879 to 1883. He entered into YMCA work after surviving eight days afloat at sea off the Newfoundland coast. Crediting his survival to prayer, Ober decided to devote himself to Christian work. Later, Ober's interest in the Young Men's Christian Association developed further during his association with George Williams, and in 1882 he was made assistant to Robert R. McBurney, secretary of the New York City YMCA. In 1883, he became state secretary of the Massachusetts YMCA, a position he held in 1883 and 1884. From 1884 to 1890 Ober was involved in the association's college movement and helped organize the Northfield Student Conference and the Student Volunteer Movement for Foreign Missions. In 1890 Ober was made field secretary of the International Committee and traveled throughout the United States in this capacity until 1910, when he conceived the Fellowship Plan for training qualified college students as secretaries. During the First World War Ober served as a YMCA special secretary in France and England. From 1910 until his retirement in 1923 he traveled extensively, visiting colleges and universities, actively recruiting for the association. Ober was the recipient of an Honorary Master of Art from Williams College in 1935 in recognition of his "interest and long-continued faithful services among college young men." He was the author of several works relating to his work in the YMCA. For more information, see Charles K. Ober Papers, Kautz Family YMCA Archives, University of Minnesota, and James Terry White, *The National Cyclopedia of American Biography* 37 (New York: J. T. White, 1951), 429–30, with picture.

zation. . . . He suggested, in the main, the flexible, yet comprehensive scheme of organization under which the movement has been working."[25]

Critics of the movement's organizational structure believe that it was a major cause of the SCM's post–World War I decline. Too much power was placed in the hands of those organizations that supplied the personnel for the SCM, such as the YMCA and YWCA.[26]

Though never fully explained by participants or later historians, the SCM's national and international leadership structure can best be visualized as three concentric circles. The three jobs that made up these circles from the center out are committee member, secretary, and pioneer. While the extent of authority granted decreased from the inner to the outer circle, the number of persons found in each circle increased. Often the fame of SCM leaders was more prominent for members of the outermost circle, the pioneer. Women served in all three capacities.

The first two circles, committee member and secretary, can best be described as "leadership by official position" because these were constitutionally established positions that made up the movement's core bureaucracy.

COMMITTEE MEMBERS

Committee members were at the core of the movement's power. These committee members came in several types.

One kind supervised local, regional, national, and international divisions of the SCM. Although the movement used different terms for these groups, such as executive committee, general committee, committee, and executive, the term "executive committee" will be used. These working groups had regular members and officers, chairs, vice-chairs, treasurers, and secretaries. Membership consisted of students, senior friends, and a small number of professional staff.

On the local, national, and international level, executive committee members dealt with questions of general policy, including establishing movement regulations and membership requirements, approving membership requests, dealing with budgetary items, hearing reports, and planning future extensions of the movement, conferences, and special meetings.

Executive committees also decided what staff was needed, haggled over salaries and benefits, heard reports, and received resignations from movement personal. Meetings were held monthly, quarterly, or during major

---

25. John R. Mott, *History of the Student Volunteer Movement for Foreign Missions*, Student Volunteer Series 1 (Chicago: SVMFM, 1892), 15–16.

26. Wallstrom, *Creation*, 87.

student conferences. They followed a similar order of business: prayer, reading the minutes of the preceding meeting, hearing the treasurer's and subcommittee reports, handling new business, and closing with prayer.

Over time, executive committees tended to grow in size. As one example, the SVMFM began with only three members, increased to six (1898), then to thirty (1920). Similarly, the WSCF started with five members in 1895 and grew to thirty by 1918. These committees had a high rate of turnover, and the number of women was never equal to the number of men. Gender ratios can be demonstrated through statistics for the SVMFM and the WSCF.

In the SVMFM between 1889 and 1898, one of three executive committee members was a woman; between 1901 and 1906, two of six members were women; in 1910, one of five was a woman; in 1914, two of six were women; and in 1920, nine of twenty-eight were women.

In the WSCF, in 1895, no women and ten men were executive committee members, and in 1900, 1905, and 1907, no women and twenty-two men were committee members. Beginning in 1909, women served as member of the WSCF executive committee. That year, four women and twenty-four men were in the group; in 1911, five women and twenty-four men served; in 1913, seven women and twenty-six men served; and finally in 1920, ten women and seventeen men served.

Another category of committee was formed to offer counsel to these executive committees. The SVMFM called their board the SVM Advisory Committee. This group was composed of several persons, some ordained and some lay. Five came from a variety of Protestant denominations, one from the YMCA, and one from the YWCA. These individuals were generally college graduates or people who never went to college. Before taking any major steps, the younger SVMFM executive sought advice from the older group.[27]

SECRETARIES

The secretary was the second circle of authority within the SCM. The term "secretary" has its own SCM definition. In the movement, a secretary was not employed to handle correspondence or do routine office work, such as taking dictation, typing, and filing. The SCM secretary focus was on spiritual development of individuals, and the term's

---

27. For more information on the purpose, duties, and personnel of this committee, see *The Advisory Committee*, Archives of the WSCF, Record Group 46 (Box 60, Folder 480), 1–2, Special Collections, Yale Divinity School.

equivalent was pastor or chaplain.[28]

Executive committees determined what qualifications the position required and what tasks were performed. The qualifications and tasks for a secretary evolved from 1880 to 1920. In the movement's earliest years, the job descriptions were rather simple. Filled with an enthusiasm for mission, the secretary visited different institutions to recruit students for missionary work. The secretaries also fostered spiritual development in individuals and small groups. Beyond this, there was no clear conception of the secretary's qualifications, training, or tasks. Hardly any evaluation of the success or failure of the secretary's ministries took place.

However, by 1920, the secretarial task evolved and had become more complex. Although the primary function of a secretary was still pastor or chaplain, secretaries were beginning to take on other tasks. For some secretaries, these other tasks, in particular administrative and executive ones, became predominant. This is perhaps because of the overwhelming need for these added tasks.

In that year, a subcommittee of the WSCF Executive, the Committee on the Enlisting and Training of Secretaries, outlined the qualifications and training required for the position.[29] This group was made up of seven individuals, three women (Hermine Baart de La Faille, Bertha Condé, and Suzanne de Dietrich) and four men with a male convener (Fritz de Rougemount).[30] This subcommittee said that secretaries were needed not only where the SCM already existed, but also in new places. Given the growing complexity of SCM work, the committee also called for a greater variety of these personnel: administrative, biblical, social, traveling, boys' and girl's work, and foreign student secretaries.

Along with a "well-rounded Christian character and personal experience of Christ," the committee said the secretary should possess a practical knowledge of the Bible (preeminently of the life, work, and teaching of Jesus Christ) so that they "may fulfill his most important function—leading students to understand and follow him." The secretary needed to be familiar with devotional literature and religious biography.

In addition to spiritual qualifications, this person had to be prepared academically, by studying church history, systematic

---

28. Tatlow, *Story*, 267.

29. "Enlisting and Training Secretaries," *Minutes of the Meeting of the General Committee of the WSCF*, St. Beatenburg, Switzerland, July 30–August 7, 1920), 13–16, Archives of the WSCF, Record Group No. 46 (Box 7, Folder 55), Special Collections, Yale Divinity School Library.

30. For more information on Bertha Condé, see chapter 3 and for more information on Suzanne de Dietrich, see chapter 12.

theology, applied psychology, sociology, comparative religions, and the policies and history of the SCM itself. Secretaries should possess a basic knowledge of business practice, organization, and methods. A university degree or equivalent was required and, if possible, a second degree. In the same year, John Mott said that the secretary had to have an "astonishing combination of qualities—administrative, promotive, scholastic, pastoral, teaching, inspirational, and prophetic. All these qualities should be exercised with the evangelistic aim in view."[31]

The secretary was under the authority of the executive committee, which appointed, paid, and evaluated those hired. Committees also determined duration of employment and compensation levels. Employment periods ranged from one month to twenty years, depending on the branch of the SCM. For example, traveling secretaries with the American SVMFM worked from one month to fifteen years. Their employment ran roughly in accordance with the school year, from September 1 to July 16 (prior to December 3, 1901, and after 1917) or from August 31 to July 15. In the American SVMFM, records demonstrate that experience, family size, and length of appointment rather than gender determined salary levels. All inexperienced, single workers, male and female, received the same amount ($500.00 a year in 1905, $600.00 a year in 1917). The number of secretaries when compared to the actual numbers of SCM members was always quite small. There was also a perennial shortage of women candidates.

Of the several types of secretaries, the two most significant were general/assistant general secretaries and traveling secretaries because they served the two major components of the movement—the SCM's headquarters and its field operations at college associations with students and university authorities.

PIONEERS

The third circle can best be called "leadership by task" since it was defined by the tasks carried out and not by its constitutionally established position. This position was called the pioneer. Whether by design or accident, women pioneers worked with both men and women.

Achieving almost mythic status in SCM groups were those hearty men and women called pioneers, whose story captured the spirit of the pre-1920 period of the SCM. Wilmina Rowland, who wrote about

---

31. John R. Mott, *Addresses and Papers of John R. Mott 2: The World's Student Christian Federation* (New York: Association Press, 1947), 217.

Ruth Rouse, felt that if people understood the "situation, methods, and results of pioneer work," they would capture the true spirit of the first twenty-five years of the WSCF's history.[32] This pioneering intent was so pervasive that Rouse observed, "The procession of pioneers will halt only at the Federation's tomb."[33] Pioneers embodied the ethos of the pre-1920 SCM because they carried out the central mandates of the movement: to reach out to all students around the world and, through time, to transform the world.

In very simple terms, Rouse described pioneers as those who "surveyed, mapped and occupied" new fields.[34] Pioneer outreach was not only linked to geography but also involved the world of women students, student migrations, and foreign students in the successive regions of thought and activity, social and ecumenical.[35]

Even though pioneers and traveling secretaries had many common traits, they were still very different. The two roles were similar in that they provided opportunities for travel, the thrill of campus visits, the chance to influence students, and, finally, the chance to have a professional career. In fact, traveling secretaries shared the pioneer role because much of their work involved visits to unreached campuses. They also visited universities and colleges to develop and advise student associations. Formally, however, pioneers and traveling secretaries were quite different roles in the SCM. Pioneers had a great deal of independence and could be self-funded or movement-funded. Traveling secretaries were tightly controlled by executive committees, which hired and paid them and evaluated their performance. Also, understanding themselves as discoverers and developers, the pioneers' main job was to explore new fields and establish new ministries. Traveling secretaries served as direct links between home offices and existing associations, seeing themselves as conduits for information between these two parts of SCM life.

Between 1880 and 1920, the pioneer role expanded into three distinct types as the SCM grew in sophistication: basic pioneers, specialized pioneers, and theoreticians.

As either short-term or long-term leaders, basic pioneers investigated untouched or underdeveloped locations, making initial contacts with individuals or groups. Later, these workers established ministries for students.

---

32. See Wilmina M. Rowland, "The Contribution of Ruth Rouse to the World's Student Christian Federation" (MA thesis, Yale Divinity School, 1937), 153–54.

33. Rouse, *World's Student Christian Federation*, 73.

34. Ibid., 81.

35. Ibid., 80, 165.

After successes with basic pioneering, specialized pioneers targeted specific groups for outreach, such as art students, conference workers, or church leaders.

With basic and specialized pioneering launched, a third type of pioneer, the theoretician, worked in the realm of ideas instead of directly with students, chewing over contemporary intellectual and social issues. Many of these individuals challenged the SCM to deal with these things.

2

The "Whys" of SCM Women Leaders

Despite Edith Wiley's assertion that she had no outside influences beyond her call to become a leader of the Student Christian Movement (SCM), in fact she did have other influences. And the same is true for all SCM women leaders. Whether they were conscious of these things will never be known. But still they existed.

Since these women served in a Christian movement, it might be better to say that there were many reasons, known and unknown to them, why women served as leaders, but of these the most important one was the call from God.

The rise of women leaders in the SCM was also due to a mixture of other factors: the SCM's guiding principles, constitutional guarantee, gradualism, World War I, the role of the SCM's men, and the traits of the SCM's women.

THE GUIDING PRINCIPLES OF THE SCM

From its inception, certain guiding principles marked the SCM. These principles established the fundamental approach taken by the movement's local, national, and international bodies throughout the movement's history. Each of these working assumptions contributed in its own way to the emergence of women leaders in the SCM.

As its first principle, the SCM adopted an *interdenominational policy*. Instead of having student members from only one Christian denomination or making them drop their denominations, the movement felt that students should bring the strengths of their denominations to the SCM. Tissington Tatlow, the head of the British SCM, summed up this approach:

The SCM is interdenominational, in that while it unites persons of different religious denominations in a single organization for certain definite aims and activities, it recognizes their allegiance to any of the various Christian bodies into which the Body of Christ is divided. It believes that loyalty to their own denomination is the first duty of Christian students and welcomes them into the fellowship of the Movement as those whose privilege it is to bring into it, as their contribution, that they as members of their own religious body have discovered or will discover of Christian truth.[1]

This interdenominational approach meant that the policies of different Christian groups in regard to women's roles became part of the SCM. In particular, while most Christian groups in the Victorian era did not allow women to lead men or be ordained, there were some notable exceptions.[2]

As a second principle, the SCM established itself as a *lay-led* instead of a clerically led organization. This was epitomized by John R. Mott, a Methodist layman, who was considered the central leader of the international movement. Having lay leadership gave women, who were largely unordained, the opportunity to become leaders. These women did not challenge existing ecclesiastical structures with demands for ordination status.

The SCM's third principle was that the SCM was established as a *federation*. In contrast to earlier student groups with centralized authority structures, each local, national, and international body within the SCM was self-directed. The movement's central leadership served in an advisory capacity only. For women's ordination, this meant that if a particular SCM group permitted women's leadership with men, there was nothing a central governing authority could do to inhibit that.

As a fourth guiding principle, the SCM considered itself an *experimental laboratory* for new ideas. Instead of inheriting a fossilized structure within which members had to work, the movement let members try new things, experiment, and even fail if necessary. Ruth Rouse observed that members were "freer to try experiments and to take risks. . . . If their experiments succeeded, the Churches could profit

---

1. Ruth Rouse and Stephen Charles Neill, eds., *A History of the Ecumenical Movement, 1517–1948* (London: SPCK, 1954), 2:342–43. Reverend Canon Tissington Tatlow, DD (1876–1957), served as the British SCM's General Secretary from 1898 to 1900 and from 1903 to 1929. He was a graduate of Trinity College, Dublin. Tatlow also served the SCM as SVMU traveling secretary (1897–1898) and editor of the *Student Movement* (1900–1908); and he was vice-chair (1922–1928), chair (1929–1933), and honorary chaplain (1933–?) of the WSCF. Tatlow was chair of the I.S.S. (1926–?). He served as a rector in London and was named an honorary canon of Canterbury Cathedral.

2. See chapter 10 for Reverend Barbara Ellen Groenendyke's ministry in the SVMFM.

by their success; the failures of these foolish young things the Church could disclaim."[3] Because of this freedom, different SCMs developed new structures for governance, such as with women leaders.

WOMEN LEADERS CONSTITUTIONALLY GUARANTEED

Constitutional guarantee in several constituent groups of the SCM established women as leaders in these groups, even at the highest levels. The most prominent example of constitutionally established women SCM leaders was found in the American Student Volunteer Movement for Foreign Missions (SVMFM). The SVMFM's constitution from its inception stipulated that a representative from the YWCA serve on its executive committee along with representatives from the YMCA and the Inter-Seminary Alliance. Because these women were leaders in women's groups, they became leaders of mixed groups. The former gave them valuable training, experience, and confidence, which they brought to combined groups. The first of many YWCA women to serve on the SVMFM executive was Nettie Dunn Clark.

NETTIE DUNN CLARK (1863–1948)

Even though Elizabeth Wilson called Nettie Clark the "pioneer traveling secretary for the YWCA," Clark's most significant role was not the one that focused on women's work with the YWCA.[4] It is more significant that Clark sat on the SVMFM governing board alongside the men who represented the other groups in the movement, such as the YMCA. Recalling her work with the SVMFM during its earliest years, Clark later wrote, "As a new national secretary of the YWCA beginning my work in November of that year (1886), I had much to do with this new missionary movement in the colleges, being one of the first volunteers, and then often helping in the special missionary meetings held by Mr. Wilder and Mr. Forman."[5]

Clark was the daughter of the Reverend Dr. Ransom Dunn (1818–1900), an abolitionist, professor, fund raiser, and president of Hillsdale College, Hillsdale, Michigan (1852–1900). He served as moderator

---

3. Rouse and Neill, *History*, 2:601.

4. Elizabeth Wilson, *Fifty Years of Association Work among Young Women, 1866–1916: A History of the Young Women's Christian Association in the United States of America* (New York: YMCA, 1916), 318.

5. Robert Parmelee Wilder, *The Student Volunteer Movement for Foreign Missions: Some Personal Reminiscences of Its Origin and Early History* (New York: Student Volunteer Movement, 1935), 45.

Nettie Dunn Clark
(Archives, Hillsdale College, MI)

of the Free Will Baptist Church. Clark was one of three daughters of Ransom Dunn and his second wife. The senior Dunn had three children from his first wife, meaning that Clark came from what today would have been called a "blended family."

According to Hillsdale College records, Nettie Clark matriculated as a student in 1875 and earned a PhB in 1882 and a PhM in 1885. While at Hillsdale College, she was a member of the Ladies Literary Union. She was also involved with the Beethoven Society, the first music organization on campus, and she was the recording secretary for the YMCA. Clark also served as the first YWCA National Secretary (1886–1891).

In 1887, Clark felt a call to missionary service after attending a meeting conducted by Robert Wilder during his travels following the 1886 Mt. Hermon Conference.[6] Missionary work became her life's work; she emphasized this ministry in all she said and did. Thinking about the SVMFM later in life, Nettie Clark said, "One reason for the great impression created by the Movement was that it made a clear,

---

6.   For more information on Robert Wilder, see chapter 9.

definite appeal for one cause only, and . . . a great mistake would be made if (it) would now [be] made to cover both foreign and home missions, or the enlistment of young people for anything other than definite missionary work."[7]

Clark served as a missionary in India from 1893 to 1932, mostly in the Punjab region under the auspices of the Presbyterian Board of Foreign Missions. She married Reverend Walter Jackson Clark in 1893 and at the time of her death, she had one son and two daughters. Clark died in Mysore, India, in 1948 of "old age" according to her doctor.[8] She was buried there.

WOMEN'S LEADERSHIP THROUGH GRADUALISM

Although the approach taken by the American SVMFM brought men and women into combined leadership, a majority of SCMs took a gradual approach to men and women's combined leadership on all levels.

An example of this approach could be found in the British movement. Though many men and women in this branch of the SCM wanted men and women to serve as co-equal leaders, they took an incremental approach, where men and women learned to work together over time. Tatlow summarized this approach when he said, "It must not be supposed, however, that the men leaders in Great Britain were advanced feminists. Both the men and women were feeling their way very slowly and cautiously in the matter of joint work at this time."[9]

The WSCF provides another example of a movement taking the gradualist approach. The history of the rise of women leaders in the WSCF was chronicled by Una Mary Josephine Saunders.[10] Her comments were cited in a few studies on WSCF history, notably by Ruth Rouse, Wilmina Rowland, and Johanna Selles.[11]

---

7. Wilbert R. Shenk, *Write the Vision: The Church Renewed* (Eugene, OR: Wipf and Stock, 1995), 108.

8. Nettie Dunn Clark, *Report of Deaths of American Citizens Abroad, 1835–1974*, NARA Inventory 15, Entry 205, 1910–1962, Box 1700: 1945–1949.

9. Tissington Tatlow, *The Story of the Student Christian Movement of Great Britain and Ireland* (London: SCM Press, 1933), 68.

10. Una Saunders, "Women in the WSCF," *Evangel* 18, no. 179 (1906): 13–14. For more details on Una Mary Josephine Saunders, see chapter 14.

11. See Ruth Rouse, *The World's Student Christian Federation: A History of the First Thirty Years* (London: SCM Press, 1948), 99–107; Wilmina M. Rowland, "The Contribution of Ruth Rouse to the World's Student Christian Federation" (MA thesis, Yale University, 1937), 47–51; and Johanna M. Selles, "Women's Role in the History of the World Student Christian Federation, 1895–1945: An Essay Commissioned to Commemorate the Centennial of the Founding of the WSCF," *Yale Divinity School*

Since the WSCF was founded primarily as a men's group, women were at first virtually ignored. Later, some women's groups were affiliated with the WSCF through a men's group. In 1905, women were invited as visitors to that year's WSCF conference, where they tried to act in a way that would gain the men's approval for their leadership. Saunders described what she and the other women went through at the 1905 meeting of the WSCF:

> We tried to behave very well and prove ourselves worthy; we lived submissively in a village a mile away from the men. We attended only such meetings as were open to us, and trooped out obediently when they were over. We tried to win over the implacable enemies of women students by being very discreet and "womanly," and keeping silence as to any ideas that might be seething in our heads.[12]

The women must have swayed the WSCF's male leaders because at the conference two women's leadership positions were established: membership on a woman's cooperating committee and a woman leader for women. Beginning in 1907, women attended meetings of the WSCF as official representatives of their national movements and as members of the cooperating committee. They sat on the WSCF General Committee in 1909 for the first time. Movements could have one woman and three men as committee members. At this time, the cooperating committee was dissolved and a women's subcommittee was appointed as an official small group of the executive. Today's WSCF makes a point of stating that there should be two representatives from each national movement on the executive committee and at least one should be a woman.

WORLD WAR I AND SCM WOMEN LEADERS

Women became SCM leaders because of the outbreak of World War I. The SCM's continued existence demanded that women become movement leaders when almost all able-bodied men were fighting at the front. By default, women assumed almost all the main tasks of many movements, such as committee chair and general secretary. They were assisted by men who could not serve in the military for age or health reasons.

Library Occasional Publication 6 (New Haven, CT: Yale Divinity School Library, 1995), and *The World Student Christian Federation, 1895–1925: Motives, Methods, and Influential Women* (Eugene, OR: Pickwick, 2011).

12. Saunders, "Women in the WSCF," 13.

Two examples of World War I's influence on the role of women are featured later in this book. These are the stories of Leo Viguier (chapter 4) in France and Dora Ivens Pym (chapter 3) in Great Britain.

THE ROLE OF SCM MEN IN WOMEN'S LEADERSHIP DEVELOPMENT

Simply put, women became SCM leaders because for the most part the men supported this. Although there were exceptions, John R. Mott and the men of the SCM generally supported the ministries of women with men and women. And because of this support, women became the leaders they did.

The key figure here was Mott. He was the head male leader of the entire SCM, and how he handled the question of women's leadership affected others, especially the other men.

Mott's approach to women leaders had several aspects. First, Mott focused more on men and their ministries than on women and their ministries. Annie Caroline Macdonald thought Mott had a limited interest in ministries with women in Japan and elsewhere.[13] She hoped to "startle Mr. Mott within an inch of his life. . . . [She wanted him to understand that] half of the population of Japan is women." Much later, Hopkins stated that John R. Mott was "perhaps a bit unappreciative of the role of women in the ecumenical movement."[14]

The fact that he was like this has led people to say he did not support the ministries of women. Yet just because he focused on men's ministries does not mean that he did not support the SCM's women leaders. In fact, in word and action Mott did support the women leaders.

Despite her harsh words, Mott supported Macdonald's ministries in Japan and encouraged her ministries with the WSCF. He also supported the leading woman of the movement, Ruth Rouse. Although Rouse was appointed as a woman's leader, she worked extensively with and served as a leader of men. And he appeared to have no issue with that.

Another significant example was Mott's enthusiastic support of Mary Geraldine Guinness Taylor's ministry with men at the 1894 SVMFM Conference in Detroit, Michigan. Having left London on February 14, 1894, Taylor was on her way to missionary service in China with her future in-laws, Hudson and her stepmother Jane Elizabeth "Jennie"

---

13. For more information on Annie Caroline Macdonald's SCM ministries, see chapter 15.

14. C. H. Hopkins, "The Legacy of John R. Mott," *International Bulletin of Missionary Research* 5, no. 2 (April 1981): 71.

Faulding Taylor, when she gave two speeches.[15] In both cases, Taylor spoke to large crowds of men and women. She shared the podium with John Mott and Hudson Taylor. She also received their wholehearted endorsement. For example, introducing her first speech, Mott said:

> We count all joy tonight that we have Miss Geraldine Guinness, of the China Inland Mission, who has also come from England to be with us during this convention, and who will speak to us now as we carefully listen, as in the presence of him who has sent her.[16]

Mott's unswerving backing here makes it clear that he supported women in their public ministries with men. He said God had sent this woman to speak to the audience, which should listen carefully.

Finally, although Mott's relationship with Elizabeth Clark was a difficult one and might suggest that Mott did not support women leaders in the movement, the fact that Clark also had relational difficulties with Ruth Rouse suggests that there was something more going on there. Johanna Selles explores the relational dynamics between Clark and Mott and Rouse in a rather lengthy discussion.[17]

However, male support for women SCM leaders was not unanimous. An example of this was a close friend and fellow SCM leader,

---

15. The Taylors had left Liverpool on February 14, 1894, and arrived at Ellis Island, New York, on February 24, 1894. After attending this conference, they left immediately for Shanghai, China, and arrived there on April 17, 1894. James Hudson (1832–1905) and his second wife, Jane Elizabeth "Jennie" Faulding Taylor (1843–1904), were Protestant missionaries to China. They spent fifty-one years there and founded the China Inland Mission (now OMF), a nondenominational missions organization. This group was responsible for bringing over eight hundred missionaries to China. It started 125 schools and had more than 300 work stations, 500 native helpers, and over 18,000 conversions. The Taylors had several creative features of their missionary work: an unusually high sensitivity to Chinese culture, which led them to wear Chinese clothes, a zeal for evangelism, and the use of working-class, single women, and multinational recruits. Taylor worked against the opium trade. For more information on the Taylors, see *The Story of the China Inland Mission* 1 and 2 (London: Morgan and Scott, 1893); Frederick Howard Taylor and Mary Geraldine Taylor, *Hudson Taylor in Early Years: The Growth of a Soul* (London: Morgan and Scott, 1911); and Mary Geraldine Taylor, *Hudson Taylor and the China Inland Mission: The Growth of a Work of God* (London: Morgan and Scott, 1918). For sources outside the family, see Ralph R. Covell, "Taylor, James Hudson," in *Biographical Dictionary of Christian Missions*, ed. Gerald H. Anderson (New York: Macmillan, 1998), 657–58.

16. Max Wood Moorhead, ed., *The Student Missionary Enterprise: Addresses and Discussions of the Second International Convention of the SVMFM Held at Detroit, Michigan, February 28 and March 1, 2, 3, and 4, 1894* (Boston: T. Metcalf, 1894), 54.

17. For more information on Elizabeth Clark, see Selles, *World Student Christian Federation*, 139–53, 257, and chapter 8.

William Paton, who told Dora Ivens Pym that British committee leadership was too much for a woman.[18] On a larger scale, concerning the WSCF, Rouse observed, "Revolt against the 'monstrous regiment of women' appeared in more than one country, to which the men leaders returned from the war to find 'our Movement' in the hands of women students, young boys and foreigners."[19] Yet even Paton served with Pym, and in different countries, movements still had women leaders working with men.

THE TRAITS OF SCM WOMEN

The final reason why the SCM had women leaders had to do with the women themselves. The SCM's women leaders broadly construed had similar backgrounds and lifestyles, which prepared them to assume leadership roles in the SCM. They were all part of a fast-changing global society that equipped them for new roles unheard of in previous generations.

Between, 1865 and 1914, the Second Industrial Revolution transformed the global landscape. New technology was quickly replacing outmoded ones. These were very beneficial changes for SCM women leaders. Because the first commercially generated electrical current was readily available beginning in the 1870s, SCM women could go safely to well-lit evening meetings. Telephones (1876), transatlantic cables (the Atlantic, 1886; the Pacific, 1902), and radio waves (1901) made communication easy, cheap, and intercontinental for these women. Finally, transportation changed dramatically with automobiles (1886) and with larger, safer, quicker steel ocean-going vessels replacing slower sail and steam ships. This made local, national, transcontinental, and

---

18.   Writer, preacher, broadcaster, and SCM worker, William Paton (1886–1943) was a graduate of Pembroke College, Oxford, and Westminster College, Cambridge. He served as central volunteer and mission study secretary for the SVMU (1911–1913), assistant general and mission secretary (1911–1919), and mission secretary (1919–1921) for the British SCM. Ordained a Presbyterian hastily so that he could escape prison as a pacifist, he went to India. Paton was very involved in the world ecumenical movement. Paton became general secretary of the National Christian Council of India, Burma, and Ceylon (1922–1927), secretary of the International Missionary Council, and editor of the *International Review of Missions*. In World War II, he argued for the use of military force against fascism and anti-Semitism. For more information on Paton, see E. M. Jackson, "William Paton," in *Mission Legacies: Biographical Studies of the Leaders of the Modern Missionary Movement*, ed. Gerald H. Anderson et al. (Maryknoll, NY: Orbis Books, 1994), 581–90 and Margaret Sinclair, *William Paton* (London: SCM Press, 1949).

19.   Rouse, *World's Student Christian Federation*, 219. Tatlow later observed that around 1918, "The men were optimistic on the whole while the women were pessimistic, unsettled and dissatisfied." They were tired. This phase lasted about a year and a half and then "disappeared." Tatlow, *Story*, 641–42.

international travel available for SCM women to use to develop national and global intercollegiate relationships.

THE NEW MIDDLE CLASS

The Second Industrial Revolution helped create a new middle class. Most SCM women leaders came from this group. Some also came from upper-class homes. No women leaders featured in this book came from lower-class homes.

At the top of this new middle class were the most successful businessmen, industrialists, bankers, and merchants. The larger center of this class was composed of the less successful, but still comfortable, businessmen, industrialists, and merchants, and members of the new professions, such as architecture, accountancy, law, medicine, and civil service. At the lower end of the middle class was a new group of white-collar workers: traveling salesmen, bookkeepers, bank tellers, telephone operators, department store salespeople, office secretaries, and stenographers. The top two sections of this new middle class led solid and comfortable lives in large brownstones in major cities or in large clapboard houses in the burgeoning suburbs and small towns. They had disposable income to spend on fashionable clothes and global travel.

This new middle class dominated turn-of-the-century life, and their values were the standards by which everyone and everything was to be judged. Those in the middle class taught their children, both boys and girls, the importance of individual self-effort, hard work, progress, science, and the value of education. They instructed their offspring in the dominant Protestant faith, which emphasized propriety ("the right way of doing things"), respectability, and church-going. Middle-class parents passed on assumptions about the fixed nature of social structures with each part having its expected role. The traditional family was the central institution of society with male and female roles long established.

More often than not, the parents of the SCM's women had advanced degrees at a time when only a small minority had them. One example would be Ransom Dunn, Nettie Dunn Clark's father, already described in this chapter. Around 1840, he attended Baptist Seminary in New Hampton, New Hampshire, and in 1873, Dunn received an honorary doctorate from Bates College in Maine, which was connected to the seminary.[20]

---

20. Baptist Seminary has also been called Cobb Divinity School, Bates Theological Seminary, and the Free Will Baptist Bible School. It was founded in 1840 and was part of Bates College from 1870 to 1908 when it merged with the college's religion department.

The parents of the SCM's women leaders were community and religious leaders, successful businessmen, planters, doctors, academicians, and lawyers. For example, Lilian Stevenson's father was a minister of a prominent Presbyterian Church in Dublin and the moderator of the General Assembly of the Irish Presbyterian Church.[21] In a highly unusual situation, Addie Waites Hunton's father owned an oyster and shipping business as well as an all-black amusement park in segregated Norfolk, Virginia.[22] Because of their parents, SCM women belonged to families with close connections to the main corridors of economic, social, political, and religious power.

Typical of these women was Canadian Margaret Christian Wrong, born into a prominent Toronto family as an Anglican. Her well-connected, imperial-minded family gave her social training, graces, and contacts. Wrong was the daughter of George Mackinnon or McKinnon (1860–1948) and Sophie Hume Blake Wrong (1859–1931), the daughter of Edward Blake, the second premier of Canada, leader of the Canadian liberal Labor Party and a member of the British House of Commons. Wrong's father was an ordained Anglican clergyman, a professor and head of the Department of History at the University of Toronto and a Round Table enthusiast. She had three brothers and one sister. One brother, Humphrey Hume Wrong (1894–1954) became a historian at Magdalen College, Oxford, and a Canadian ambassador to the United States.[23]

As middle- and upper-class women, most SCM women leaders were members of prominent Protestant denominations. In her analysis of the prominent American women of 1914, Barbara Kuhn Campbell stated that the following churches were the most dominant and established Protestant faiths at this time: Anglican/Episcopal, Presbyterian, Congregational, the Methodist Episcopal Church, South, the African Methodist Episcopal Church, Quakers, and the Reformed Churches.[24] The SCM's women leaders were members of these faith communities. Examples here included Anglicans Ella Cara Deloria and Michi Kawai. Annie Caroline Macdonald was a Presbyterian, and Edith Wiley and Dr. Mary Pauline Root were Congregationalists.

This means that Ransom Dunn was a member of one of the first classes of this institution.

21. For more information on Lilian Stevenson and her family background, see chapter 8.

22. For more information on Addie Waites Hunton and her family background, see chapter 13.

23. For more information on Sophie Hume Blake Wrong, see chapter 12.

24. See Barbara Kuhn Campbell, *Liberated Woman of 1914: Prominent Women in the Progressive Era,* Studies in American History and Culture 6 (Ann Arbor, MI: UMI Research Press, 1979).

Perhaps even more interesting here are the religious roots of some for these women. Michi Kawai came from a 2,000-year line of Shinto priests and converted to Christianity. Ruth Rouse was a member of Charles Spurgeon's London congregation, but later switched to Anglicanism.

By the turn of the century, this same middle class inadvertently fostered the development of a new lifestyle for women. This came as a shock to many middle-class parents, who had a difficult time figuring out what was happening to their daughters and why it was occurring. As Peter G. Filene observed, "Many parents during the last third of the nineteenth century were sitting late at night and asking in worried tones, 'What is the matter with our Mary, our Minnie, our Maude? Why is she so reckless, so rebellious, so intent upon disgrace?'"[25]

Two important facets of this change for SCM women were access to higher education and an independent spirit. The first was the direct result of their parent's wealth and support, and the second was partially the result of this educational process.

ACCESS TO EDUCATION

Increasing numbers of daughters of the new middle class had the desire, parental support, and financial wherewithal to attend high school and college. This choice to pursue higher education meant that a woman turned her back on the assumption that after high school, a woman was to remain in her parent's home until a proper suitor could be found.

Many SCM women had the support of parents or legal guardians to pursue educational opportunities. The parents of Ruth Rouse provide a good example. They invited Adelaide Anderson, an 1887 Moral Sciences Tripos graduate of Girton College, into their home when Rouse was eleven years old. Her parents' forethought assured that Rouse would at least see a role model of an educated woman.[26] Suzanne de Dietrich's

---

25.   Peter Gabriel Filene, *Him/Her/Self: Sex Roles in Modern America* (New York: Harcourt Brace Jovanovich, 1974), 21. For a very good sense of the angst women felt, see Filene, *Him/Her/Self*, and Carolyn Forrey, "The New Woman Revisited," *Women's Studies* 2, no. 1 (January 1, 1974): 37–56.

26.   Adelaide Anderson (1863–1936), later Dame Anderson, was a British civil servant and labor activist. She was interested in child labor practices in China. Anderson was the HM Principal Lady Inspector of Factories from 1897 to 1921. While her Wikipedia article makes no reference to Anderson's possible Christian connections, other references do. See Adelaide Anderson, *Humanity and Labour in China: An Industrial Visit and Its Sequel, 1923–1928*, which was published by the SCM in 1928. See also Adelaide Anderson, *Women in the Factory: An Administrative Adventure, 1893–1921* (London: Murray, 1922).

legal guardian believed that she should receive the same education as a man, and he praised her for her intelligence.

The supreme example of a parent's support for a daughter's education was Ume Tsuda's father, Sen Tsuda. From personal experience, he knew how much an exposure to America and its education system would broaden his daughter's opportunities.[27] So Sen Tsuda allowed his daughter to participate in the experimental education program that sent her to the United States in 1871 at age six.[28]

By 1900 over 80 percent of American colleges and universities and professional schools admitted women. Acknowledging this fact in a 1905 speech, Ruth Rouse argued that Christian work with women collegians had become a necessity because their numbers had increased markedly.[29]

In a report at the same time, Ruth Rouse offered some statistics to back up her point. Starting from either no women students or negligible numbers, she said that United States had 40,000 women college students by 1905. In Great Britain, the number had jumped from 2,500 in 1895 to 5,000 in 1905.[30]

Using percentages instead of numbers, a recent scholar, Nancy Woloch, noted similar statistics for the women of the United States:[31]

	1870	1880	1890	1990	1910	1920
17-year-old high school grads	2.0	2.5	3.5	6.4	8.8	16.8
high school grads, women	56.3	54.6	56.8	60.0	59.6	60.5
18- to 22-year-olds in college	1.68	2.72	2.99	3.91	4.99	7.88
undergrads, women	21.3	32.7	35.9	35.9	39.6	47.3
BA or BS degrees awarded to women	14.7	19.3	17.3	19.1	22.7	34.2
PhD women	0	5.6	1.3	6.0	9.9	15.1

27.   Sen Tsuda traveled to the United States in 1867 with Tomogoro Ono, the treasurer of the Shogunate, who was sent to demand the delivery of a warship Japan had purchased from an American shipbuilder. He was struck with the advanced state of American science, technology, and agricultural methods. Tsuda was also impressed with American democracy.

28.   For more information on Tsuda, see chapter 14.

29.   Ruth Rouse, "Extracts from Report on Women's Work under the WSCF, Presented at the Women's Section of the Conference at Driebergen, Holland, May 5, 1905," in *Report of the Conference of the WSCF Held at Zeist, Holland, May 3–5, 1905* (New York: WSCF, 1905), 121–33.

30.   Ibid., 121–22.

31.   Nancy Woloch, *Women and the American Experience* (New York: Alfred A. Knopf, 1984), 543.

SCM women leaders were part of these statistics. Almost all had high school diplomas or undergraduate degrees at a time when they were a statistical minority of men and women and highly privileged. Undergraduate degrees came from many of the world's most prestigious private and public institutions, such as Smith College, Cornell University, Johns Hopkins University, Occidental College, Oberlin College, Columbia University, Bryn Mawr College, University of Toronto, Girton College, Cambridge, Newnham and Somerville Colleges, Oxford, Queen Margaret College, Glasgow, Leipzig University, and University of Lausanne.

Even more astounding than the number of SCM women with undergraduate degrees, is the number who had graduate degrees or graduate study. This was at a time when having these degrees or opportunities for study was even rarer than having an undergraduate education.

These women attended graduate schools of theology (Bertha Condé, Michi Kawai, and Edith Wiley), general studies (Margaret Wrong), medical school (Drs. Mary Pauline Root and Emmeline Stuart), and law school (Olga Kuleshova). Graduate degrees came from the Women's Medical College of Pennsylvania, University of Zurich, and an unnamed law school in St. Petersburg, Russia. A few spent an extra year or two in specialized study. Ruth Rouse and Agnes de Selincourt were students in a one-year program of Sanskrit study.

AN INDEPENDENT SPIRIT

Besides access to higher education, another aspect of the change in women's lives was the development of an independent spirit.

Suzanne de Dietrich stands out in this regard. She chose a different path from the one presented to her as a child, which in itself was unique for a woman at the time. Born into a wealthy family, Suzanne de Dietrich's family assumed that their offspring, even the women, interestingly enough, would be involved in their metal-foundry business. As a result, she studied engineering in a pre-college course at an all-boys school and at the University of Lausanne, she was one of three women in a class of eighty.

However, armed with an independent streak, de Dietrich chose her own career with the SCM. Her family accepted her decision, though they were not happy about it. Looking back on this vocational choice in a 1971 interview, she said, "I worked extremely hard to get a diploma in engineering which I never used, and I have not done enough study for what is now my life work."[32]

---

32. Hans-Ruedi Weber, *The Courage to Live: A Biography of Suzanne de Dietrich* (Geneva: WCC Publications, 1995), 21.

NEW CAREERS

Many middle-class women began to establish themselves as "prominent" in society. This prominence was due to their efforts, not the efforts of the men in their lives. And many of these women were self-supporting. Thus by 1914 some nine thousand American women were considered eminent enough by an editor familiar with the standards of prominence for men, to warrant inclusion in a literal who's who of prominent women.[33]

As part of this, women began to enter many professional fields, including the most esteemed professions of law and medicine.[34] According to Woloch, the percentage of women in the professions of law, academia, nursing, and social work all increased between 1870 and 1920. To take just one example, in 1870, 12 percent of all academics were women, but by 1920, the number had risen to 26.3 percent.[35]

Many SCM women leaders had long-time professional positions within the SCM, such as secretaries like Zoe Barbara Fairfield and pioneers like Olga Kuleshova, Almira Leavitt, Suzanne de Dietrich, and Annie Caroline Macdonald. Although appointed to work exclusively with women, many of these professionals developed extensive ministries, sometimes exclusive ministries, with men. Other professionals worked with men from start to finish.

Many of the SCM's women leaders launched their careers in the movement, but moved to new positions outside the SCM after extensive periods of SCM work. The movement had provided them with valuable experience and had taught them leadership skills. They took these credentials into other ministries or into nonministry positions.

Examples here were Rena Carswell Datta, Bertha Condé, and Ruth Rouse. Joining the rising numbers of new office workers, Datta

---

33. Campbell, *Liberated Woman*, xi.

34. For women's efforts to enter traditionally male professions, see Clara Collet, *Educated Working Women: Essays on the Economic Position of Women Workers in the Middle Classes* (London: P. S. King and Son, 1902), and Edith Morley, ed., *Women Workers in Seven Professions: A Survey of Their Economic Conditions and Prospects* (London: G. Routledge and Sons, 1914). For more recent studies, see Roy Lubove, *The Professional Altruist: The Emergence of Social Work as a Career, 1880–1930* (Cambridge, MA: Harvard University Press, 1965); D. Kelley Weisberg, "Barred from the Bar: Women and Legal Education in the United States, 1870–1890," *Journal of Legal Education* 38 (1977): 485–507; Mary Roth Walsh, *Doctors Wanted: No Woman Need Apply* (New Haven, CT: Yale University Press, 1977); Barbara Harris, *Beyond Her Sphere: Women and the Professions in American History* (Westport, CT: Grenwood Press, 1978); and Rosalind Rosenberg, *Beyond Separate Spheres: Intellectual Roots of Modern Feminism* (New Haven, CT: Yale University Press, 1982).

35. Woloch, *Women and the American Experience*, 543.

was employed as Rouse's personal secretary until she married.[36] Bertha Condé, after over twenty years of SCM work, became an evangelist to educated, agnostic women in the 1920s and 1930s. After more than twenty-five years of SCM-related work, Rouse directed student relief efforts after World War I, held influential posts in the Church of England, and was the World's YWCA President during World War II.

Other women featured in this book had careers outside the SCM and interacted with the movement many times. For example, before, during, and after giving speeches and traveling for the SVMFM, Mary Geraldine Guinness Taylor carried out her missionary work in China and authored many books and articles. Between working with SCM groups, Jane Addams developed and became director of Hull House and was an activist in the peace movement, suffrage work, and labor relations.[37]

NEW VARIETIES OF INTIMACY

The women leaders of the SCM chose a variety of intimate relationships, each rejecting the traditional view that women were happiest when innocent, submissive, and domestic, the wife of a dominant man and the mother of many children.

---

36. For several years, Alexandrina McArthur "Rena" Carswell Datta (1886–1978) was Rouse's personal secretary, and in 1933 she was secretary of the WSCF's International Student Service. She was born in Glasgow, Scotland, to Malcomb (1856–1892) and Elizabeth Forsyth (1861?–?) Carswell. Her father was a timber merchant. She had two sisters. Datta graduated from Greenock Academy and Hillhead High School, Glasgow, and Queen Margaret College, Glasgow, with a bachelor of arts degree in 1908. Although she had a long formal name, Datta is repeatedly called Rena in records. During her college years, she was treasurer from 1905 to 1906 and president of her college union from 1906 to 1908. After college, Datta was intercollegiate secretary for Glasgow from 1908 to 1909 and traveling secretary for the SVMU from 1909 to 1910. In the 1911 British Census, she was listed as an SCM secretary, living in West Sussex, south of London on the coast. Datta supported the work of her husband, Surendra Kumar Datta, whom she married in India in 1919. They were married for fifty-eight years and had one child. She spent many years in Lahore, India (now Pakistan), because of her husband's work at Forman Christian College. There he was a lecturer from 1909 to 1914, principal from 1932 to 1942, and president beginning in 1942. Forman had been founded by a Presbyterian missionary, Charles William Forman, whose son John Newton Forman was one of the founders of the Student Volunteer Movement. During the 1930s, Rena Datta organized European tours for Indian women students. The two Dattas have been honored with a statue at Forman Christian College. A 2003 article titled "FC College: A Pandora's Box," states, "The tall ponderous and stately figure of Principal S. K. Datta and his equally well-built Irish wife, were almost omnipresent on the college premises." See archives.dawn.com (June 1, 2003), Pakistan Herald Publication, Karachi, Pakistan. Later in life Rena Carswell Datta was appointed by the National Birth Control Association to organize birth control services in India. She died at age ninety-one in Kensington, West End, London.

37. For more information on Jane Addams, see chapter 15.

One group chose new ways of handling marital life. Though Addie Waites Hunton and Edith Wiley assumed the role of helper and assistant to their husbands, they still did some things quite differently than most of their predecessors.

Rather than staying solely in the domestic realm, Hunton combined YMCA and YWCA work, women's club activities, and motherhood (she had four children). She often traveled with her husband, and acted as his secretary, handling trip details, correspondence, and his magazine. Hunton edited *The Messenger*, even though a male was the official editor. She gave speeches and sat on organizational boards.

Wiley was originally appointed as a joint missionary with her husband; so in the early years they did missionary work together. Subsequently, she assumed the role of a pastor's wife on the mission field. Later in life, Wiley became an active nondomestic missionary again. In her retirement, she and her husband were both declared "missionary emeriti."

Another group formed companionate marriages. Popular at the time, husband and wife acted as co-equal partners in all decisions and were good friends. Dora Ivens Pym had this type of marriage with Thomas Wentworth Pym. She was married while chair of the British Executive Committee and led a meeting only five days later. In their first apartment, they each had a study; hers was the larger of the two. After they had children (two sons and two daughters), Pym continued to work outside the home on a part-time basis. Thomas Pym believed that every father should be actively involved in the raising of children and that every man should consider the impact a move to a new position would have on his wife's profession. As her husband became increasingly debilitated with sclerosis, Pym courageously assumed the burden of family support by working full-time outside of the home.[38]

A third and quite large group of SCM women leaders never married or had children. In fact, most of the women featured in this book remained single. Just a few examples are Zoe Barbara Fairfield, Bertha Condé, Winifred Sedgwick, Ella Cara Deloria, and Ume Tsuda. Studies show that if a woman had a college education at the turn of the century,

---

38. Anglican clergyman, theologian, and writer Thomas Wentworth Pym (1885–1945) was the son of Right Reverend Walter Ruthven Pym, Anglican bishop of Bombay, India. He was educated at Bedford School and then Trinity College, Cambridge. He served as a chaplain there. During World War I, Pym was assistant chaplain-general to the British Third Army. In 1922, he was appointed chaplain to King George V; in 1925, canon of Southwark Cathedral; in 1929, canon of Bristol Cathedral; and in 1932, chaplain and fellow in Theology at Balliol College at Oxford. In 1917 Pym was invested as a Companion of the Distinguished Service Order, a military decoration for meritorious service in wartime, typically in actual combat, by military officers. For more information on Dora Ivens Pym, see chapter 3.

she decreased her chances for marriage because of the lack of appropriate suitors for a college-educated woman. In addition, it was often held that marriage was incompatible with a career.[39]

These women chose to remain single or never had the opportunity to marry. Tsuda refused to have an arranged marriage, believing that one married for love only. Rouse never married because of her view of marriage as a refuge in which one was "sheltered and cared for and happy."[40]

To make up for the lack of emotional bonding that marriage provided, these women formed networks with other professional women inside and outside the SCM.[41] Sexual or not, women's same-sex relationships were especially popular at this time.

In 1902, Tsuda set up a household with female friends with herself as head, a symbolic feminist gesture in nineteenth-century Japan. The closest suggestion for same-sex relationships comes from Jane Addams. She considered Ellen Starr and Mary Rozet Smith her closest confidants. The latter lived with Addams for over forty years and became her most treasured intimate and constant companion. According to Woloch, Jane Addams "became the confidante of Ellen Starr, whose support and affection surpassed what any man could offer."[42]

Even though SCM women leaders such as Wiley attributed their ministries to calls from God, these women joined men in the central corridors of movement power for other reasons. Because of the SCM's guiding principles, the constitutions of different movements, gradualism, World War I, and the movement's men, and the women themselves, this notable group of women became leaders of women, men, and in mixed groups of men and women.

---

39. Joyce Antler, "The Educated Woman and Professionalization: The Struggle for a New Feminine Identity, 1890–1920" (PhD diss., State University of New York, 1977).

40. Ruth Franzén, "The Legacy of Ruth Rouse," *International Bulletin of Missionary Research* 17, no. 4. (October 1993): 156.

41. See "The Female World of Love and Ritual: Between Women in Nineteenth-Century America," in Carroll Smith-Rosenberg, *Disorderly Conduct: Visions of Gender in Victorian America* (New York: Alfred A. Knopf, 1985), 53–76.

42. Woloch, *Women*, 257.

3

Committee Members and Officers

In the February 9, 1930, edition of the *Syracuse Herald*, sixty-nine-year-old Bertha Condé, the well-known Student Christian Movement (SCM) committee member, world traveler, inspirational speaker, and author, said for the first time why she had chosen her career track. Condé told of a childhood dream or message that she felt impelled her to preach to women. Even though the primary subjects of her messages were women, her life was full of joint leadership experiences with men.

Using the same words over and over again in this interview, Condé said, "Focus your life on Jesus." To her, "For each person to focus his or her life on Jesus is the practical thing which makes for happiness and a radiant life." Continuing, she said, "Focus your life on Jesus and on service, and the picture of your life will remain clear and sharp and gorgeously colored in the minds and hearts of your friends and leave lasting impressions on every soul you meet."[1]

Committee member Bertha Condé's inspiration for SCM work was mirrored in the lives and ministries of other SCM women. As Christians in committee leadership, they were called to serve Jesus Christ and to challenge those around them to do likewise. They worked with men and women.

Of all the committees that the SCM had, the two most important were the executive committee and the advisory committee. The work of women executive committee members will be explored first through the ministries of American and British women on the American Student Volunteer Movement for Foreign Missions (SVMFM) and British SCM executive committees. The ministry of women on the American SVMFM Advisory Committee will be described through the life of Abbie Bullock Child.

SCM executive committees also had officers, chairs, vice-chairs, treasurers, and secretaries to direct these small groups. No woman served as an officer of the American movement between 1880 and 1920, during

---

1. "Lives Her Own Doctrine after Dream during Childhood Spent in Auburn, World Traveler," *Syracuse Herald*, February 9, 1930, sections 3, 4, and 5, with photo.

World War I, probably because John Mott, the chair, was too old to join the military and served in this capacity.

Outside of North America, only a handful of women held these posts between 1880 and 1920. They served between 1914 and 1920 solely because of the absence of men during World War I. Because of her visibility as head of the British SCM, arguably the most prestigious SCM in the international movement, Dora Ivens Pym is the best example of a woman serving as a chair of an entire movement's committee.

AMERICAN SCM EXECUTIVE COMMITTEE MEMBERS

Two examples of American SCM women committee members were Bertha Condé and Dr. Mary Pauline Root. They both served on committees that included men and women. and their committee work shows the wide range of ways women understood their role in these leadership groups.

BERTHA CONDÉ (1871–1944)

Bertha Condé had a reputation as a world traveler, religious worker, and inspirational speaker. She was also an author, evangelist for women in secular organizations, pastor of men and women, and SCM committee member. A typical assessment of Condé was made when her book *What's Life All About? A Key for Those Who Ask the Question*[2] was announced. The *Oakland Tribune* stated, "Out of her experiences of speaking to people she has formed an opinion of what they wish. She knows men and women, what they seek and how to answer their problems."[3]

The events of Condé's life and professional career can be pieced together from a combination of SVMFM executive committee minutes, YWCA records, newspaper clippings, and her articles and books. This can be done despite Rouse's judgment that little would be remembered about Condé because she did not leave any papers. One official paper, titled "Correspondence of John R. Mott with Miss Bertha Condé (U.S.A) July 15, 1899–February 28, 1925," reports "in the whole of this correspondence, there is singularly little of interest, considering that for twenty years, Miss Condé was the leading student secretary in the U.S.A."[4]

---

2. Bertha Condé, *What's Life All About? A Key for Those Who Ask the Question* (New York: Scribner, 1930)

3. Bertha Condé, "What's Life All About? Bertha Condé Answers," *Oakland Tribune*, July 6, 1930, 10-S.

4. Ruth Rouse, Archives of the WSCF, Record Group 46 (Box 44, Folder 326), Special Collections, Yale Divinity School Library.

Bertha Condé
(Special Collections, Yale Divinity School)

Condé was born in Auburn, New York, to Reverend Samuel Lee (1837–1919), a minister, and Edith Collier Condé (1833–1918). She had two sisters and lived with one in New York City for part of her life. She was a direct descendant of the French Huguenot family of de Condé, conspicuous in French history. After graduating from Smith College (1895) with BA in natural sciences, Condé became a professor at Elmira College, Elmira, New York (1895–1897). Later she worked at the Christadora Settlement House, where Rouse later would claim she discovered her in 1898.[5] Condé later studied, but did not graduate from, the Free Church of Scotland School of Theology, Glasgow, Scotland.

Condé visited leading universities and colleges to promote Christian work in America, Western Europe, Asia, and the Balkan States. She gave addresses in almost every college in the United States on subjects relating to Christian faith and service, and enlisted many students for Christian social service at home and abroad.

---

5.   For more details on the Christadora Settlement House, see chapter 15.

An example of Condé's speaking ministry was her 1930 speech to the Girls' Friendly Society, an organization that empowered girls and young women to develop their gifts and talents. It was founded by English Anglicans in 1875 to address the problems of working-class out-of-wedlock pregnancies through Christian values.[6] Condé's audience of over three hundred included a small number of men. She talked about values that were based on Jesus Christ as the key to success and happiness.

She also helped organize the Central Club for Nurses in New York City, and she was a member of the Woman's University Club.

Although early in life a Presbyterian, later on Condé had associations with the Protestant Episcopal Church. Her funeral was held in Boston, and it was conducted by an Episcopal curate, the Reverend Peter Blynn, Church of the Advent, an Anglo-Catholic parish. Her obituary accompanied with a picture appeared in the Episcopal Church's denominational magazine, *The Living Church*.[7] Condé supported women's suffrage. She never married. She died in 1944 at age seventy-three after a seven-year illness and was buried in Redding Ridge, Connecticut.

Condé's writings include *The Business of Being a Friend*; *The Human Element in the Making of a Christian: Studies in Spiritual Evangelism*; "Hopeful Signs," *Spiritual Adventuring: Studies in Jesus' Way of Life*; *The Way to Peace, Health and Power: Studies in the Inner Life*; and *Spiritual Adventures in Social Relations*.[8]

BERTHA CONDÉ AND
THE SVMFM EXECUTIVE COMMITTEE

Rouse used the term "yeoman" for Condé's SCM service. This was an interesting choice of terms, but it was not clear why she used it.[9] However, what is known about Condé is that in her lengthy profes-

---

6.   Bertha Condé, "Ideals Essential to Radiant Living, GFS Told," *Syracuse Herald*, February 4, 1930, 3, with photo. For more information on the Girls' Friendly Society, see Elizabeth Vaughan Jones, *One Hundred Years of the Girls' Friendly Society, 1875–1975* (Bristol, England: Girls Friendly Society, 1975).

7.   Deaths: Bertha Condé, *Living Church* 109, no. 10 (September 3, 1944): 21.

8.   Bertha Condé, *The Business of Being a Friend* (Boston: Houghton Mifflin, 1916); *The Human Element in the Making of a Christian: Studies in Personal Evangelism* (New York: Charles Scribner's Sons, 1917); "Hopeful Signs," *Fisk University News* 6 (February 1918): 30; *Spiritual Adventuring: Studies in Jesus' Way of Life* (Nashville, TN: Cokesbury Press, 1926); *The Way to Peace, Health and Power: Studies in the Inner Life* (New York: Scribner, 1930); and *Spiritual Adventures in Social Relations* (Nashville, TN: Cokesbury Press, 1931).

9.   Ruth Rouse, *Bertha Condé (USA)*, n.d., Archives of WSCF, Record Group No. 46 (Box 84, Folder 681), 1, Special Collections, Yale Divinity School.

sional SCM career, this single woman served on the SVMFM executive (1899–1920), the WSCF executive (1909–1920), and the council for the North American Student Movements (1914–1920).[10]

Condé held her SVMFM committee post longer than any other woman and all but two men. Only John R. Stevenson as committee vice-chair (1898–1920) and John R. Mott as committee chair (1888–1920) served longer than Condé.[11]

Besides her committee work, Condé served as YWCA secretary (1898–1920), eventually becoming the senior student secretary for that group. She was a delegate to the WSCF Conference in Constantinople in 1911.

As an SVMFM committee member, Condé was quite outspoken. She participated and facilitated discussions with men and women.

The group's minutes show that Condé offered more prayers and more motions than any other member. For example, on December 10, 1902, speaking on behalf of the American YWCA, she made a motion that General Secretary Fennell Turner attend an upcoming YWCA secretary's conference in his official capacity with the SVMFM. As with most of her motions, this one was approved.

Condé served on numerous subcommittees, such as those dealing with budgetary issues, annual conference preparation, and staff. She and two men were appointed on January 29, 1913, to decide if a man named Murray could officially represent the American SVMFM at an upcoming German SVM convention. This last role demonstrates that Condé was not limited to dealing with only women's issues.

An even more obvious indication of Condé's leading role in committee work came with her actions to create consensus. No one else, male or female, was mentioned as having a similar impact in the 1880–1920 minutes. Consensus was the approach taken for significant concerns before the SCM. From personal experience, English committee member Eric Fenn described this process:

> The process of forming a common judgment that shall be true to facts and fair to the different points of view is a complicated business, and in most organizations it is almost always cut short by majority vote. I have never known an important

---

10. The Council for the North American Student Movements was a short-lived committee (1914–1920) with representatives from all North American SCMs. It published the *North American Student* (1914–1919) jointly with the YMCA.

11. John R. Stevenson later become president of Princeton Seminary (1914–1936) and represented the modernist position during the Fundamentalist-Modernist controversies of the 1920s and 1930s.

decision taken, in the Movement, in that way. Discussion and prayer have always gone on until the decision reached has carried the active assent of all parties—and that seldom by vote, and almost always by the chairman putting to the meeting a line of policy which met with general approval, and which was yet not a compromise which meant nothing at all. And such a method means not only that, on the whole, sound decisions are reached for the policy of the Movement, but that members of the committee are continually being educated in co-operative thinking and action, so that the minority opinion never feels it is being coerced.[12]

Committee minutes suggested Condé directed this consensus building when dealing with two issues. In one instance, on September 3, 1910, during a discussion of what changes were necessary to improve the movement's effectiveness, Condé helped the group decide that a thorough investigation of the actual reasons for the falling off in the numbers of volunteers be carried out before any changes were actually made.

On a second occasion, in a series of discussions on what kind of journal the SVMFM should have, Condé guided the committee to publish a mixed-gender SVMFM journal. She made it quite clear that she wanted a journal that represented the interests of all movements linked with the SVMFM, both men and women. On September 23, 1907, Condé said it was hard to get students (i.e., women students) interested in the *Intercollegian* because other student periodicals existed and the magazine's whole preparation was "from the standpoint of men."[13]

Thanks to Condé and the ensuing discussion, the executive voted to have one broader student newspaper representing all student movements in North America (YWCA, YMCA, SVMFM, and the Canadian YWCA). Plans were made to negotiate with these movements about the upcoming periodical. The committee also wanted to have a strong editor with no gender specified.

Three years later, on September 13, 1910, the failure of the *Intercollegian* as the sole SCM magazine was again discussed, where it was made clear that neither the YWCA nor the SVMFM liked this arrangement. During this discussion Condé made two motions that the minutes recorded were carried "decisively." Condé moved that the SVMFM terminate its present arrangement of publishing a joint YWCA/

---

12.   Eric Fenn, *Learning Together* (London: SCM Press, 1939), 22–23.

13.   The *Intercollegian* was published in 1887–1891, 1893–1912, and 1918–1930. Condé was dealing with the fourth series printed from October 1898 (21, no. 1) to December 1912 (35, no. 3). This series was published jointly by the YMCA and the SVMFM.

Mary Pauline Root
(Special Collections, Yale Divinity School)

SVMFM journal, and instead publish a more comprehensive journal with an editorial board representing the different organizations. Condé also moved that if this arrangement did not work, the SVMFM should begin to publish its own magazine separate from these organizations. The former approach was taken, and finally in 1913, *The North American Student* was launched with George Irving as editor (appointed November 19, 1912).

MARY PAULINE ROOT (1859–1944)

What most people know about mid-nineteenth-century American women physicians comes from the popular 1990s TV show, *Dr. Quinn, Medicine Woman*. Actress Jane Seymour played Dr. Michaela Quinn, a fictional 1860 graduate of the Women's Medical College of Pennsylvania who practiced medicine in Colorado Springs, Colorado.

A real life Dr. Michaela Quinn was Dr. Mary Pauline Root. Root served on the American SVMFM Executive Committee during the 1897–1998, 1900–1902, and 1903–1904 school years.[14] Like the fictional Dr.

---

14. For more information on Root, see Catharine MacFarlane, "Account of Dr.

Quinn, Root traveled far from home to practice medicine. One place where Root served was India.

Mary Pauline Root was born in Providence, Rhode Island, and her parents were Harry Theodore (1830–1914) and Mary Evelyn Lake (1835–1876) Root. According to the 1880 United States Census, she was the eldest of nine offspring. Root's father was a dealer in quality furniture. Root was a member of the Congregational Church.

Root graduated from Ingham University, LeRoy, New York, and was an early graduate of the Woman's Medical College of Pennsylvania (1883). Her March 15, 1883, Commencement Bulletin noted that her special focus was Pathology of Tubercule.

Root held a postgraduate Blockley Scholarship from Blockley Hospital, Philadelphia (1883–1884). This scholarship was earned through a competitive exam and resulted with her appointment as the first woman resident and physician. She was one of thirty-seven applicants for Philadelphia Hospital (Blockley) in 1883, and she was one of twelve appointed. Many women interns and doctors followed Root's footsteps.

In her career, Root was director of a women's hospital in Madura, India (1885–1891) under the American Board of Commissioners for Foreign Missions, a medical doctor at Cornell Medical Center (1904–1906), a resident medical doctor at Smith College (1906–1909) and at the Bennett School, Millbrook, New York (1909–1911). Root was a member of the Rhode Island Medical Society.

Root never married. At eighty-five years of age, she died and was buried in South Bristol, Maine.

Records indicate that Root said very little at executive committee meetings, while men and other women spoke. When she did speak, Root gave opening or closing prayers alone or with another man on September 4, 1901, and June 6, 1902. She was appointed to a committee to find female secretarial candidates on March 3, 1902, and April 16, 1902. Root gave a report to the committee on her efforts on June 6, 1902.

Mary Pauline Root's Admission to Blockley Hospital." Root told MacFarlane this story as they were driving along Maine roads on August 23, 1929 (SC, Folder 18, and Mary Pauline Root Papers, Related Materials to Catherine MacFarlane, ACC 257, Catharine MacFarlane Papers, Manuscripts, College of Medicine Legacy Center, Drexel University http://dla.library.upenn.edu); "Mary Pauline Root" ("Accession 257, Collections: Guide to the Women in Medicine Collections, Accessions, 241–60, Archives and Special Collections, Drexel University College of Medicine, http://archives.drexelmed.edu); The College of Physicians of Philadelphia, *The College of Physicians of Philadelphia*, The Images of America Series (Mt. Pleasant, SC: Arcadia Publishing, 2012); and "Mary Pauline Root," in *Woman's Who's Who of America, 1914–1915: A Biographical Dictionary of Contemporary Women of the United States and Canada*, ed. John Williams Leonard (New York: American Commonwealth, 1914), 701.

Even though her participation was less significant than Condé's, Root's committee work was still trend-setting. She was willing to work as a leader with men, and was theoretically and legally equal with men. Her background, education, career, and marital status suggests that she represented a new outlook on women's lives. Yet when combined with Root's opposition to women's suffrage, this suggests that her work with men in the public arena had boundaries.

BRITISH SCM EXECUTIVE COMMITTEE MEMBERS

The British Movement had very vocal women in committees of men and women as well as in committees made up of women only. For example, in 1893, one year after the establishment of the British SCM, a woman student volunteer proposed "out of the blue" that women be permitted to sit on the then all-male Student Volunteer Missionary Union executive at the mixed SVMU convention held at Keswick. The men readily agreed, but told them that they would have preferred to have heard that request privately. At this point, the women also decided to appoint one woman to speak for them.

But things changed in just a few short years. Instead of the 1893 request that women bring their concerns to the men in private and through one woman's voice, women were asked to fully participate in all committee discussions. In 1904, in a vigorous debate between men and women over the tone and spiritual impact of the movement's conferences, the committee decided that each woman should speak for herself with no one woman speaking for the rest. From the women's perspective, it took a great deal of courage to speak freely and make motions in this combined setting thereby going against the existing power relations.

British SCM chroniclers Tissington Tatlow and Wilmina Rowland both claimed that this unknown woman who spoke up in 1893 was Agnes de Selincourt.[15]

AGNES DE SELINCOURT (1872–1917)

Agnes de Selincourt was a missionary, educator, author, and SCM leader. Known to be extremely bright, she was reputed to have a working knowledge of fourteen languages. De Selincourt was known

---

15. Tissington Tatlow, interview with Wilmina M. Rowland, January 1937. In Wilmina M. Rowland, "The Contribution of Ruth Rouse to the World's Student Christian Federation" (MA thesis, Yale University, 1937), 51. For more information on de Selincourt, see "Agnes de Selincourt," *Girton Review* (Michaelmas Term 1917): 7–9.

Agnes de Selincourt
(From Tatlow, The Story of the Student Christian Movement, *76)*

to be a good speaker and a person who not only created fresh ideas but also carried them out to fruition.

De Selincourt was born in London to Charles Alexandre (1835–1900), a naturalized British citizen of French derivation, and Theodora Bruce Bendall (1842–1913) de Selincourt. In the 1891 British Census, Charles Alexandre was listed as a cloth and silk merchant. Agnes had five brothers and two sisters. A younger brother, Ernest de Selincourt was a literary scholar and eventually became the vice principal of the University of Birmingham.

With her best friend, Ruth Rouse, de Selincourt was educated at Dover, Notting Hill High School, and Girton College (1894 with a First Class in Medieval and Modern Language Tripos). Between 1895 and 1896, she spent one year's study of Asian languages at Somerville College, Oxford. After college, de Selincourt taught for one year at Sheffield High School.

De Selincourt was active in SCM circles at many different times in her life. Joining Rouse, she established and directed the Girton College

Christian Union. The two women helped several independent SCMs in British women's colleges join the British SCM.

Later, she went with three other British women to Bombay, India, to establish the Missionary Settlement for University Women. These institutions served as hostels for Indian women students. They would offer medical, educational and evangelistic services.

Forced to leave Bombay because of poor health, de Selincourt moved 723 miles northeast to be the first principal of Lady Muir Memorial College, Allahabad, India (now Pakistan). She remained there from 1899 to 1909. There she was "'intensely interested to watch the development of these girls whose commitment to intellectual pursuits were an 'encouragement for the future' and the students' 'fellow-countrywomen.'"[16]

In 1900, she accompanied Mary Fraser on a walking tour of the Kula Valley in Northern India.

Recurring poor health compelled her to return to England, where she worked as a British SCM traveling secretary (1909–1913). In 1911, de Selincourt served with men and women on the executive committee for the Second Missionary Conference on Behalf of the Mohammedan World, held in Lucknow. There she argued for a women's ministry to upper-class Muslim women.

De Selincourt succeeded Constance Maynard as the principal of Westfield College, London, from 1913 to 1917.[17] She was the first person to use the word principal. At Westfield, she launched public lectures on popular topics and invited the public to attend. She died in 1917 at age forty-five from the effects of a tetanus shot after a bicycling accident in the vicinity of Westfield College. De Selincourt left an estate of £5,829 which would have been worth £455,827.80 in 2016.

Westfield College honored de Selincourt by establishing Selincourt Hall and the Agnes de Selincourt Scholarship in mathematics. The Agnes de Selincourt Fund of the British SCM was named after her. A memorial plaque to De Selincourt was placed in the chapel at Girton College, Cambridge.

---

16. *Girton College Review* (May 1904).

17. Constance Maynard (1849–1935), a committed Christian, author, and educator. She was the first head of Westfield College (1882–1913) and a pioneer in women's education. Maynard was the first woman to read Moral Sciences (Philosophy) at the University of Cambridge. She was awarded an MA from Cambridge in 1928. For more information on Maynard, see Pauline Phipps, *Constance Maynard's Passions: Religion, Sexuality, and an English Educational Pioneer, 1849–1935* (Toronto: University of Toronto Press, 2015).

ABBIE BULLOCK CHILD (1840–1902)

Although their numbers cannot be verified, older women worked with the SCM and its committees. It was a daunting task that these older adults took on because of the large age gap between them and the student community. At first glance, older workers also went against the movement's fundamental directive that the SCM be student-led. Yet these individuals had lifetimes of experience and good connections. So the SCM sought these people out and appointed them to advisory committees. Some of these individuals were former student members, but most were not. However, whether they were former students or not, these women made significant contributions to the SCM.

Abbie Bullock Child (more often known as Abbie B. Child) was characterized as a missionary stateswoman with an unusual knowledge of missions, who had a judicial temper "inherited perhaps from her father." Child worked on a variety of committees, some of which were SCM-sponsored.[18] Child is remembered as a visionary with the ability to bring things dreamed to pass.

Child was born in Lowell, Massachusetts, to Linus (1803–1870) and Berinthia Mason (1808–1872) Child. Her father was a lawyer, politician, and the manager of a large manufacturing firm there. Linus Child had a commitment to theological education and missions. For many years, he was a member of the Prudential Committee of the American Board of Commissioners for Foreign Missions, and a member of the Board of Trustees of Andover Theological Seminary. Abbie Child had one sister and one brother. She did not attend college like her father and brother, who both graduated from Yale University. She never married. Child grew up in comfortable circumstances. This was suggested by the presence of two Irish domestic servants in the 1865 United States Census and the acknowledged success of Linus Child in legal circles.

Child was a very active leader in missionary organizations with both men and women. She served as home secretary of the Woman's Board of Missions of the Congregational Church and developed fifteen auxiliaries and many local branches of the board. Child was editor of *Life and Light for Women* from 1870 until her death.

In June 1888, Child presented a paper on women in missions at the Centenary Conference on Protestant Missions of the World. At this meeting with women from the United States and Canada, she helped

---

18. For more information on Child, see "Death of a Woman's Board Leader," *Intercollegian* 25, no. 3 (December 1902): 69, and *In Memoriam Abbie B. Child April 8, 1840–November 9, 1902* (Boston: Woman's Board of Missions, 1902).

establish the World Missionary Committee of Christian Women. Child was selected to be chair.

Child guided this committee to hold a conference of women's missionary societies during the World's Congress of Missions in Chicago in 1893. Her group also prepared sessions on women's work for the 1900 New York Ecumenical Missionary Conference. Child's committee created the central committee of the United Study of Foreign Missions. This group created study materials on missions for all women's missionary boards and local associations of these boards. Finally, Child instituted a weekly hour of prayer, from five to six o'clock each Sunday, for all missionary groups in the World Missionary Committee. Her leadership in this prayer time encouraged other groups to sponsor days of prayer around the world.

As one of the few women members of the SVM's Advisory Board, she joined several older, mostly male, members to work largely behind the scenes giving advice, seeking financial supporters, and acquainting those outside the SVMFM about the movement.

Two world journeys to visit mission fields in Turkey and Spain in 1888 and in China, Japan, and India in 1895–1896 rounded out Child's lengthy career.

Child died suddenly in Boston in 1902.

DORA OLIVE IVENS PYM (1890–1980)

Dora Olive Ivens Pym served as chair of the British SCM executive committee during World War I. Extensive materials on Pym's background, education, family, career, and contributions exist. These include Girton College and SCM records as well as her own articles and books.

Pym was the daughter of upper-middle-class timber merchants and farmers, William (1830–1905) and Sarah (1852–?) Ivens. At his death, William Ivens left £27,680. This would have been worth £3,044,800 in 2016. Dora was first educated by a governess at home, then at King Edward VI High School for Girls, Birmingham, and Girton College (1910–1915, 1916–1918). Pym married Reverend Thomas Wentworth Pym on July 15, 1918, and the couple had two sons and two daughters. Her husband was a member of the peerage, the British nobility.[19]

At Girton College, Pym won the prestigious Barbara Leigh-Smith Bodichon Scholarship, the Agnata Butler Prize (1912, 1913), the French Year Scholarship (1913, 1914), the Old Girtonians' Scholarship (1914–1915), and the Gamble Prize for her essay "Origin as Apologist" (1916).

---

19. Darryl Lundy, *The Peerage, Person Page* (October 16, 2016), 14070.

Trained as a classical scholar, Pym devoted her life to helping men and women learn the classics. She was a temporary classical lecturer at Westfield College, London (1916), under Agnes de Selincourt, resident classical lecturer at Girton College (1917–1918). Pym did educational and canteen work in France during World War I with the YMCA.

With her husband's increasing debilitation due to sclerosis, Pym began to work as much as she could. She became visiting classical mistress at St. Brandon's School (1929–1940) and at Clifton High School, Bristol (1930), and visiting lecturer in classics method for the Department of Education (1933–1945) and in English method (1942–1945) at the University of Bristol. At the same time, she taught evening classes in Greek in Bristol and Towbridge. After World War II, Pym helped develop the Bristol Institute of Education by chairing committees in its Department of Education.

After her husband's early death in 1945, Pym became a full-time lecturer in education at the University of Bristol and chief examiner for candidates for state scholarships, for science boys at Marlborough and for the Wiltshire II-Plus.

In 1962, Pym helped established the Joint Association for Classical Teachers, a national organization. During the summers of 1969 and 1970, Pym taught summer school classes for the Summer School of Ancient Greek at Dean Close School, Cheltenham. She was a member of the Court of Governors of St. Saviour and St. Olave's Schools, Southwark (1921–1929 on and off) and a member of the Governing Body of St. Brandon's School, Clevedon.

Pym died in London at the age of eighty-nine. She left an estate in 1980 worth £10,280. That amount would have been worth £46,979.60 in 2016.

Pym wrote *Readings from the Literature of Ancient Rome from English Translations*; *Readings from the Literature of Ancient Greece in English Translations*; *Outlines for Teaching Greek Reading*; and *Tom Pym: A Portrait*.[20]

DORA OLIVE IVENS PYM AND
THE BRITISH SCM EXECUTIVE

In her SCM ministry, Pym was first elected committee chair on March 27, 1917, in the absence of the regular chair the Reverend L.

---

20. Dora Pym, *Readings from the Literature of Ancient Rome from English Translations* (New York: Harcourt, Brace, 1923); *Readings from the Literature of Ancient Greece in English Translations* (New York: Harcourt, Brace, 1924); *Outlines for Teaching Greek Reading* (London: J. Murray, 1946); and *Tom Pym: A Portrait* (Cambridge: Heffer, 1952).

W. Grenstad, and was elected chair again on July 25, 1917, though she was at the Western Front working as a YMCA canteen worker.[21] Pym was elected chair on September 26–28, 1917, though still at the front, on December 18–20, 1917, and on July 20, 1918, when present at the meeting. Pym's resigned the chairmanship on March 8, 1919, and Ronald D. Rees was elected chair.

As chair of the British Executive, Pym presided over committee meetings, such as a May 27, 1917, gathering, where hymns were sung, prayers offered, minutes read, and topics were discussed, including finance, summer conferences, Bible study, publications, theological students, the impact of the war, fine arts, the basis for SCM membership, missions, social service, traveling secretary salaries, and women's issues.[22]

On July 20, 1918, Pym served as the chair even though it was only five days after her wedding. She was also chair for the September 1918 meeting, which was crucial for the SCM's future development. This meeting set the movement's postwar agenda. Pym opened with an address titled "Our Gospel" and then led a discussion titled "The Experience of Christianity as a Working Force, Tested and Purified by the Experiences of Men and Women in France and England." The meeting went on to deliberate the movement's aim and basis for membership. The basis for membership was extremely important because a variety of Christian groups were asking to join the movement. Defining the essence of Christianity in a way acceptable to these different denominations proved to be a challenge. Pym presided successfully over these discussions, and more and more Protestants, ranging from evangelicals to high churchman, became SCM members. Speeches were given by J. H. Oldman, W. E. S. Holland, and Baron Frederick von Hugel. Holland spoke on Christianity's social responsibility, and Von Hugel on institutional Christianity.[23]

---

21. For details on the actual dates and days of Pym's committee chair leadership, see *SCM Executive Minutes, 1914–1917 (SCM/M32) and 1917–1920 (SCM/M33, Records of the Student Christian Movement)*, Cadbury Research Library, Special Collections, University of Birmingham.

22. *SCM Executive Minutes, 1914–1917* (SCM/M32, Records of the Student Christian Movement), 246, Cadbury Research Library, Special Collections, University of Birmingham.

23. See Tissington Tatlow, *The Story of the Student Christian Movement of Great Britain and Ireland* (London: SCM Press, 1933), 613–14. Joseph Houldsworth Oldham (1874–1969) was a Scottish missionary in India, an author, a significant ecumenical leader, and a layman. He was never ordained in the United Free Church of Scotland as he had hoped. Oldham was a noted missionary statesmen and editor of the *International Review of Missions*. He was the son of Lieutenant-Colonel George Wingate Oldham, RE (1840–1923) and Eliza (Lillah) Houldsworth Oldham (1845–?). Oldham was born in Bombay where he lived until age seven when he moved to back to Scotland. He attended Trinity College, Oxford and then in 1897, went as a missionary for the Scottish YMCA

As part of her tasks as chair, Pym also accepted and signed committee minutes.[24]

Committee members such as Bertha Condé, Dr. Mary Pauline Root, Agnes de Selincourt, Abbie Bullock Child, and Dora Olive Ivens Pym served faithfully. They not only led women-only groups, but they served jointly with men on a variety of SCM committees. Each in their own way navigated the dynamics of relationships between men and women SCM leaders.

---

in Lahore, India. In 1898, Oldham married Mary Anna Gibson Fraser (1875–1965), the daughter of an Indian civil servant and the lieutenant governor of Bengal. In 1901, he and his wife returned to Scotland due to typhoid. His work with the emerging ecumenical movement was wide-ranging. He served for example on the International Missionary Council and with the World Council of Churches. And he was heavily involved with the reconstruction of Europe after World War I. W. E. S. Holland was an expert on Christian social policy and had just been called back from India by the Archbishop of Canterbury to lead a missionary recruiting crusade. Baron Frederick Von Hugel (1852–1925) was a Roman Catholic philosopher, mystic, and writer. Although born in France, he went to England at age fifteen and lived there the rest of his life. He was a baron of the Holy Roman Empire, an avid student, and a master of seven languages. Von Hugel was a spiritual mentor to many individuals and a supporter of the modernist movement in Roman Catholicism.

24.   As committee chair, Pym approved and signed the minutes of meetings on several occasions. Some of these include the March 27, 1917, minutes for the December 19, 1916, meeting, *SCM Executive Minutes, 1914–1917* (SCM/M32, Records of the Student Christian Movement), 245; the December 18, 1917, minutes for the September 19, 1917, meeting, *SCM Executive Minutes, 1917–1920* (SCM/M32, Records of the Student Christian Movement), 303; the December 22, 1917, minutes for the September 19, 1917, meeting, *SCM Executive Minutes, 1914–1917* (SCM/M32, Records of the Student Christian Movement), 198; and the September 24, 1918, minutes for the May 23, June 17, and July 20, 1918, meetings, *SCM Executive Minutes, 1917–1919* (SCM/M33, Records of the Student Christian Movement), 64, 70 and 71.

4

General and Assistant General Secretaries

It was a most impressive gathering and I assure you that whatever YMCA and YWCA may do, the YWCA is going to do the right things and work on the right lines in Europe and elsewhere. The American women impressed me a good deal more on the whole than the American men. I do not think this entirely feminist prejudice and I think Mr. Carter is probably stronger than any of the women.[1]

Assistant General Secretary for Women Students in the British Student Christian Movement (SCM), Zoe Barbara Fairfield penned these words in 1919. And almost one hundred years later they still reveal some of the traits that marked this remarkable woman and her ministry. She comes across as articulate, decisive, insightful, visionary, understanding, straightforward, and able to work with both men and women. Fairfield is just one example of a small group of women who served as SCM general and assistant general secretaries.

As mentioned in chapter 1, the terms "pastor" or "chaplain" defined the ministry of an SCM secretary. These individuals had spiritual leadership, and they did not work as a secretary in an office taking dictation, typing, filing, and answering phone calls.

However, this focus on "primary function" of a secretary as pastor or chaplain minimized the other tasks that a typical secretary like Fairfield might carry out. For some secretaries, these other tasks, in particular administrative and executive ones, became predominant. This was perhaps because of the overwhelming need for these added tasks.

The SCM secretary was the second circle of authority within the movement. This individual was under the authority of the executive committee, which appointed, paid, and evaluated those hired. Committees determined duration of employment and compensation levels.

---

1. Zoe Barbara Fairfield, *Report* (1919), *SCM Staffing and Staff Reports, 1916–1920* (SCM/A58, Records of the Student Christian Movement), 2, Cadbury Research Library, Special Collections, University of Birmingham.

53

Of all the types of secretaries, the two most significant were general secretaries and traveling secretaries. These two were most important because they served the two major components of the SCM—the movement's headquarters on the national and international level and its field operations with college and university students and university authorities.

Examples of general and assistant general secretaries will be discussed in this chapter. Chapter 5's topic is the traveling secretary.

GENERAL AND ASSISTANT GENERAL SECRETARIES

The typical general or assistant general secretary wore three hats. This person was administrator, diplomat, and pastor.

First, as administrative officers, the general and assistant general secretary were called "the unseen power that moves all."[2] They kept different departments of the movement working together smoothly and harmoniously. To carry out their administrative work, the secretary had to know the history, objectives, methods, and current condition of the SCM, and the staff and policy decisions of executive committees. They had to lead or, at least, be a member of a variety of subcommittees. All these administrative tasks were crucial because executive committees only met a few times a year.

Second, given the federated nature of the SCM, the secretary helped different movements communicate with each other and worked to balance the needs of different SCM groups. To carry out these diplomatic responsibilities, the general and assistant general secretary met with a variety of Christian leaders and groups, and hosted gatherings. They also worked with organizations outside the SCM.

In their third and most important function, as SCM pastor, the secretary encouraged the spiritual life of the SCM through evangelism, Bible study, personal counseling, manners and morals instruction, conference work, and clergy recruitment.

Only a few individuals, male or female, ever became general and assistant general secretaries. The American and British movements had only a few general secretaries prior to 1920, all of whom were male.[3]

---

2. Eula Bates, "The Importance of the Secretaryship," in *The 1889 Report of the Second National Convention of the YWCAs*, Bloomington, IL, April 11–14, 1889, 35. YWCA of the USA Records, Sophia Smith Collection, Smith College, Northampton, MA.

3. Fennell P. Turner served as the American SVMFM's General Secretary from 1897 to 1919. During the same period, the British movement had several general secretaries: Crayden Edmunds (1894–1895), Rev. Canon L. B. Butcher (1895–1896), John H. Oldham (1896–1897), Rev. Harry C. Dunce (1897–1898), Rev. John M. B. Dunce (1901–1902), Rev. W. W. Williams (1902–1903), Rev. Canon Tissington Tatlow (1898–1900, 1903–1929).

Two women will serve as examples. Leo Viguier took over the reins of the French SCM during World War I and relinquished it at the end of the war. Zoe Barbara Fairfield served as assistant general secretary for women students for the British SCM from 1909 to 1929.

In one way, these two women were very different. Viguier assumed her role in the midst of war and gave it up when World War I ended. Fairfield was appointed to a position that she held for twenty years before, during, and after World War I.

Yet Viguier and Fairfield were much alike. They led different national movements and made significant contributions to their maintenance and development. Because a general secretary or assistant general secretary was a movement's most important leader, Viguier and Fairfield had great authority and power that was limited only by the authority of different executive committees. They both used their talents as administrators and pastors. Like male secretaries, Viguier and Fairfield had to be qualified for their work with strong Christian convictions, education, and business sense. There is no record that either woman faced rejection in their leadership role because they were women. And finally, even though these women served as chaplains, neither was officially ordained.

FRENCH SCM GENERAL SECRETARY LEO VIGUIER

Leo Viguier took over the leadership of her national movement during the darkest hours of World War I. Most eligible men were in the army, and the popular French general secretary Charles Grauss had been killed, along with a sizable number of active SCM members.[4] About women like Viguier, Ruth Rouse wrote, "On the women students and all women lies practically all the responsibility for carrying on various forms of Christian service in France just now."[5] With women's leadership so central to the French SCM, it was decided to move the group's headquarters to what had been the woman's center prior to the war.[6]

Little is known about Viguier, except from reports by Rouse and comments by Wilmina Rowland. Rouse and Rowland disagreed on the actual position Viguier held at the outbreak of the war. Rouse said she was a stenographer or office secretary for the French SCM and YMCA,

---

4. Grauss died on April 29, 1918, on the battlefield. He was being groomed for future leadership in the WSCF.

5. Ruth Rouse, *The World's Student Christian Federation: A History of the First Thirty Years* (London: SCM Press, 1948), 219, 222–23. For more information on the French Student Movement (FFEC), see Archives of the WSCF, Record Group No. 46 (Boxes 139–53), Special Collections, Yale Divinity School.

6. Hans-Ruedi Weber, *The Courage to Live: A Biography of Suzanne de Dietrich* (Geneva: WCC, 1995), 72.

whereas Rowland said she was an office secretary for the French SCM general secretary.[7]

Viguier carried out the general secretary's three major responsibilities. Her administrative tasks included handling staff concerns. For example, she helped hire a WSCF representative to handle foreign student work in France at the war's end. As an intermediary, Viguier corresponded with the candidate, the WSCF, and the French movement. Acting as a diplomat during the war years, Viguier also hosted open houses, called "At Homes," every Sunday evening in Paris for men and women of different nationalities and Christian faiths.[8] Most important, she fostered spiritual development by "almost single-handedly" editing, publishing, and distributing the movement's periodical, *Le Semeur*, and writing personal notes of encouragement to many individuals, including soldiers in the trenches. These included spiritual tidbits, which were meant to encourage her readers to draw closer to God.

After World War I, Viguier along with her husband, Albert, directed the *Correspondance Mensuelle*, a peacetime journal sponsored by the French SCM.

BRITISH SCM ASSISTANT GENERAL SECRETARY ZOE BARBARA FAIRFIELD (1878–1936)

Although there are significant gaps in the information concerning Zoe Barbara Fairfield, enough material exists to study her as the prime example of a woman appointed as an assistant general secretary. Fairfield was the British assistant general secretary for women from 1909 to 1929. Typical of assistant general secretaries, she was appointed to work with one gender but worked with both men and women.

Fairfield became a well-respected, knowledgeable leader in SCM circles, particularly among her fellow male leaders. After Fairfield started working for the SCM, Tatlow observed:

> People soon realized that a first-class mind was being brought
> to bear on the problems of the movement. There was no side of
> its thought and work in which she did not share at one time or

---

7. Ruth Rouse, "Belligerent Nations," in *Notes on Work amongst Students in Europe in War-Time*, 1, Archives of the WSCF, Record Group No. 46 (Box 8, Folder 67), Special Collections, Yale Divinity School Library; and *WSCF*, 205; and Wilmina M. Rowland, "The Contribution of Ruth Rouse to the World's Student Christian Federation" (MA thesis, Yale University, 1937), 236.

8. See Rowland, "Contribution of Ruth Rouse," 236; and Rouse, *World's Student Christian Federation*, 205.

Zoe Barbara Fairfield
(From Tatlow, The Story of the Student Christian Movement, *674)*

another; and no man or woman who has served the movement has been her equal combining range of thought, independence or judgment and creative capacity.[9]

Writing in 1958, J. Davies McCaughey stated that Fairfield's "creative mind and human wisdom have become a legend passed on by faithful oral traditions from eye-witnesses."

Zoe Barbara Fairfield was born in the Hanover Square area of west London to a retired civil servant, Irishman Arthur (1856–1915) and his English wife Sophia Louise Blew (1857–1936) Fairfield. She had one sister. She was baptized at the parish church of Chelsea, St. Luke's.

Fairfield was raised in comfortable surroundings, demonstrated by British Census records which show that the family had many servants through the years. In the 1891 census, the Fairfields had five servants: one governess, one cook, one nurse, and two housemaids.

Fairfield graduated from Notting Hill High School, London, and then attended the most prestigious art school in Great Britain—the

---

9. Tissington Tatlow, *The Story of the Student Christian Movement of Great Britain and Ireland* (London: SCM Press, 1933), 337.

National Art Training Center (the Slade School of Fine Art) in 1897–1898 and 1899–1900. This institution was established in 1817 to offer an education in fine arts in the context of a liberal arts university. In offering female students education on equal terms as men from the outset, the Slade played a key part in the introduction of women to University College London. Since its inception, the Slade has been at the forefront of developments in the field of contemporary art and has welcomed students from all over the world.

The purpose of Fairfield's education at the "Slade" was to receive instruction and have ample practice in a variety of art-related subjects, such as freehand, architectural and mechanical drawing, practical geometry, perspective, painting in oil, tempera, and watercolors. The overall purpose of this education was to prepare men and women to become art teachers.

Fairfield leaned toward Anglo-Catholic Anglicanism with a modernist bent. Fairfield supported women's right to vote. An early death at fifty-eight years of age in London was a loss to the SCM. Her will labels her a spinster and states that she left £6,777, a good sum for 1936. This would have been worth approximately £434,405.00 in 2016.

THE SCM CAREER OF ZOE BARBARA FAIRFIELD

Fairfield's lengthy SCM career included being chair and then secretary of the London women's committee (1898), organizer and general secretary of the Art Students' Christian Union (1902–1909), a regular member and officer of the British executive (1909 to at least 1929), assistant general secretary for women for the British SCM (1909–1929), British representative at the WSCF Conference at St. Beatenburg (1920), and general secretary of the auxiliary movement (1929–1933?). She was active in the British and world YWCA as well.

Fairfield carried out the three tasks of the assistant general secretary: administration, diplomacy, and most important, spiritual development.

To start with, Fairfield possessed the most important aspect of the administrative task, having a good working knowledge of the movement. According to William Paton, she had "a complete and unconscious mastery of the religious vernacular of the SCM."[10] In addition she brought confidence to her administrative work. According to Tatlow, "Zoe Fairfield fought no battle, but simply took her place in the councils of the Movement with complete ease."[11] In 2007, Robin Boyd agreed, noting that "Tissington Tatlow would never have been

---

10. William Paton, "Zoe Fairfield," *Student Movement* 3, no. 1 (1933): 206.
11. Tatlow, *Story*, 236.

able to achieve what he did without Zoë Fairfield, whom colleagues called the brain behind the movement, while 'T squared' was the brilliant administrator."[12]

With this working knowledge, Fairfield was able to carry out her duties. Two of Fairfield's most important executive tasks were helping to manage the central office and leading committees or subcommittees. Her daily office work included normal office responsibilities, such as handling a considerable amount of correspondence, talking on phones, keeping records and files, and dealing with many drop-in visitors.[13] She interviewed applicants, negotiated salaries, and placed new employees.[14]

Fairfield's skills in negotiation were demonstrated in the way she handled her own employment contract. When it was about to expire in September 1913, she came to terms with the British executive based on her desires and only after careful negotiation. Even though the committee wanted to extend her contract indefinitely, Fairfield wanted only a six-month contract. In order to keep her, the executive agreed to her stipulation. In its official minutes, however, the group expressed its enthusiastic approval of Fairfield's leadership despite the contract's short time frame.

As Paton later noted, Fairfield also had a talent for placing staff:

> She had a great skill in fitting people into jobs. In some ways, this has been the chief of all her services to the movement. She was quite uncannily good at it, and it nearly always involved seeing rather deeper into personality than most people do, and judging what a personality was capable of in the future as well as in the present.[15]

Staff placement was important for movement development. Having the right person in the right location helped the movement expand.

---

12. Robin Boyd, "The Witness of the Student Christian Movement," *International Bulletin of Missionary Research* 31, no. 1 (January 2007): 4.

13. In her November 19–22, 1917, report, Fairfield wrote, "Correspondence has been pretty heavy, too." Fairfield, "Report" (1917–1918), 3. In 1918, she again mentioned, "correspondence heavy all term." Fairfield, "Report" (1918), 3.

14. In her official reports from 1917–1919, Fairfield mentioned interviews over and over again. She interviewed secretaries and "others" (October 14, 1918), 1; conducted "various interviews" (October 16–17, 1918), 2; "several interviews" (October 18, 1918), 2; "various interviews" (October 31, 1918), 2; "several interviews" (November 13, 1918), 2; "various interviews" (November 23, 1918), 2; and finally, "I had several interviews" (January 18, 1919), 2.

15. Paton, "Zoe Fairfield," 205–06.

According to many observers, she was effective in her role of leading many committees and subcommittees:

> Someone once described ZBF as the ideal secretary of a sub-committee. It hits off part of her intellectual ability very well. She is very versatile, first-rate at the preliminary skirmishing round a new subject, never afraid of new and unconventional ideas, readier to listen to shy and unaccustomed speakers and new hands than to those either glib or orthodox. Herself the possessor of a strong and active intelligence, she was a great believer in corporate thinking, and if the student movement has given to many of us a belief in the reality of corporate thinking and prayer, as something different from and richer from that of the individual, it is no small measure due to Zoe's influence.[16]

During her SCM tenure, Fairfield sat on many committees, including the theological students' committee, the social service committee, the basis commission, the commission on the SCM staff, and the British and WSCF executive committees. These committees were important to the SCM because they dealt with some of the most pressing issues that the movement faced. Fairfield also led the committees that founded the Nurses' Missionary League, the Art Students' Christian Union's lecture series, and the Auxiliary Movement.

To carry out the assistant general secretary's diplomatic task, Fairfield reached out to foreign students and worked with different SCMs. Paton felt that Fairfield's main interest and gifts were international ministry because for her, this ministry was personal (i.e., she knew men and women by name and need) and connected (i.e., she recognized the international character of the SCM, and she enjoyed working with foreign students):

> It seemed to me that her heart was most of all in international relationships, which characteristically meant for her not abstractions, but dealing with Pierre, Fritz, Gopal, etc., and their sisters. . . . During all the time I have known the movement there has never been a secretary to whom the most sensitive, sore and indignant foreign student would go so readily as to Zoe; I have known any number of causes of this, for she somehow conveyed

---

16. Ibid., 206.

to them that though entirely uncosmopolitan, she was also devoid of national prejudice, and human enough to understand genuine feeling of any kind.[17]

As part of her diplomatic tasks, Fairfield worked with SCM-related organizations, which due to the federated nature of the movement acted autonomously, even though interconnected.

For example, Fairfield was considered the chief arbitrator between the SCM in Ireland, Wales, and the British movement's headquarters. Her work was fortified by her regular visits to Ireland. On one 1917 visit, Fairfield spoke to a joint meeting of the auxiliary and the Irish Fellowship in Dublin. This was after what she called a "horrible journey" through which she "got a cold which lasted me about two months."[18]

Typical of a general and assistant general secretary, the most important aspect of Fairfield's work was spiritual development. Though a layperson and a woman, Fairfield functioned as an elder and pastor for the British movement. To this aspect of her ministry, she brought "sort of intuitive theology . . . [which was] her favorite intellectual milieu."[19]

Fairfield's spiritual leadership was demonstrated in a variety of ways. Fairfield provided pastoral care for a large number of men and women. Paton reported that she gave them something practical to do in their troubles, instead of "merely holding their hands."[20] Agreeing with this observation, Tatlow wrote that her counseling had an "astringent quality."[21] Fairfield also challenged students through the printed word to have genuine faith, a faith inspired by Bible reading and prayer. If a student had this type of faith, his or her life would reach "its true and fullest development," where visions would be fulfilled and difficulties overcome. Victory, not defeat in temptation, would mark their lives.[22]

Fairfield's spiritual leadership was demonstrated in her ministry with meetings and conferences. Although the SCM's conference ministry will be fully investigated in chapters 9 and 10, what can be noted here is that conferences contributed to overall spiritual development through

---

17. Ibid.

18. Zoe Barbara Fairfield, "Secretary's Report" (1917), 1. The British SCM was divided into three national groups by World War I: The English and Scottish branch, the Welsh branch, and the Irish branch. This setup was ahead of the secular government, which was still struggling with Irish independence.

19. Paton, "Zoe Fairfield," 206.

20. Ibid., 205.

21. Tatlow, *Story*, 852.

22. Ibid., 287–89.

themes selected, inspirational speeches given, and relationships established between those in attendance. Fairfield dominated these programs for more than twenty years. Her ministry began in 1909, when she joined Dorothy Eda Brown and several men to plan summer conference programs.[23]

Fairfield's agenda with her conference and meeting ministry caused considerable problems. For example, she ran into trouble with her selection of speakers for SCM meetings. This criticism was just one part of the growing split between conservatives and liberals within the movement and global Protestantism. In his analysis of the growing rift between conservatives and liberals in the British movement, Douglas Johnson observed that beginning around 1909, evangelicals began to object to conference themes and speakers. He believed that evangelicals felt that their spiritual and intellectual interests were not being represented.[24] This was just one small part of the international fundamentalist-modernist split which would later tear the SCM in two.[25]

---

23.   Dorothy Eda Brown attended Dulwich and Brambly High Schools and Girton College, Cambridge). At Girton, she earned a BA in mathematics Class II in 1905. Brown received a BA from the University of Dublin (1906). She earned a teaching certificate in 1907. During college, she was secretary (1904) and president of Girton College Christian Union (1904–1905). After college, Brown served as traveling secretary (1907–1909) and executive committee member (1909–1910) for the British SCM. She was also secretary of the Overseas Committee of the British YWCA.

24.   Douglas Johnson, *Contending for the Faith: A History of the Evangelical Movement in the Universities and Colleges* (London: Inter-Varsity Press, 1979), 69–71.

25.   This growing division involved more than Fairfield's choice of speakers and topics. Conservatives felt that the SCM had abandoned its biblical moorings on the centrality of the atoning work of Christ, biblical infallibility, and evangelization. In 1919, when talks between conservatives and liberals reached an impasse, an official split took place. The result was two separate organizations, the Universities and Colleges Christian Fellowship (originally known as the Inter-Varsity Fellowship of Evangelical Unions) and the SCM.

For more information on the evangelical branch of the British movement, see Inter-Varsity Christian Fellowship, *A Brief History of the Inter-Varsity Fellowship* (London: IVFEU, 1929); J. H. Oldham, *Old Paths in Perilous Times* (London: Inter-Varsity Press, 1932); Donald Coggan, ed., *Christ and the Colleges: A History of the Inter-Varsity Fellowship of Evangelical Unions* (London: IVFEU, 1934); Johnson, *Contending for the Faith*; J. C. Pollock, *The Cambridge Movement* (London: John Murray, 1953), and *The Keswick Story: An Authorized History of the Keswick Convention* (Chicago: Moody Press, 1964); and Steve Bruce, "The Student Christian Movement and the Inter-Varsity Fellowship: A Sociological Study of Two Student Movements" (PhD diss., University of Stirling, 1980).

For the nonevangelical branch of the British SCM, see Tatlow, *Story*, 385–88 and J. Davis McCaughey, *Christian Obedience in the Universities: Studies in the Life of the SCM of Great Britain and Ireland, 1930–1950* (London: SCM Press, 1958).

See chapter 12 for a specific instance of this growing division.

A good example of this issue with Fairfield's choice of speakers occurred when she invited a popular and controversial woman preacher, Agnes Maude Royden, to speak at several SCM meetings.[26] She said that it was obvious that Royden was a prophetess with a real spiritual message. But Fairfield's support of Royden was not universally embraced. In a February 7, 1920, message to SCM headquarters, an Irish woman, Elfridals Johnson, expressed in the strongest terms her disapproval of Royden as conference speaker:

> I want to make a strong appeal against the teaching given by Miss Maude Royden under the "SCM," speaking to students and others at the University of Dundee last month. It is hardly fair for me to attempt to report what she said without being able

---

26. Agnes Maude Royden (1876–1956), later known as Maude Royden-Shaw, was a preacher, suffragist and SCM worker. Royden was born into a financially and socially comfortable Anglican Liverpool family, whose money had been made in shipping. She was educated at Cheltenham Ladies' College (1896) and Lady Margaret College, Oxford, and earned Second Class Honors in History. In 1931, she became the first woman in England to earn a Doctor of Divinity degree. She had no financial need to work, but she longed to make herself useful. Maude suffered all her life from lameness, and when it was eventually diagnosed as dislocated hips, there was little that could be done. Her success in conquering this handicap throughout her life was remarkable, but it did at times overtax her strength.

After college, Royden worked in the Victorian Women's University Settlement in Liverpool. In 1902, Royden went to work for the Reverend Hudson Shaw, who later in 1944 became her husband. Since he was involved in the Oxford University Extension Movement, he recruited her to be the first woman teacher for this program.

Royden worked in several churches. First, in 1917, she became assistant pastor at the City Temple (Congregational), London, and then in 1920, along with the Reverend Percy Dearmer, an Anglican curate, created the Guildhouse, where she preached regularly. This was not a church but a group of Anglicans and non-Anglicans with worship services, study groups, and social service ministries. During this era, Royden became a popular preacher and speaker as well as radio host. She toured Great Britain, the United States, New Zealand, Australia, India, and China.

Royden's popular causes were world peace and women's rights. Royden was a pacifist until World War II. At that time, she renounced her pacifism in light of the evils of Nazism.

Royden died in 1956 in London and was buried at St. John the Divine Church, Frankby, near Liverpool where she was raised.

An author of many books, articles and speeches, some of Royden's works include *"Votes and Wages": How Women's Suffrage Will Improve the Economic Position of Women* (London: National Union of Women's Suffrage Societies, 1912); *Women and the Sovereign State* (New York: Stokes, 1916); *Beauty in Religion* (New York: G. P. Putnam's Sons, 1923); *Women at the World's Crossroads* (New York: Woman's Press, 1923); *Christ Triumphant* (New York: G. P. Putnam's Sons, 1924); and *The Threefold Cord* (New York: Macmillan, 1947), her autobiography. For more information on Royden, see Sheila Fletcher, *Maude Royden: A Life* (Oxford: Blackwell, 1989).

to quote her words exactly, which I cannot do; but the trend of her thoughts was just that which is popular to-day about "God is everybody!" and a good thought or good decire [*sic*] was an evidence of this, and of the soul seeking after God in its own way. She clearly stated that all the religions of the East were some manifestations of Him. "The heathen in his blindness bows down to wood and stone." The unregenerate state of the human heart apart from the New Birth, conversion through faith in the atonement of our Lord Jesus Christ—These evangelical truths seem to be ignored by her. As one who takes a public stance as a teacher of the Word of God, I felt it incumbent upon me to offer some word of protest.[27]

Nowhere in this letter is Fairfield's name mentioned specifically in connection with the selection of Royden as a speaker at the University of Dundee. However, since Fairfield had endorsed Royden on other occasions, this most likely contributed to the University of Dundee's invitation. It is interesting to note that objections to Royden's speech at the University of Dundee were theological, not gender-based. It is also worth commenting that the University of Dundee has no record of Elfridals Johnson ever being a student there.

In addition to her other pastoral duties, Fairfield's spiritual leadership led her to help recruit and train new clergy to spread the Gospel. This included active involvement with the British SCM's theological department's committee. In 1892, the British SCM had subdivided into three related groups, all of which had their own executives and representatives on the main British executive committee: the general, missionary, and theological departments. Fairfield related so well with theological committee members that they eventually made her the committee's secretary.[28]

Fairfield and Rouse were the lone women along with sixteen men of different denominations appointed to a special commission on clergy recruitment sponsored by the theological department committee. Since Rouse was never able to attend, Fairfield was the only woman present at the commission's three meetings. The commission met on December 14, 1914, February 15, 1915, and March 23, 1915.

Frustrated by the shortage of suitable male candidates, at a February 15, 1915, commission meeting, Fairfield asked, "What would happen if

---

27. Elridals Johnston to Tissington Tatlow, February 7, 1920, *SCM, 1919–1920, General Correspondence* (SCM/A66, Records of the Student Christian Movement), Cadbury Research Library, Special Collections, University of Birmingham. Johnston calls herself a reader, YWCA.

28. Tatlow, *Story*, 800.

Agnes Maude Royden
(From www.roydenhistory.co.uk; used by permission of Mike Royden)

a number of women want to become ministers?" The minutes record, "Mr. Lloyd thought that it was for the Free Churches to experiment, but the Commission gave no conclusion on the matter."[29]

Fairfield had a large share in planning the first postwar theological students gathering, "A Conference for Theological Students and Others," held April 12–17, 1926. The conference had worship, speakers, private devotions, and small group discussions. Topics included belief in God, the presentation of the Christian faith, worship, and the church in action.

As opposed to earlier theological student conferences, which were solely the domain of men, this conference was primarily organized by this laywoman without any formal theological training. She arranged for speakers and prepared and passed out materials for conference delegates to discuss prior to the meeting.

Fairfield's subjects for small group discussions point to a high level of theological sophistication on her part. For example, under the general

---

29. *Minutes of the Theological Commission held at "Annandale" on Monday, the 15th February 1915, from 2:30 to 5:30,* Archives of the WSCF, Record Group No. 46 (Box 206, Folder 1550), Special Collections, Yale Divinity School Library.

topic "Belief in God," one question for discussions asked, "What is the difference between immanence and incarnation?" In another example, under the topic, "The Presentation of the Gospel," small group members were asked to debate, "Does the real distinction between the Traditional and Modernist (Liberal) position turn upon a 'literal' as opposed to a 'metaphorical' interpretation of the creeds?" or "How far do you understand the Marxian philosophy of history and its challenge? Has Christianity a philosophy to put forward which is capable of substantiating its truth in the face of this challenge?"

Lest it be forgotten, Fairfield dealt with organizations outside the SCM. She worked with groups from her church, the women's movement, the peace movement, and patriotic associations. Fairfield mentioned the following groups in her 1916–1920 reports: the Challenge; the Archbishop's Committee on the Teaching Office of the Church; the Army and Religious Enquirer; the Women's Movement; "a group of people thinking about Preparation for Peace, which Dr. Hodgkin has rather adroitly shifted from his own shoulders to mine, and which I am now endeavoring to shift to others!"; the Central Committee; the Women's Church Work; Nurse's Missionary League, the Order of the Kingdom; and the League of Faith and Work. Fairfield was secretary for the Guild of Helpers (1907–1909). She also spent a great deal of time with YWCA and YMCA leaders. Discussions concerning joint projects were main items at these meetings. They were as simple as "having lunch at the YWCA to talk about the relations with the YMCA," or more substantive, such as meeting with the World's YWCA Committee to discuss postwar developments in Europe. She was interested in ecumenical relations and was a prolific author. Both of these are discussed later in this book.

5

Introducing the Traveling Secretary

Between the years 1898 and 1914 while serving as a YWCA traveling secretary on the Pacific Coast, Frances Cousens Gage faced a problem that needed solving, and she set out to fix it. Gage found that girls under her care could not ride a particular steamboat because it was not safe. So she went straight to the headquarters of the steamboat company and told the company's president directly, "Your boats aren't safe for my girls to ride on." When the president said he agreed and said "Tell them not to use them," she responded quickly, "You've got to make your boats safe for my girls." And the president dutifully did what she demanded.[1]

This story of Gage's ministry is but one example of the work of the traveling secretaries of the Student Christian Movement (SCM). Traveling secretaries like Gage were often seen as the great heroes of the SCM. Perhaps this was because these SCM employees ministered on the front lines, working on college campuses with campus associations, individual collegians, and university authorities. For all intents and purposes, they were the "Face of the SCM." And while they most likely had been appointed to work with members of their own gender, they often crossed over and worked with the other one.

Appointment as a traveling secretary was one of the most coveted positions in the SCM hierarchy. This position gave recent college graduates the thrill of travel, new friendships, and professional ministry opportunities as a representative of a vibrant movement. For many women, the positive side far outweighed the negative. It afforded them an unprecedented opportunity to break out of older gender roles in professional work.

Employing recent graduates proved to be a significant factor in the movement's appeal on college campuses. It was believed that these young men and women were closer to the student experience than older

---

1. "Some Women," *Woman Citizen: The Woman's National Political Weekly* 3, no. 23 (November 2, 1918): 474.

67

personnel. Also as younger people, they "represented instead of professional efficiency, the attraction of definite commitment and contagious enthusiasm."[2]

Prerequisites for being a traveling secretary included a love for travel and the physical and mental stamina to handle the rigors associated with it. Ruth Rouse was a case in point here. Wilmina Rowland observed that she "loved to wander and confessed that she never tired of travel." Rather humorously, Rouse claimed that she loved to travel because she was descended from a "race of naval people and engineers on one side and from the highland clansmen and cattle thieves on the other."[3] She also had the ability to withstand the physical and mental pressures of travel. Reminiscing about her in 1936, a former SCM leader, Frederick W. S. O'Neill wrote, "Ruth Rouse had several remarkable qualities . . . [including] physical endurance, enabling her to sleep in any position, an important adjunct to travel."[4]

At the same time, there were all sorts of problems associated with traveling work. Tissington Tatlow observed:

> Traveling secretaries do often feel worn; it is a very exacting life. The traveling secretary is almost invariably a man or a woman who has started work immediately after graduation. He is plunged into a continual stream of engagements: addresses, committee meetings, talks with individuals; always trying to lift a situation on to a higher plane; expected by every new college to be fresh and concerned alone with its problems; hampered all the time by correspondence; constantly packing and unpacking his luggage and making journeys; always meeting new people. There are probably few people in the Student Movement who are more lonely at times then traveling secretaries.[5]

That women SCM workers often traveled unchaperoned raised eyebrows, and the journeys of these individuals also and perhaps more importantly raised important concerns for personal safety.

---

2. William M. Beahm, "Factors in the Development of the SVMFM" (PhD diss., University of Chicago, 1941), 107.

3. Ruth Franzén, *Ruth Rouse among Students: Global, Missiological and Ecumenical Perspectives* (Uppsala: Swedish Institute of Mission Research, 2008), 26.

4. The Very Reverend Frederick W. S. O'Neill, letter to Wilmina Rowland. In Wilmina M. Rowland, "The Contribution of Ruth Rouse to the World's Student Christian Federation" (MA thesis, Yale University, 1937), 70.

5. Tissington Tatlow, *The Story of the Student Christian Movement of Great Britain and Ireland* (London: SCM Press, 1933), 54–55; and Rowland, "Contribution of Ruth Rouse," 70.

Alone during an 1897 late-night stopover at a small village on the border of Norway and Sweden, Rouse was compelled to find lodging with the help of a man she did not know and whose language she did not speak. Writing later about the experience at the town's small boarding house, Rouse said: "I reflected that if they meant to rob and murder me they would do it whether I waited up for them or not, so I went to sleep very comfortably, and did not even meet a flea. Next morning I noticed a small door in the wall! Picture the situation for anyone with nerves."[6]

Added to this, though exciting, turn-of-the-century travel could be dangerous. Trains could wreck and ocean-going passenger liners could sink.[7] This was highlighted by the tragic sinking of the great passenger liner, the *RMS Titanic* with over 1,500 lives lost on a chilly April 1912 night after striking an iceberg. The *Titanic* sinking might have directly affected SCM circles because John R. Mott had been offered free first class passage on this ship, which he didn't use. Odds are, he would have perished in the sinking, and his death would have been deeply felt in the movement.

Wars also posed special problems. Rouse traveled for the World Student Christian Federation (WSCF) across the U-boat-filled Atlantic Ocean even after the tragic sinking of the *RMS Lusitania* in May 1915, which sank in just eighteen minutes with 1,198 souls lost. Yet Rouse traveled extensively by boat between 1916 and 1918, going to the United States, Canada, Latin America, Switzerland, and France.

Rouse was severely wounded while on a speaking tour in France in July 1918. After giving a speech in Étaples in Northern France, an air raid began when Rouse and three companions were about to leave.

During World War I, Étaples was the most important depot and transit camp for the British Expeditionary Force. It served as a central railway location with connections across France. Étaples was one of several locations with a variety of support services for soldiers, such as canteens and YMCA Huts for food, entertainment, and educational opportunities.

Étaples also had hospitals for battlefront wounded. During the war, the German military bombed and machined-gunned these institutions. In the bombing of one hospital, "One ward received a direct hit and was blown to pieces, six wards were reduced to ruins and three others were severely damaged. Sister Baines, four orderlies and eleven patients were killed outright, whilst two doctors, five sisters and many orders,

---

6. Rowland, "Contribution of Ruth Rouse," 83–84.

7. Even Wikipedia chimes in here with a list of the most well-known and tragic train accidents between 1900 and 1929. https://en.wikipedia.org.

and patients were wounded."[8] The military cemetery in Étaples has the graves of 11,658 British and Allied soldiers.

In Rouse's case, when the raid began, her car stopped, and its passengers sought refuge in the bushes at the side of the road. As the raid ended, several shells burst near them, showering them with earth and bits of shrapnel. One passenger was killed, and Rouse and others were wounded. Rouse had to go through three operations, spend nine weeks in the hospital, and endure a lengthy period of convalescence. Later, she discovered that had the shrapnel hit her just a little closer to a main artery, she would have died instantly.

GRACE HELENA SAUNDERS

As a traveling secretary, Grace Helena Saunders toured the war zone during the Balkan Crisis of 1912–1913.[9] Two conflicts occurred just prior to World War I, the First and Second Balkan Crises. In the first Balkan Crisis (1912–1913), a loosely affiliated group of Balkan states kicked the Ottoman Empire out of most of Europe. In the Second Balkan Crisis (1913), the formerly allied Balkan states fought among themselves for former Ottoman territory and property.

The Balkan Wars caused huge causalities. The Bulgarians lost about 65,000 men, the Greeks 9,500, the Montenegrins 3,000, and the Serbs at least 36,000. The Ottomans lost as many as 125,000. Thousands of civilians died from disease and other causes. Horrible atrocities happened in every theater of these wars.

In an article for the *North American Student*, Saunders described in realistic and vivid detail what she saw when she helped in a front-line hospital:

> We found the streets full of pale, hollowed-eyed men, unshaven and half starved, wandering from one hospital outpatient department to another to try and get their wounds dressed. . . . Surgeons and amateur nurses were hard at work dressing wounds and extracting bullets. In one hospital the pressure at the door was so great that a pistol had to be discharged over the heads of the crowd to keep them back, and everywhere, in every house in the city, thousands of wounded were located, just lying there in

---

8. E. J. King, *The Knights of St. John in the British Empire: Being the Official History of the British Order of the Hospital of St. John of Jerusalem* (London: St. John's Gate, 1934), 201.

9. For more information on Grace Helena Saunders, see chapter 11.

their muddy uniforms and on the bare floors. . . . We dressed a large numbers of wounds every day. . . . Bullets were extracted without any anesthetic.[10]

Saunders even had the highly unusual and dangerous experience of going to the actual front line at a battle at Tchatalja, which was the last line of defense for the Ottoman capital, Constantinople. The language she uses, such as "privilege" and "chatted," seems a bit quixotic. Saunders appears to have been caught up in the romance of the situation without regard to practicality:

We had the unique privilege of two days' visit to the battle front at Tchatalja, during the last armistice, though up to this time, no ladies and no foreign correspondents had been allowed. . . . We not only inspected the trenches and underground huts, but actually chatted with two of the enemy's soldiers at the half red, half white flag which marked the center of the neutral zone.[11]

This has to be one of the most unusual moments that women had with men in all SCM history.

FRANCES COUSENS GAGE (1863–1917)

The story of Frances Cousens Gage was one of the most hair-raising tales in SCM history.[12] Gage was a YWCA student traveling secretary in North America and Turkey. Her focus was women's work, but she worked with men many times and in many challenging situations.

Gage's desire to "get the job done" in ways thought impossible resulted in the loss of her life. She became the first overseas America YWCA missionary to die while in service to the YWCA and the SCM.

Because of who she was and what she did, Gage was very popular in life and in death. A measure of just how popular and highly respected Gage was can be seen by all the laudatory comments made about her after her death. She was called "one of the brightest stars among Minnesota's

---

10. Grace Helena Saunders, "Red Cross Work in the Balkans," *North American Student* 2, no. 1 (October 1913): 16–17. The article includes a picture of Saunders, but it is of very poor quality.

11. Ibid., 8.

12. For more information on Frances Cousens Gage, see Elizabeth Wilson, *The Road Ahead: Experiences in the Life of Frances C. Gage* (New York: Woman's Press, 1918).

heroic missionary daughters."[13] Later that year, a similar brief article stated in somewhat hagiographic style:

> Among the women who deserve to be held in remembrance by their sisters, is Frances C. Gage, who has laid down her life in Turkey since the war began. Miss Gage was a Y. W. C. A. worker in Marsovan. . . . In the story of her life briefly written by Elizabeth Wilson, *The Road Ahead* [Woman's Press], there are many incidents which show Miss Gage as a path breaker in the woman movement. A feminist? Yes, of the old-fashioned pioneer sort, like Frances Willard and Susan B. Anthony, women who pushed the world along until it has become almost safe for women.[14]

Gage might have wondered who all these writers were talking about if she had had the opportunity to read their words. She was modest in assessing her gifts. Considering herself a very ordinary person, Gage said, "I am not very brave, but I realize that a missionary's life is by no means an easy one, and after looking at the matter in the face, I believe, God helping me, I can meet the emergencies He may send me."[15]

Frances Cousens Gage was the eldest of three children (two girls and one boy) born to George (1834–1910) and Elizabeth Webber (1835–1899) Gage in Quincy, Massachusetts. George Gage was an educator. His career took him to Mankato, Minnesota, between 1868 and 1872. There he was the president of Mankato State Normal School (now Minnesota State University, Mankato). At the time, the area had a small population. This little town had been one of the locations of the bloody Dakota War of 1862. After, it was the setting for the hanging of thirty-eight participants on the Dakota side, the largest mass execution in American history. Residents fled during the war, and some returned after it. This was about the time the Gages, including Frances, moved in.

In 1872, the family moved to St. Paul, Minnesota, for two years, where George Gage became the superintendent of the public schools. After that, the Gage family moved to Portland, Oregon.

Gage attended Carlton College, a small Christian college affiliated with the Minnesota Conference of Congregational Churches in Northfield, Minnesota. Carlton had been founded in 1866, and it graduated its first class in 1874. During her college years, Gage was a charter member of the Gamma Delta Literary Society. She graduated as valedictorian

---

13. *Mission Studies* 36, no. 1 (January 1, 1918): 27

14. "Some Women," *Woman Citizen*, November 2, 1918, 474.

15. *Mission Studies* 36, no. 1 (January 1, 1918): 28.

Frances Cousens Gage
(Courtesy Carleton College Archives, Northfield, MN)

with a BS in 1890.

Despite being raised in a Christian home, Gage later claimed that she did not want to become nor did she become a Christian at that time. Then because of the lives led by some Christian students and faculty at Carlton College, she committed her life to Christ. The impact of this may be what a later report noted about Gage's college years. Gage was said to have "inspired interest in missions among the students, all of whom admired her fine intellectual abilities, her earnest spirit of consecration and her beautiful and attractive personality."[16]

After college, Gage was elected to Phi Beta Kappa as an alumni member.

Between 1890 and 1891, Gage was a teacher at St. Paul's High School, St. Paul, Minnesota. At this time she decided, "I would rather teach girls than boys." But her life story would tell a different tale.

In 1893, the Women's Board of the Interior (a Congregational overseas missionary society) appointed Gage and another woman, Martha King, to work at the Girls' School in Marsovan, Turkey.

---

16. Ibid., 27.

In 1840, Bebek Seminary was established outside Constantinople by the American Board of Commissioners for Foreign Missions. In 1862, this school was transferred to Marsovan. In 1886, the Anatolia College was established there. Students were mainly Greek and Armenian. Most were boarding students because they came from outside Marsovan. Students quickly numbered 115, and in 1893, a girls' school was founded.

After a bon voyage party on July 18, Gage and King left for Turkey. The Ladies' Aid Society of the Atlantic Congregational Church, St. Paul, Minnesota, supported their Turkish ministry. The Atlantic Congregational Church had been founded in the early 1880s. Its first meeting was held in the Gage home on November 21, 1882. The church does not exist in 2016. The support Gage received from the Ladies' Aid Society can be seen in a thank-you letter sent to the society. Gage expressed appreciation for some flannel nightgowns and an apron. In the letter she also explained the ministries she was carrying out, such as helping needy women, education, and working with children. Gage also explained how she did the laundry.[17]

On arriving in Turkey, Gage was witness to what has become known as the Marsovan Massacre. That year, Ottoman troops took many Armenian students and faculty to jail and damaged some college buildings in reaction to the posters Armenian activists posted near the school. The Turks accused some of the school's Armenian students and faculty of colluding with the activists. Later, the Ottoman government gave funds to rebuild the damaged campus.

A *Los Angeles Herald* article in 1895 included a description of the massacre's events very close to the school from an unidentified person at the school.[18] This person might have been Gage herself, but since the source is unidentified, no one will ever know.

The article said, "A storm broke over Marsovan." The article's witness said that slaughter, shrieks, and yells could be heard close to the school. "Bullets came humming and struck the girls' school." The noise of soldiers banging on nearby doors could be heard also. The cries of a wounded woman could be heard just outside the school gates one entire day. About twenty-five soldiers guarded the institution, and no one was permitted to attack the school or harm the students or staff. Students and staff were huddled in a room. Several years later, Gage would recall praying for protection in that room during the massacre.

---

17. Letter, Frances Cousens Gage to Mrs. John Bell, October 6, 1896, Minnesota State Historical Society Library.

18. "Massacre at Marsovan," *Los Angeles Herald* 45, no. 58 (December 8, 1895): 2.

In the fall of 1898, Gage came back to the United States, and she was not sure she would ever return to Turkey. The combination of her teaching load, the death of Martha King, and the massacres had taken their toll.

Once back in the United States and after a time of recovery, Gage worked for the YWCA Student Department in Washington, Oregon, and Idaho. She was a traveling secretary in Oregon and the executive secretary for the North West Field Committee of the YWCA. Even though she worked hard in these roles, one observer noted, "The outlook of her heart was toward Turkey."[19] While Gage was in the United States, Clarissa Spencer of the World's YWCA and Ruth Rouse of the WSCF visited Turkey's women's groups. Ernest Otto Jacob, the YMCA secretary, worked with women's groups as well until Gage returned.

Gage responded to the call to return to Turkey in 1913 or 1914, depending on the account one accepts. Listed as a secretary for the YWCA's foreign department for the years 1913–1916, Gage returned to Turkey as a YWCA traveling secretary. In addition to her experience of Turkey, she understood the Turkish language.

The foreign department of the YWCA employed more than eight hundred secretaries throughout the world between 1895 and 1970.[20] Many of these individuals were sent as career professionals by the foreign divisions of the American, Canadian, English, and World's YWCA and YMCAs.

During her first months back in Turkey, Gage spent eleven weeks traveling, checking out local associations, and examining the conditions of Turkish women. This trip included ten days of sea travel, twenty by wagon, two by horseback, and twelve by rail. All in all she traveled over 2,500 miles. She visited Orthodox, Roman Catholic, and Protestant believers as well as member of other religions. Gage had to be sensitive to the beliefs and practices of all these groups.

---

19. Wilson, *Road Ahead*, 55.

20. For more information on the American YWCA's foreign work, see Nancy Boyd, *Emissaries: The Overseas Work of the American YWCA, 1895–1970* (New York: Woman's Press, 1986). From 1894 to 1941, the Foreign Division of the American YWCA sent 250 women to develop YWCAs in China, Japan, the Near East, and Latin America. Of these, at least half the men and 68 of the women spent time in student work. Rouse identified some of these men and women, all of whom had SCM connections: Mary Bentley (India), Grace Coppock (China), Annie Caroline Macdonald (Japan), and Frances Gage (Turkish Empire). For more details, see Ruth Rouse, *The World's Student Christian Federation: A History of the First Thirty Years* (London: SCM Press, 1948), 79; Boyd, *Emissaries*; and Kenneth Scott Latourette, *World Service: A History of the Foreign Work and World Service of the Young Men's Christian Association of the United States and Canada* (New York: Association Press, 1957).

During her travels, Gage generally spoke on "The Preciousness of Womanhood" to large audiences. In local associations, she gave evangelistic and inspirational speeches, and she spoke in Armenian, Greek, Turkish, Catholic, and secular schools.

In 1916, Gage was a member of the General Committee of Christian Associations in the Turkish Empire along with YMCA workers. Typical of Gage's work with men and women, she was known to speak up when she disagreed with the men around her, even when it was to her disadvantage. She said, "When I asked Mr. ______ what he thought my traveling allowance should be for a year, he said $1,000, but that is a man's estimate and is too large, of course."[21]

World War I changed the dynamics of Turkey. Gage's traveling work became rare, and she was always faced with how to handle the immense needs of women at this time.

In 1915, Gage was caught up in what we now know as the Armenian Genocide (or the Armenian Holocaust, Armenian Massacres, or the Medz Yeghern, in Armenian, the "Great Crime"). This was the Ottoman government's systematic extermination of its Armenian population. Victims are estimated to number 800,000 to 1.5 million. April 24, 1915, is considered the first day of this genocide. On that day, the Turkish government rounded up, arrested, and deported between 235 and 270 Armenian intellectuals and community leaders. The majority of this group were later murdered.

This extermination program was conducted during and after World War I. The first part involved the killing of able-bodied males through massacre or forced labor. Then women, children, the elderly, and the infirm were sent on death marches to the Syrian desert. These individuals did not have food or water and were subject to robbery, rape, and massacre.

Gage's heroic part in the Armenian Genocide occurred in 1915 when the genocide came to Marsovan.[22] With the assistance of fellow teacher Charlotte Willard, her actions were considered to be "one of the most thrilling stories of women's work during the war." To many, it made her and Willard real-life heroes. Even in this work, Gage was a leader of men.

One day in the summer of 1915, a force of Turkish soldiers came into the school compound. The Armenian men and boys had already

---

21. Wilson, *Road Ahead*, 78.

22. For a blow-by-blow account of events in Marsovan, see Bertha B. Morley, *Marsovan 1915: The Diaries of Bertha Morley*, 2nd ed., ed. Hilmar Kaiser, Armenian Genocide Documentation Series 3 (Ann Arbor, MI, and Princeton, NJ: Gomidas Institute; and Reading, Eng.: Taderon Press, 2000). Gage's role is included.

been taken. This time they came for the Armenian women and girls. Depending on which account is to be believed, sixty-two or sixty-three were taken in fourteen open carts. Gage herself went to the classroom mentioned in the 1895 account. She prayed and then reasserted her belief that she had to defend all girls not just the ones being taken.

So Gage and Willard set out to get the kidnapped women and girls back. They had to wait around six days to get travel permits. But once they got these, they were off on the 113-mile journey. Gage and Willard passed large groups of refugees as soldiers let them pass. The roads were crowded, dusty, and dangerous. Gage and Willard telegraphed the governor of Sivas, an upcoming town, and asked him to hold the kidnap victims there. About an hour after their arrival there, most of the women and girls appeared. Typical of Gage's work with men, she had a "momentous interview" with the governor of Sivas and the soldiers.[23] In the end, forty- eight would return with Gage and Willard to Marsovan.

Recalling how the men listened to her and Willard, Gage would later say. "You might say that the Boli courteously gave us back fifty girls." But to her intimate friends, she said, "The result was directly of God, nothing we could do was even slightly adequate, so many had tried and failed. This was just one of God's miracles."[24]

Gage died on July 15, 1917, in Marsovan at the age of fifty-one and was buried the next day before a crowd of over 300 men and women in a small cemetery next to her good friend Martha King.[25] After her death, the Portland YWCA started the Frances Gage Club and established the Frances Cousens Gage Memorial Fund.

Very quickly different ideas about why Gage died circulated. Suggestions ranged from typhus to eating unwholesome and "brittle" food.

---

23. The man referred to as the "governor" or "vali" may have been Ahmed Muammer. He was the governor of the Vilayet of Sivas from 1913 to 1916. A vilayet was the term used for an administrative district in the Ottoman Empire. Muammer has been accused of complicity in the killing of the Armenians, which would make him particularly dangerous to Gage and Willard.

24. Wilson, *Road Ahead*, 99–100. Sivas was a town in north central Turkey located in the Sivas Vilayet, one of the six Armenian districts of the Ottoman Empire. It is located southeast of Marsovan. Gage's use of the term "boli" is unclear, and why she used it may never be known. However, there are at least three possibilities for its use. Boli is the older name for the Bolu Province northwest of Marsovan, the term "boli" is slang for confirming a person agrees with something someone else is saying (i.e., someone being "dead right" or "on point"), or the term is a misspelling of the word "vali," or governor.

25. See James L. Barton, "American Colleges in Turkey," *Student World* 11 (1918): 5–11. For more information on Gage, see Wilson, *Road Ahead*.

In *The Road Ahead*, author Elizabeth Wilson described an exhausted person: "It would come to pass that Frances Gage's nervous reserve was exhausted and could no longer spur on her flagging physical forces."[26] A hagiographic account suggested that like Jesus she "hath borne the griefs and carried the sorrows of her beloved people."

---

26. Wilson, *Road Ahead*, 109.

6

The Ministry of the Traveling Secretary

One day, two Russian men who were probably theological students came to see a woman leader of the Student Christian Movement (SCM). It is not clear where or when this meeting occurred. Was she alone with them in a private room or in a public place? These men were part of a local preaching society whose members created and then criticized each other's sermons. These talks would then be given in local churches. The woman suspected a trap when they asked what she thought about Charles Spurgeon. After all, the SCM leader observed, it was commonly held that Baptists like Spurgeon were carrying out "evil doings." To her surprise, one of the men said he liked Spurgeon. The two had been passing out copies of his "Lectures to Young Preachers" to every theological student. The men then asked her for help in spiritual matters and with their preaching. They were very anxious for this assistance. The SCM leader offered some advice, and afterward sent some materials to these men.[1]

This SCM leader was Ruth Rouse. Her personal work with these two individuals was an important part of the overall task of this type of secretary. In her description of this encounter, no mention was made of Rouse's gender or that she met with the men by herself. Given that Rouse was raised in Spurgeon's church in London, one wonders if she brought that up.

Rouse was just one example of women traveling secretaries doing one of the tasks that this ministry included. These women worked extensively with men even though in most cases, they were appointed to work with women.

---

1. Ruth Rouse, *Talks with Russian Students*, Russia IV (October 7–November 25, 1911): 6, Archives of WSCF, Record Group No. 46 (Box 44, Folder 363), Special Collections, Yale Divinity School.

THE MINISTRY OF A TRAVELING SECRETARY

In any given year, the traveling secretary visited too many institutions to count and took a remarkable number of trips by carriage, car, rail, or steamship. Travel was by first and second class. Occasionally, traveling secretaries went third class for special reasons.[2]

Most visits occurred during the school year, August to June. As an example, during the 1917–1918 school year when the United States was rationing all travel due to World War I, a handful of American Student Volunteer Movement for Foreign Missions (SVMFM) traveling secretaries made an astounding 800 visits to 516 schools, attending nine summer conferences for men, eleven summer conferences for women, and thirty-one special student conferences.

During the summer months, traveling secretaries kept quite busy, with only brief times for vacations. The SVMFM required them to read materials published inside and outside the movement. In a June 17, 1913, letter to Edith Wiley, Fennell P. Turner advised her to read the Bible and as many books on missions as possible. He suggested Arthur Judson Brown, *The Foreign Missionary: An Incarnation of a World Movement*; *Counsel to New Missionaries from Older Missionaries of the Presbyterian Church*; and *The Call, Qualifications and Preparation of Missionary Candidates: Papers by Missionaries and Other Authorities*.[3]

Although the last book covered topics that would be of interest to both men and women, such as the missionary call and missionary and spiritual development, it also contained topics of special interest to women. Subject matter here included qualifications for a women's missionary, what "outfit" a woman missionary needed, and other practical preparations for women intending on missionary work.

However, despite the fact that women were clearly doing many things traditionally ascribed to men in the SCM, the book instructed women to prepare for ministries typically ascribed to women, such as working with children, teaching, nursing, and the domestic arts. It even suggested that women take up needlepoint.

Traveling secretaries also attended summer student conferences and secretaries' training conferences as the school year began. For example,

---

2. See chapter 11 for Grace Saunders's choice to travel steerage from Canada to England.

3. Arthur Judson Brown, *The Foreign Missionary: An Incarnation of a World Movement* (New York: Fleming H. Revell, 1907); *Counsel to New Missionaries from Older Missionaries of the Presbyterian Church* (New York: Board of Foreign Missions of the Presbyterian Church, 1905); and *The Call, Qualifications and Preparation of Missionary Candidates: Papers by Missionaries and Other Authorities* (New York: SVMFM, 1906).

in 1903, a conference for training secretaries was held in Princeton, New Jersey.[4] Those in attendance included thirty men and six women (Pauline Root, Bertha Condé, Susie Little, M. L. Blount, Harriet Taylor, and Dorothea Day). The subject matter for both men and women here was the Watchword, recruitment of missionary candidates, increasing attendance in missions study groups, SVMFM accomplishments, and spiritual development.[5]

The traveling secretary's main goal was to visit institutions of higher learning to stimulate existing Christian activity or develop new groups. As John Mott wrote:

> [Traveling secretary work] consists in organizing, educating, developing, quickening and setting at work the volunteers in the different institutions, and in extending the movement, not only among previously visiting institutions, but also among those as yet untouched.[6]

Traveling secretaries also sought to link local associations with national and international student movements. Visits were necessary to supplement the literature provided by movement headquarters.

Visits of traveling secretaries included pre-visit arrangements, the visit itself, and tasks to be done afterward.

PRE-VISIT TASKS

Before any visit, movement headquarters informed the traveling secretary of the date and place of upcoming appointments. Once notified, secretaries wrote leaders of the local groups at least two days in advance to announce their arrival times, approximate schedules, and needs. Traveling secretaries also made unannounced visits a few times during the school year.

TASKS DURING VISITS

Tasks done during each visit became so standardized that they came up repeatedly in literature published throughout the SCM community.

---

4. *Conference of Secretaries of the SVM, Princeton, New Jersey, September 12–14, 1903,* Archives of the SVMFM, Record Group No. 42 (Box 449, Folder 5256), Special Collections, Yale Divinity School Library.

5. Ibid.

6. John R. Mott, *Addresses and Papers of John R. Mott: The Student Volunteer Movement for Foreign Missions* (New York: Association Press, 1946), 1:27.

For example, analyzing a 1907 survey of expectations for traveling secretaries by British students, Tatlow observed, "Most colleges seem to expect much the same thing, to address one or more meetings, visit Bible circles, meet the committee, meet as many individuals as possible with a view of doing personal work."[7]

Traveling secretaries usually gave an astounding number of speeches during the average visit. Tatlow estimated that British workers gave between one and five a day during the average semester to mixed and separate gatherings of men and women.[8]

Two SCM stand out as prime examples of a traveling secretary: Mary "Minnie" Geraldine Guinness Taylor and Clara Ruth Rouse.

MARY "MINNIE" GERALDINE GUINNESS TAYLOR (1865–1949)

Today when an individual hears the word "Guinness," they think of a very popular and well-known brewery in Dublin, Ireland. Tourists flock to the Guinness Storehouse for tours and souvenirs in its rather large gift shop. The story of the history of beer, this beer company, and the Guinness clan has been explored in Stephen Mansfield's recent book *The Search for God and Guinness: A Biography of the Beer That Changed the World*.[9] Inside this text is a reference to and a picture of a popular SCM traveling secretary, Mary Geraldine Guinness Taylor. With a little further study beyond Mansfield the careful student of the Guinness clan will find that the family had bankers, politicians, beer makers, religious leaders, and missionaries. She was part of the last category of Guinness.

Taylor was a popular author, Protestant missionary to China, and global speaker.[10] She has been hidden in the shadow of famous men

---

7. Tissington Tatlow, *Memorandum on the Work of Traveling Secretaries and the Training of Local Leaders, prepared for the Commission, October 1907*, SCM and SVMU Staffing and Staff Reports, 1907–1910 (SCM/A18, Records of the Student Christian Movement), 3, Cadbury Research Library, Special Collections, University of Birmingham.

8. Tissington Tatlow, *The Story of the Student Christian Movement of Great Britain and Ireland* (London: SCM Press, 1933), 375.

9. Stephen Mansfield, *The Search for God and Guinness: A Biography of the Beer That Changed the World* (Nashville, TN: Thomas Nelson, 2014).

10. Taylor prepared many articles for the *Regions Beyond*, her father's missionary school's periodical, and for publications of the China Inland Mission. Taylor also wrote several books including: *In the Far East* (London: Marshall, Morgan and Scott, 1889); *One of China's Scholars: The Culture and Conversion of a Confucianist* (London: Morgan and Scott, 1900); with Frederick Howard Taylor, *Hudson Taylor in Early Years: The Growth of a Soul* (London: Morgan and Scott, 1911); *Hudson Taylor* (London: China Inland Mission, 1918); *The Call of China's Great North-West* (London: CIM, 1923); *Hudson Taylor's Spiritual Secret* (London: CIM, 1923); *Guinness of Honan*

Mary "Minnie" Geraldine Guinness Taylor
(Courtesy Michele Guinness)

and women: her father, Henry Grattan Guinness (1835–1910), a notable preacher, missionary, educator, and author; her father-in-law Hudson Taylor, founder and director of the China Inland Mission; and her mother, Fanny Emma Fitzgerald Guinness (1831–1898). Fanny Guinness was Honorary Secretary of the London Institute for Home and Foreign Missions and author of *The New World of Central Africa: With a History of the First Christian Mission on the Congo* and *Congo Recollections: Edited from Notes and Conversations of Missionaries.*[11] Taylor's mother believed that women should be able to work outside the home and should be able to discuss fine points of theology as comprehensively as men. She took her daughter to a small, all-male dinner

---

(London: China Inland Mission, 1933); *Margaret King's Vision* (Philadelphia: CIM, 1934); *The Triumph of John and Betty Stamm* (Philadelphia: CIM, 1935); with Howard Taylor, *By Faith* (Philadelphia: CIM, 1938); and *Behind the Ranges* (London and Redhill: Lutterworth Press and China Inland Mission, 1944).

For Taylor's conference ministry, see chapter 10.

11. Fanny Guinness, *The New World of Central Africa: With a History of the First Christian Mission on the Congo* (London: Hodder and Stoughton, 1890); and *Congo Recollections: Edited from Notes and Conversations of Missionaries* (London: Hodder and Stoughton, 1890).

meeting at Charles Spurgeon's home, and the two Guinness women were active in the theological discussions. Inspired by Catherine Booth of the Salvation Army, Fanny Guinness became a street preacher with audiences of men and women. In 1858, she wrote, "Women (the daring of it!), *women* began to take part in the revival meetings, with trepidation at first, and after long searchings of heart and much anguished prayer. There was an outcry, of course, but the broader minded among the revivalists soon came to see that resistance to such compelling sincerity would be in vain."[12]

Geraldine Guinness Taylor was educated by a governess at home by a Miss Gardner from an early age and then attended Mrs. Pennefather's School run by Catherine King Pennefather, the wife of the Reverend William Pennefather. Taylor was then tutored by Florence Maude Charlesworth (who later became Mrs. Ballington-Booth, the daughter-in-law of William and Catherine Booth, founders of the Salvation Army) and then went to boarding school for only six weeks before dropping out. Taylor continued her education briefly in China. There she studied intensive Chinese at a China Inland Mission School, but quickly dropped out, saying she could learn Chinese living among the people.

Though fiercely independent, Taylor married Dr. Howard Taylor in 1894.[13] She felt she should do this because of an early morning experience in prayer when she was alone in a barn. Guinness had gone there to pray during a day set aside as a special day of prayer for the China Inland Mission. While on her knees, she told God that she would go anywhere. Immediately, Guinness heard an inner voice, "Go anywhere, Geraldine? Do anything? Even marry Howard Taylor?" Despite immediate protestations, Guinness did feel a growing attraction and soon was engaged and married. She lost her only child in a miscarriage. Guinness gave her inheritance away to her stepmother, Grace Alexandra Ruth Hurditch Guinness, who as a widow had two young boys to care for, John Christopher Guinness and Paul A. Grattan Guinness.

---

12.   Fanny Guinness, "She Spake of Him," in *Being Recollections of the Loving Labors and Early Death of the Late Mrs. Geraldine Dening, an Essay by Fanny E. Guinness* (1872), in *Genius of Guinness: The Enduring Legacy of an Irish Dynasty*, by Michele Guinness (Belfast: Ambassador International, 2005).

13.   Frederick Howard Taylor (1862–1946), MRCS (Member of the Royal College of Surgeons), was the second son of the founder of the China Inland Mission, James Hudson Taylor and his first wife, Maria Jane Dyer (1837–1870), who are featured in chapter 10. After graduating from the Royal London Medical College in 1888, he served in China starting in 1890. He was a speaker and author. For details on her relationship with her husband, see Michele Guinness, *Genius of Guinness.*

Taylor also did not like housework and only did that starting around age sixty. Guinness chronicler Michele Guinness remembered when her father-in-law became engaged, Taylor asked his fiancée the following, "Jean, dear, can you sew? Jean dear, can you cook? Jean, dear, can you type?" Later after marriage, the woman told Michele, "Blooming cheek really, she'd never done any of those things in her life. Howard always did them for her."[14] This observation was characteristic of their life as a couple. Taylor was typically in the limelight with her writing and public speaking while her husband, who was shy and self-effacing, was in the background looking after her.

Working in missions her entire life, Taylor started her ministry at her parents' missionary training school. In her youth, she taught a Bible class for women factory workers and provided pastoral care for them in London's East End. Taylor taught men and women. Her men's groups grew to over one hundred students. She was assigned the "beginners and drunkers." One male student observed, "I can see her now, standing on the platform with her white handkerchief on the rostrum. She was like an angel."[15] In the mid-1880s, she and a friend posed as factory workers and temporarily moved to the East End where they lived and worked in factories to see what life was like for those in their ministry.

Because her leadership gifts were so evident, Taylor interviewed prospective pastors for the mission hall in her early twenties. She attended meetings as a deaconess in the East End of London.[16]

Taylor was interested in personal evangelism. Michele Guinness noted this after she brought her father-in-law to Christ and then made it possible for him to speak at the Canadian Keswick. Guinness said, "As an elderly lady, she would introduce this young man in her plumy English accent (which the Americans loved) as 'my brother' to everyone's astonishment."[17]

Taylor spent the bulk of her career serving with her husband as a missionary in China (1888–1941). She went there because of a sunrise experience on a beach. Guinness observed later that while watching a beach sunrise at Rathdrum Rectory in Ireland, she saw two lights. One was a strange orange light that slowly lit up the sky. A second light filled her "inner grey" and despondency over life. Because of the second light, she was absolutely sure that she should go to China.

---

14. Email from Michele Guinness to Thomas Russell, May 10, 2016.

15. These kinds of observations about Guinness would be noted on several occasions.

16. For more information on the deaconess community, see chapter 12.

17. Email from Michele Guinness to Thomas Russell, May 10, 2016.

She went to China in 1888. Her journey took her through Gibraltar, Naples, the Straits of Messina, Ceylon, Singapore, Hong Kong, and Shanghai. Taylor traveled with other missionaries bound for China.

In Shanghai, Taylor exchanged her European clothes for typical late-nineteenth-century Chinese clothes. This was a practice that separated her from other missionaries. Most missionaries wore late-nineteenth-century European or American clothing.

After Shanghai, Taylor went to Chinkiang and then after a barge ride of six hours, she arrived at Yang-chau. After training in China, she eventually was stationed in Honan Province.

The last years of her and her husband's life were as exciting as the earliest years. They lived in close proximity of the epicenter of the devastating 1920 earthquake in Lanchow, so they helped with its aftermath. Then they were ambushed and kidnapped. To get their release, the kidnappers let Taylor go alone to another city to negotiate their release. Before they were freed, the political situation changed, so they were both freed. But before they were, Howard had led the chief kidnapper to Christ. After returning home to England, Taylor wrote a book on her adventure called *With P'u and His Brigands*.[18]

In 1946, Taylor's husband died, and she suffered a stroke around that time. She died in 1949 in her eighty-fourth year in Tunbridge Wells, England. Her estate was valued at £5,487, which would have been worth £213,993 in 2016.

The SVMFM invited Taylor and her husband to serve as traveling secretaries between November 1900 and April 1901. In SVMFM history, this campaign was considered one of the most notable for its successes. Taylor gave many speeches during visits to public and private colleges, medical schools, nurses' schools, and training schools with her husband or a female traveling companion.[19] She visited about as many sites as her husband separately (he visited seventy-seven schools) and focused on the women's colleges in the eastern United States. Traveling together for part of this time, the Taylors visited the western United States and Canada. Since they were so successful, the SVMFM invited the Taylors to repeat their 1901 visit in 1912.

---

18. Mary Geraldine Guinness Taylor, *With P'u and His Brigands* (Philadelphia: Sunday School Times, 1922).

19. For more information, see "The Missionary Campaign of Dr. and Mrs. Howard Taylor," *Intercollegian* 23, no. 8 (May 1901): 180–82. For more information on Guinness, see Joy Guinness, *Mrs. Howard Taylor: Her Web of Time*, 1st ed. (London: China Inland Mission, 1949); Michele Guinness, *The Guinness Legend* (London: Hotter and Stoughton, 1989); and Patricia Barr, *To China with Love: The Lives and Times of Protestant Missionaries in China, 1860–1900* (London: Secker and Warburg, 1972).

Taylor's visit to Bryn Mawr College, cited in this book's introduction, is worth repeating here. In a December 20, 1900, note, M. Carey Thomas, the college's president, seemed very happy to have Taylor speak.[20] She wrote:

> I am very much pleased that you can arrange for Mrs. Howard Taylor to preach to our students on Wednesday, March 6th. This date suits us perfectly and we shall understand that Mrs. Taylor will be with us at that time. When you write Mrs. Taylor, will you not tell her that $25.00 is appropriate for the traveling expenses of each of our speakers at these evening meetings.[21]

Taylor's speech was significant because it provides a vivid picture of women's traveling secretary work with men. In it Taylor spoke to an all-male audience:

> [One] story . . . describes an incident of this tour when Geraldine was to address a gathering of men students. Possibly under

---

20. Martha Carey Thomas (1857–1935) was an American educator, suffragist, linguist, and second president of Bryn Mawr College (1894–1922). Thomas attended Holland Institute, Cornell University (BA, 1877), Johns Hopkins University (one year's study of classics), Leipzig University, and finally the University of Zurich (PhD, Summa Cum Laude, 1892, the first foreigner and woman to do so).

At her request in 1885, Thomas was appointed dean and professor of English at the newly opened Bryn Mawr College. By 1892, she was acting as president, and in 1894 she was officially named as such. Thomas remained president until 1922. She made Bryn Mawr as rigorous as any Ivy League institution and believed that the strongest women's colleges in America could produce an elite corps of women who were men's equals and who could change the world. She never married, but instead had female lifetime companions, namely Mamie Gwinn and later Mary Elizabeth Garret.

Thomas felt that a woman could be married, have children, and have a full-time professional career. She was active in progressive causes, such as Teddy Roosevelt's Bull Moose Party, pacifism, and feminism. Thomas helped found the College Equal Suffrage League (1906) and by 1908 was its president and a widely traveled speaker. Her most important role was an example of a militant, individualistic, career-oriented, competent woman.

For more information on Thomas, see Marjoram Houspian Dobkin, ed., *The Making of a Feminist: Early Journals and Letters of M. Carey Thomas* (Kent, OH: Kent State University Press, 1979); and Helen Lefkowitz Horowitz, *The Power and Passion of M. Carey Thomas* (New York: Alfred A. Knopf, 1994).

21. This is the only reference to Taylor's visit in the M. Carey Thomas Papers at Bryn Mawr College, Papers of M. Carey Thomas, Reel 97: 75. Taylor's visit was also mentioned in a report by "F.S.S." of the campus Christian Union in the *Lantern*, a campus magazine: "The Union has been addressed this year by the following speakers: Miss Weitzel on "The Advantages of Mission Study," Mrs. Howard Taylor on her work in China, Miss Abby Irk on "Miss Tsudo's Work in Japan," and Mrs. Gilco on "The Educational Condition of Girls in Spain, "Christian Union," *Lantern* 10 (June, 1901) [Philadelphia: Anvil Printing Company, 1901]: 76.

the impression that it was a secular lecture, they settled down to listen with their feet on the backs of the chairs in front of them. The outlook from the speaker's point of view was an audience of soles. It was a little disconcerting, but Geraldine rose to the occasion, and addressed herself to their "souls," determined to make their "soles" disappear. She had not been speaking for fifteen minutes before almost every shoe was out of sight, and the whole audience was hanging on her every word.[22]

Taylor also had a significant impact on Thomas. Taylor's niece, then a student at Bryn Mawr College, reported that the "striking feature of Taylor's visit was the impression she made on President M. Carey Thomas. . . . Mrs. Taylor's simplicity and directness . . . her lovely English voice, beauty of her white forehead and dark hair, and her unique charm, 'held students and the President in a reverent spell.'"[23] Thomas was so moved that she invited Taylor to stay at the Deanery where she lived and provided her with a room for private talks with students. The newly renovated facility had plenty of room for guests.[24]

Martha Carey Thomas has several other connections with the SCM. In 1921, she and Jane Addams appeared on the stationery of the SCM-sponsored Student Friendship Fund.

CLARA RUTH ROUSE (1872–1956)

The roles Ruth Rouse played in SCM circles were so wide-ranging that she could be placed in any chapter in this book. She served as a committee member, secretary, and pioneer in her lengthy SCM career. This book places her in the traveling secretary position because she loved this task, and it filled up a large portion of her time and ministry. Because of her extensive ministries, Rouse said she had traveled to every continent and more than sixty nations.

---

22.   Guinness, *Mrs. Howard Taylor*, 174.

23.   Ibid., 174.

24.   The Deanery was the residence of Thomas from 1885 to 1933. Thomas had the facility enlarged for entertaining the college's important guests, students, and alumnae as well as her immediate family and friends. One of several renovations of the Deanery occurred between 1894 and 1896 just prior to Taylor's 1901 visit. In this renovation, more guest and servant quarters were added, plus a library. At first it was merely a five-room cottage, but it eventually became a forty-six-room mansion with Louis Comfort Tiffany light fixtures. The building was demolished in 1968. For more information about the facility during Taylor's visit, see Ruth Levy Merriam, *A History of the Deanery, Bryn Mawr College* (Bryn Mawr: Bryn Mawr College, 1965).

Clara Ruth Rouse
(Special Collections, Yale Divinity School)

Typical of many SCM women leaders, though officially appointed to work with women, her ministry touched men also. Concerning this, former SCM leader Annie Beatrice Glass Fraser observed, "Certain it is that men always regarded her as an equal, and that even in these early days when joint men's and women's work was somewhat new, 'quite as many young men were her disciples as young women.'"[25]

Rouse was clearly the most powerful and respected woman leader inside and outside the SCM. In her day, she was a well-known figure in global Christian circles. Princess Pauline Sulkowska of Hungary said, "She was Dr. Mott's 'man of invincible good-will' in female form."[26] In 1957, Beatrice Glass Fraser gave a good overall description of Rouse's reputation and influence:

---

25. Mrs. Alek G. Fraser, letter to Wilmina M. Rowland, January 25, 1937. In Wilmina M. Rowland, "The Contribution of Ruth Rouse to the World's Student Christian Federation" (MA thesis, Yale University, 1937), 73.

26. See Ruth Franzén, "The Legacy of Ruth Rouse," *International Bulletin of Missionary* Research (October 1993): 156–57; Karl Fries, *Mina Minnen* [My reminiscences] (Stockholm: Triangelförlaget, 1939), 100; and Rowland, "Contribution of Ruth Rouse," 175.

As a traveling secretary I think she was extremely valuable in Britain through her quiet massiveness, good looks, good clothes (as compared to women missionaries of those days), good introductions, good degree from Girton. Most heads of women's colleges then were definitely extremely afraid of religious enthusiasm and outwardly at any rate did not seem in any way to identify themselves with religion at all and they had at least to respect Ruth and listen to what she had to say.[27]

Sadly, Rouse is not well known today. This point was highlighted by what Lord George Carey, the former Archbishop of Canterbury, said in 2003, "A great woman, too bad she is unknown today. We should have a day in the Anglican annual calendar just for her for her contributions."

This single career woman was born into an upper-middle-class family in Clapham, in south London, England, the oldest of five children of George Woodford (1846–1906), a cotton broker, and Williamina Georgina MacDonald (1847–1937) Rouse. Her father came from Plymouth Brethren roots with some Evangelical Anglican connections, and her mother was a Scottish Baptist. Testimonies to her comfortable upbringing can be seen in the servants that appear in census lists in the late nineteenth century and in Rouse's mother's will in 1937 that said her estate was worth £6,340, which would have been worth approximately £403,858 in 2016.

Rouse attended Notting Hill High School (1889), Bedford College, London (where she studied mathematics, physics, chemistry, English literature, and Latin from 1890 to 1891), and Girton College, Cambridge (Classical Tripos, Pt. 1, Cl. III, Div. 1, 1893). After Girton, Rouse spent one year studying Sanskrit at the British Museum.

Rouse attended Charles Spurgeon's Metropolitan Tabernacle as a child. She claimed that she became a Christian at a Children's Special Mission as a teen. This occurred in Bournemouth while on vacation with her family. The layman directing the mission asked her to teach a swimming class for the youngest children. Watching the activity on the beach, she had a spiritual awareness that conversion was something that God initiated and not something humans could do. After her conversion, Rouse was baptized in Spurgeon's church. At age twenty-two, she became a member of the Church of England, where she was a lifetime communicant until her death in 1956.

Rouse's missionary call came through several experiences and developed over time. In college, she witnessed her good friend Agnes

---

27. Rowland, "Contribution of Ruth Rouse," 73.

de Selincourt commit her life to missionary work. She was touched by SVMFM founder Robert Wilder's mission to Cambridge University in 1891. She attended her first student conference at Keswick with 50 women and 143 men in 1894. At that meeting she met John R. Mott and Robert Speer.[28] In 1896, Rouse attended the Student Volunteer Missionary Union (SVMU) Conference in Liverpool with over 700 other students. Through these things, according to Rowland, "She began to see missions not as slavery and denial, but as a joyous task a part of which was a ministry to students in an international setting. The missionary ideal, that dominated her life was an expanding ideal, and was now becoming a flying goal before her."[29]

But in the end, Rouse recalled years later that the most important part was when she signed the Volunteer Pledge. In doing this, she committed herself to a worldwide missionary career. In an interview with her biographer, Rowland, she remembered that there was that "decisive, and unforgettable, moment when she was standing looking out of a window in her private domain at Girton and Paul's statement flashed through her mind: 'I know whom I have believed, and am persuaded that He is able to keep that which I have committed unto Him against that day.'" For Rouse accepting and keeping this pledge was totally in God's hands. It was not left to her indecision. As a result, Rouse had absolute certainty about God's purpose for her life. She might have some indecisiveness in other areas, but not with her call.[30]

The list of Rouse's SCM activities was quite lengthy, but here are a few. Rouse's SCM involvement began in college, where she helped start local associations. In 1895–1896, Rouse was editor of the *Student Volunteer*, which gave her a seat on the British executive. From 1896 to 1897, Rouse served as the traveling secretary for the British College

---

28. Robert Speer (1867–1947) was born in Huntington, Pennsylvania. He graduated from Princeton University in 1889 and then traveled for the SVMFM in 1889 and 1890. Speer studied at Princeton Theological Seminary in 1890 and 1891. He left seminary to become secretary for the Presbyterian Board of Foreign Missions. He did that job until 1937. Speer was active in the SVMFM, the Foreign Missions Conference of North America, the Federal Council of Churches, the International Missionary Council, and the Committee on Cooperation in Latin America. In 1927, he became the moderator of the General Assembly of the Presbyterian Church. He sided with the modernists in the 1920s by opposing the actions of John Gresham Machen. Speer was a preacher and authored books on missionary strategy and biography, the practical Christian life, and Bible studies. For more information on Speer, see James A. Patterson, "Speer, Robert Elliott." In *Biographical Dictionary of Christian Missions*, ed. Gerald H. Anderson (New York: Macmillan, 1998), 633.

29. Rowland, "Contribution of Ruth Rouse," 65.

30. Ruth Franzén, *Ruth Rouse among Students: Global, Missiological, and Ecumenical Perspectives* (Uppsala: Swedish Institute of Mission Research, 2008), 46.

Christian Union (BCCU) and the SVMU. From 1897 to 1899, she was traveling secretary for the American SVMFM and YWCA. In 1905, Rouse was appointed the WSCF's women's secretary. Between 1905 and 1924, she was a traveling secretary for the WSCF and secretary for its executive from 1921 to 1924. Also after World War I Rouse was the head of Emergency Student Relief, a WSCF-sponsored group. Because Mott had resigned from his position as WSCF general secretary in 1920, many have suggested that Rouse was his replacement for this four-year period.

Rouse also worked with organizations closely linked with the SCM. She served the British YWCA as a canteen worker with the British Armies from 1916 to 1918. Rouse turned down an offer to be the World YWCA international student secretary. Instead, between 1938 and 1946, Rouse was president of the World YWCA after serving as a member of its executive since 1907. She attended the 1910 World Missionary Conference held at Edinburgh, and the First Assembly of the World Council of Churches in 1948.

Outside of SCM circles, Rouse worked in several capacities. During 1900–1902, Rouse co-founded and co-led the Missionary Settlement for University Women in Bombay, India. For her efforts with the YWCA and YMCA in Le Havre, France, in World War I from 1916 to 1918, she received a British War Medal. From 1925 to 1939 she was the educational secretary of the Missionary Council of the Assembly of the Church of England.

After taking care of her sick and aging mother until her death in 1937, Rouse died in 1956 leaving an estate worth £3,600, which would have been worth £85,320 in 2016.

Rouse authored many articles and books, including *Religious Experiences and Psychological Process* (with Hugh Crichton Miller); *Rebuilding Europe: The Student Chapter in Post-War Reconstruction*; *The Commonwealth of Man*; *The Federation in the World War 1914–1918*; and *The World's Student Christian Federation: A History of the First Thirty Years*. She was the editor (along with Stephen Charles Neill) of *A History of the Ecumenical Movement, 1517–1948*.[31]

---

31.   Ruth Rouse and Hugh Crichton Miller, *Christian Experience and Psychological Processes* (London: SCM Press, 1918); Ruth Rouse, *Rebuilding Europe: The Student Chapter in Post-War Reconstruction* (London: SCM Press, 1925); *The Commonwealth of Man* (London: SCM Press, 1939); *The Federation in the World War 1914–1918* (Geneva: WSCF, 1940); *The World's Student Christian Federation: A History of the First Thirty Years* (London: SCM Press, 1948); and with Stephen Charles Neill, eds., *A History of the Ecumenical Movement 1517–1948* (London: SPCK, 1954).

CLARA RUTH ROUSE'S
TRAVELING SECRETARY MINISTRY

Meeting with the local association's executive committee, which ran the local group, was an important part of a traveling secretary's typical visit. Traveling secretaries sought to encourage, inspire, and direct these important committees. They offered insights from their personal experiences, training, and visits to other campus associations.

Rouse described her experience of meeting with three executive committees while traveling with for the WSCF in Finland in 1903. While the gender makeup of these groups is not specified, given the coeducational nature of the Finnish movement's leadership, it could be construed that she worked here with men and women:

> I had three long committee meetings with them in which ten of them went through different points of their C.U. work with me. We were at it about three hours each time!! Don't despise me, please, but remember that five languages were hurtling around the room, and that while they were developing their ideas amongst themselves in Finnish or Swedish, I was preparing weighty sentences in French or German or loading my interpreter with ammunition in English. We really reached results, and I learned more of them in that way then in any other, but it took time and patience.[32]

A final task of traveling secretary was ministry with individuals or "personal work." Traveling secretaries worked with student leaders and campus authorities. Because many of the former often felt overburdened or discouraged, they looked forward to the visit of a traveling secretary. Local leaders hoped to talk with an experienced SCM worker, who could sympathize with the difficulties they faced in campus associations. Attempting to develop a repertoire with campus authorities was

---

32. Ruth Rouse, *Report of Tour in Finland October and November*, 5, Archives of the WSCF, Record Group No. 46 (Box 45, Folder 364), Special Collections, Yale Divinity School Library. For more information on Rouse, see the Archives of the SVMFM and WSCF at Yale Divinity School; the British SCM Archives, Cadbury Research Library, Special Collections, University of Birmingham; Suzanne Bidgrain, "Ruth Rouse (1872–1956)," *Student World* 50 (1st Quarter, 1957): 73–77; Rowland, "Contribution of Ruth Rouse"; Ruth Franzén, "Ruth Rouse," in *Mission Legacies: Biographical Studies of Leaders of the Modern Missionary Movement*, ed. Gerald H. Anderson et al. (Maryknoll, NY: Orbis Books, 1994), 93–101, and *Ruth Rouse among Students*; and Johanna M. Selles, *The World Student Christian Federation, 1895–1925: Motives, Methods, and Influential Women* (Eugene, OR: Pickwick, 2011).

crucial because through this important connection, traveling secretaries could find support for further visits, local SVMFM activity, and their missionary recruitment.

Rouse felt that she was especially inspired while working with individuals. The story of one of her experiences was told at the beginning of this chapter. After a 1907 visit to Moscow, she wrote:

> The private talks revealed life after life in which there had been the clearest preparation of the spirit of God, leading up to light. . . . At first, some came merely to argue, but in the last ten days, each one came with a definite question concerning her own spiritual need. I was constantly conscious of divine help, given moment by moment to meet their strange difficulties and problems. And they were strange; never before had I to tackle student girls apparently meditating in breach of the sixth commandment.[33]

Those who knew and those who have studied Rouse have claimed that her strongest talent was evangelism through personal work. Benefiting from this, a student named Helmi Forsman observed:

> She had remarkable insight in the mentality and problems of students not only of women but also of men students who were reached by her. . . . Miss Rouse laid such stress upon personal work. She had the capacity for listening to a person in trouble, and not only that, but of deep understanding. One had the feeling that she understood and knew one. I remember wondering when I myself had a personal talk with her during one of her visits here: How can a person from England, quite strange to me, understand my difficulties so well? I would think she had known me for years. It was not perhaps easy to approach her, but when you were under the circle of her personal care, you felt her understanding love, her unselfish interest and her faithfulness surround you, and you felt you had a real friend. She gave out herself to you.[34]

Rouse's official reports are littered with observations about individual work. She met with many types of people and often with more men than women. From a Russian report, Rouse noted that she had met

---

33. Rowland, "Contribution of Ruth Rouse," 161–62.
34. Ibid., 88–89.

with the spiritually needy, those coming to argue a theological point, followers of Tolstoy, those curious about the student movement, and students from the ecclesiastical academy. Her eight-day 1907 visit to Finland included "at home daily from 1 to 2 for talks."[35] During a return visit in 1915, she was "at home for two to three hours daily to students, who wished to come and see me."[36] From Kiev, Rouse noted, "After speaking, I chatted with any who wanted to ask questions; then another hour; then last words with questioners; then supper in same restaurant between 11 and 12 o'clock. . . . After the large meeting, I have many personal talks with students, both men and women."[37]

POST-VISIT TASKS

After a visit, the traveling secretary still had tasks to do with the local campus. They maintained contacts established during a visit so that they could hear of the progress of the local ministry and plan future visits. The traveling secretary also wrote to local campus leaders, university authorities, and students at institutions to thank them for their hospitality, to pray for them, and to send them movement literature. Since the worker was the connecting link between the local school and the national or international movement, reports had to be filed detailing the visit so that executive committees could see what had transpired during the visit and assess progress made. In their reports, traveling secretaries identified campus authorities who might prove beneficial to the SVMFM.

On May 11, 1918, Edith Wiley demonstrated the benefit of having this link. Wanting to know the suitability of a possible candidate for missionary work, Ray Buearman, she wrote, "I've written to President Riley of McMinnville, asking him to write to you about him."[38] This was most likely Dr. Leonard W. Riley, the president of McMinnville College from 1906 to 1931.[39] In a similar way, in 1919, Wiley wrote that she had

---

35. Ibid., 179. Ruth Rouse, *Finland: Reports of Ruth Rouse* (November 1907), 6, Archives of the WSCF, Record Group No. 46 (Box 45, Folder 364), Special Collections, Yale Divinity School Library.

36. Rouse, *Finland: Reports of Ruth Rouse* (April 8–14, 1915): 1, Archives of the WSCF, Record Group No. 46 (Box 45, Folder 364), Special Collections, Yale Divinity School Library.

37. Ruth Rouse, "Kiev," *Russia III* (October 31-November 30, 1911), 5, Archives of the WSCF, Record Group No. 46 (Box 44, Folder 363), 5, Special Collections, Yale Divinity School Library.

38. Edith May Hazlett to Burton St. John, Candidate Secretary, May 11, 1918, 2, Archives of the SVMFM, Record Group No. 42 (Box 482, Folder 5723), Special Collections, Yale Divinity School Library.

39. In 1922, the name of the institution was changed to Linfield College. It is a

found a dean at the University of Idaho who could serve as her liaison there. She also said that she received recommendations of missionary candidates from him.[40]

Also, Wiley's post-visit reports to SVMFM headquarters contained her recommendations for potential missionaries, describing their strengths and weaknesses. In most of her letters, she suggested more men than women. This was surprising given that most American men of college age were in the armed services and most colleges had only a handful of men.

For example, on May 11, 1918, Wiley gave two men high recommendations: "[Harold Humbert seemed] very well qualified and might fit into some urgent need this year. . . . I met a very young man . . . Raymond Buearman. . . . He would seem to me to be very fine for the science department at the Honolulu High School."[41] Apparently troubled by the ratio of male-to-female recommendations, however, Wiley added in small print at the bottom of the letter, "Am writing Miss Holliday about more women."[42]

In sum, the SCM's women traveling secretaries were very important. And although assigned to women, these individuals often worked with the men. Tatlow noted just how much the SCM owed to its intrepid individuals:

All over the world there are now thousands of men and women who owe an incalculable debt to the band of men and women who, each for one, two or three years, have given their time and strength to the Student Movement as a traveling secretary before they entered upon their life work.[43]

---

private four-year institution located in McMinnville, Oregon, and with historic ties to the American Baptist Convention.

40. Edith Hazlett to Burton St. John, SVMFM Candidate Secretary, May 26, 1919, Archives of the SVMFM, Record Group No. 42 (Box 482, Folder 5722), 1, Special Collections, Yale Divinity School Library.

41. Edith May Hazlett to Burton St. John, Candidate Secretary, May 11, 1918, 2, Archives of the SVMFM, Record Group No. 42 (Box 482, Folder 57), Special Collections, Yale Divinity School Library.

42. Ibid.

43. Tatlow, *Story*, 55.

7

Basic and Long-Term Pioneers

I am simply bursting with joy and yet am scared to death. . . . But just think what it may mean! Ain't it just the guidance of God?

The joy expressed here by Winifred Sedgwick while pioneering in Switzerland in the early 1900s typifies the emotions often felt by women pioneers. Sedgwick was excited and yet scared to death. And she believed that all pioneering was done through God's guidance.

The last type of "women in leadership" post to be explored in this book is the pioneer. Pioneers made up the final circle because they were the largest group, and had the least constitutionally mandated power in comparison to committee members and secretaries.

Women SCM pioneers came in three varieties: basic, specialized, and theoretical. Each of these will be discussed in chapters 7 through 14. And in each chapter specific women will be discussed. As with all other women leaders, these women had extensive leadership roles alongside men.

BASIC PIONEERS

Basic pioneers came in two types. Using what Rouse labeled the *subterraneous method*, *short-term pioneers* were students sent to a place where they investigated the field, made initial contacts with individual students and student groups, and started small ministries in a limited amount of time. A second basic pioneer was the *long-term organizer*, who remained in one location for a long period to establish relationships with students and start and direct permanent ministries.

SHORT-TERM PIONEER: WINIFRED MARY SEDGWICK (1880–1922)

Because of the early date of her ministry and the rich sources available, Winifred Mary Sedgwick's efforts offer a substantive picture of a short-term pioneer.[1]

---

1. Sources for the following information on Sedgwick come from her correspondence,

Winifred Mary Sedgwick
(From Tatlow, The Story of the Student Christian Movement, *244)*

The World Student Christian Federation (WSCF) appointed Sedgwick to carry out the tasks of a short-term pioneer at the Universities of Geneva (1905–1906) and Moscow (1907–1909). Like other Student Christian Movement (SCM) women, she was hired to work with women only, but she also worked extensively with men.

Fellow SCM workers had nothing but praise in their descriptions of Sedgwick. Many of these comments were made after her early death.

Archives of the WSCF, Record No. Group 46 (Box 167, Folder 1194; Box 100, Folder 816, 819; and Box 210, Folder 1600), Special Collections, Yale Divinity School Library; and Tissington Tatlow, *The Story of the Student Christian Movement of Great Britain and Ireland* (London: SCM Press, 1933), 489–97.

SCM historians have cited the ministry of the American J. B. Reynolds as the prototype for pioneering efforts. After graduating from Yale in 1884, Reynolds launched a successful student YMCA in Berlin during a one-year postgraduate course of study. Later, working as a long-term organizer, Reynolds ministered to American students in the Latin Quarter of Paris, helped to organize the first German and Scandinavian student conferences, which had both men and women in attendance, and recruited European students to attend English and American conferences. For more information, see Ruth Rouse, *The Story of the World's Student Christian Movement: The First Thirty Years* (London: SCM Press, 1948), 42–43.

Ruth Rouse said Sedgwick was one of the "most brilliant and sensitive spirits we have ever had."[2]

Tissington Tatlow described Sedgwick more extensively than any other SCM leader, male or female, and his insightful comments painted a clear picture of this woman:

> Winifred Sedgwick took a prominent place in the life of the Movement. Her able mind and devoted spirit fitted her for leadership. She was a good committee member, clear and definite in discussion, with a competent knowledge of theology and the Bible and a firm hold on experimental religion. Sympathetic, tenacious and conciliatory, she could hold her own in any debate. Men and women both liked her and she always had something useful to contribute when consulted. She was one of the three or four ablest and most effective women leaders the Movement has had, and I think the best speaker of all its women secretaries and committee members. . . . One's first impression of Winifred was likely to be that she was making a mental analysis of you. She had an incisive, analytical mind and was not easily deflected by side issues, but went at once to the heart of the matter upon which her mind was at work. She was immensely interested in people, watched them, considered their motives and tried to find the principles, good or bad, on which they lived. Some found her critical mind a barrier, but her love of people was deep and true, she had a wealth of kindliness and sympathy, and students in need sought her help in large numbers.[3]

Sedgwick was born into a comfortable Birmingham, England, family. Her parents were George and Emily Newman Sedgwick. Her father was a commission agent with teas and coffees. The family's affluent lifestyle is evidenced by where (next to Farm Park in Birmingham) and how they lived. British census data list at least two servants, a cook and a domestic, throughout this era. She was the youngest biological child with five older brothers, four of whom went to Cambridge University.

Baptized into the Church of England in 1880, Sedgwick remained a devout Anglican Christian throughout her short life. Her faith involved much more than personal spiritual experiments or imitating Christ. Whenever she heard a person say Christianity could be summarized in the imitation of Christ, she argued, "Christianity is more than that. It

---

2. Archives of the WSCF, Record Group No. 46 (Box 210, Folder 1600), Special Collections, Yale Divinity School Library.

3. Tatlow, *Story*, 490.

is not what we do but God in Christ doing for us and with us what we could never do of ourselves." Faith, grace, atonement, and redemption were full of theological content for her.[4]

Sedgwick received her education at the King Edward VI School, Birmingham, or Edgbaston Church of England College, Birmingham (records indicate one or the other. Either one record is wrong or Sedgwick split her early education between these two schools), Somerville College, Oxford (1899–1903, with Honors in Modern European History, Class II), Dublin (BA, 1905), and Oxford (BA, 1921).

Inside SCM circles, Sedgwick played a variety of roles. At Somerville, Sedgwick was treasurer of the Christian Union (1901–1902) and then with the British movement, co-secretary, traveling secretary, and evangelist for women students (1903–1905 and 1909–1914), and finally, with the WSCF, a pioneer (1905–1909). She published a 1914 Bible study titled *Christ the Teacher,* for male and female students in the training colleges. One of the most important tasks of these institutions was to train elementary school teachers.

Because she had a heart for music and felt that she expressed herself best through it, she was the first student secretary to reach out to music students. Her heart for music was demonstrated by her favorite way to share the Gospel with students. This was to combine music with short talks. Tatlow observed, "After playing Chopin, Bach, Grieg, or Schubert, she would swing round on the piano seat and began talking about the Cross, or inspiration, or faith or grace, and then quite abruptly would being to play or sing again."[5]

In her ministry to music students, Sedgwick made two points: "We as music students are faced by two facts. The fact of our gift, and its demand on our life. The fact of Christ and his demands upon our life."[6] She always concluded her appeals to music students with "trust God with our art."[7]

After 1914, Sedgwick became warden of Duff House London, a YWCA training center, which offered training classes for YWCA leaders. She was honored by the British government with a British Military Medal for her service in Étaples, France, from 1917 to 1918. Working as a YMCA canteen worker, Sedgwick furnished frontline soldiers with food, fellowship, classes, and religious activities.

Sedgwick contracted influenza and died in 1922 at the young age of forty-two at Tetbury Hospital Cottage in the Cotswolds area of Glouces-

---

4. Ibid., 497.
5. Ibid., 493.
6. Ibid., 491
7. Ibid., 492.

tershire. Labeled as a spinster in her will, Sedgwick left £9,021, which would have been worth £397,826 in 2016.

WINIFRED SEDGWICK IN SWITZERLAND AND RUSSIA

Official WSCF records mention Sedgwick's appointment only a few times, and each was only a passing reference. The rationale was laid for Sedgwick at the 1900 general committee meeting where it was decided that "women correspondents be appointed in different lands having women students, to assist the committee and officers of the Federation in carrying out the objects of the Federation among the women students of the world."[8] Sedgwick's ministry was mentioned in the budget presented at the 1907 and 1909 executive committee meetings. The 1907 budget combined Rouse and Sedgwick's account under "By Expenses of Work in Women's Colleges including the salary of Miss Rouse and Miss Sedgwick, £645 and 10s."[9] The 1909 budget had a separate Swiss fund that was to pay Sedgwick £28.[10] Rouse refers to Sedgwick's Moscow ministry in a 1909 report: "One saw again and again the help which Miss Sedgwick's stay in Moscow had been."[11]

Although Sedgwick made no direct statement about the short-term responsibility of investigating a location, this aspect of her work was demonstrated through her efforts to become acclimated to Geneva and Moscow. Learning to speak a local language helped the pioneer communicate and, more important, understand her environment, since words often convey the subtleties of a local culture. In her February 22–March 6, 1908, comments, Sedgwick was forthright about her struggles with Russian: "My Russian gets on slowly, and I feel I have to give much time to it. It is an awful language. I find I often understand the gist of conversation without knowing the actual words—so that I believe the girls here think I know far more than I say—and that I understand all their conversation. It is rather a joke!"

---

8. *Minutes of the General Committee of the WSCF, held at Versailles, France, in August, 1900*, 13–14, Archives of the WSCF, Record Group No. 46 (Box 36, Folder 280), Special Collections, Yale Divinity School Library.

9. *Minutes of the General Committee of the WSCF, held at or near Nikko, Japan, April 1–2, 1907*, 75, Archives of the WSCF, Record Group No. 46 (Box 36, Folder 283), Special Collections, Yale Divinity School Library.

10. *Minutes of the Meeting of the General Committee of the WSCF, held at Oxford, England, July 13–17, 1909*, 4a, Archives of the WSCF, Record Group No. 46 (Box 36, Folder 284), Special Collections, Yale Divinity School Library.

11. Ruth Rouse, *Russia Report II, 1909*, Archives of the WSCF, Record Group No. 46 (Box 44, Folder 363), Special Collections, Yale Divinity School Library.

To fully appreciate the setting of their ministry, a pioneer like Sedgwick had to be able to distinguish between local customs and their own. Sedgwick was shocked by some varying local customs. On November 26, 1905, she observed about a fellow resident at her lodging: "She is very dear, very attractive but my stars—talk of the sex question—she is the whole sex question in herself. There are two men in this pension, to whom she is very attractive—and I can't cry 'wolf' too often, but not too much 'a l'anglaise.' The continental ideas of propriety differ from ours! Then she is a little pagan."

Given that the SCM was a religious organization, it was imperative that a short-term pioneer understand local religious beliefs and practices.

In her February 22–March 6, 1908 comments, Sedgwick described a conversation she had with a man named Bulgakov, who came to her because he thought she was an expert on English religion.[12] The two discussed the influence of the Church of England on the WSCF, and he asked her what she felt about the value of church life. Bulgakov and Sedgwick also had a heated debate about whether the statement of faith of the St. Petersburg SCM was acceptable. He felt that the words "I have repented, I have given myself to him and believe that he has accepted me" were "unwarranted daring on our part and very alien to the Slav temperament." She, in contrast, believed that this statement summarized what God expected Christians to believe. At the end, all Sedgwick could say was, "We discussed it for a long time, but I am afraid he did not understand."

In her March 25, 1908, letter to Rouse, Sedgwick gave her opinions about differences between Russian Orthodoxy and Protestant Christianity. She believed that Orthodoxy stressed modeling one's life after Christ and the saints, whereas Protestantism emphasized putting one's faith in Christ's redeeming work. To her, this meant that Orthodox Christians focused on changing outward behavior, Protestants on changing the inner spirit.

Making individual and group contacts was the most crucial task carried out by the subterraneous worker because that was usually all a short-term worker had time to do. Contact work required a certain personality type which combined friendliness and the "gift of gab" with

---

12. Even though Sedgwick does not identify Bulgakov, one wonders if this man was Sergei Nikolaevich Bulgakov (1871–1944), a Russian Orthodox theologian, philosopher, and economist with ties to the SCM inside and outside Russia before and after the 1917 Russian Revolutions. He was chair of political economy at Kiev Polytechnic Institute (1901–1906) and chair of political economy at the Institute of Commerce at Moscow University (1906–1911). This conversation appears to have occurred in Moscow when he would be in Moscow, but it is only speculation. For more information on Bulgakov, see Nicholas Zernov and James Pain, eds., *Sergius Bulgakov: A Bulgakov Anthology by Sergius Bulgakov* (Eugene, OR: Wipf and Stock, 2012).

a strong faith and courageous spirit that actively sought out new people despite the possibility of rejection.

Sedgwick's ability to develop friendships with both men and women was well known. Tatlow observed, "She had all the qualities needed for friendship at its best—steadfastness, insight, candour, patience and tenderness. Perhaps her chief characteristic as a friend was to stimulate."[13]

Her group contacts began at her residence, where she spent most of her time. In a February 22–March 6, 1908, report from Moscow Sedgwick wrote about the struggles she was having developing relationships in her pension. She felt her only point of contact was through music. Often eating alone, she observed the women around her and noticed a difference between her and other residents: "I do not feel I am getting on very well yet. I think, it has a special atmosphere of its own and a rather frivolous one—chiefly balls, and theater and young men. I think getting to know them is a slow process."

Sedgwick reported that she had met with a variety of people. In a February 28, 1906, letter to Rouse, Sedgwick said that she had met with a "cosmopolitan" woman, who confessed she was a Christian and who had nothing but contempt for the liberated women around her: "If only you had been there you would have been amused. She has a vigorous contempt for the libre-penseurs—and made me chuckle more than once by her remarks." The libre-penseurs thought themselves to be free thinkers loosed from what they perceived to be the restraints of religion and culture.

Sedgwick also tried to establish relationships with Russian students. On March 25, 1908, she felt that Russian women "generally pose themselves as being utterly indifferent." Sedgwick then gave an example, telling the story of a two-hour debate she had with a "weird specimen," who appeared to take the entire matter without any seriousness. She wrote that the two reached an understanding and then talked quite honestly, even though they got no further.

Her ministry with Russian men seems to have been more successful than her work with women. Writing to Rouse about a meeting with a man, she observed, "Last night, the President of the Society which runs this 'intranat' came here and sent for me. . . . He asked me various questions as to my reasons for coming here and I told him quite frankly. He had heard about your meetings, but did not think you had much success—but at the end of our interview, he gave me his card and asked me to call next Thursday."[14] Sedgwick's visitor was probably referring

---

13. Tatlow, *Story*, 494.

14. An internat was a student hostel, pension, or small residential house with student bedrooms and a common dining hall.

to Rouse's October 17–December 15, 1907, visit to Russia with visits to Moscow and St. Petersburg.

As part of her efforts to establish semi-permanent ministries at the Universities of Geneva and Moscow, Sedgwick joined existing small groups. Following John R. Mott's tactic, she sought out "strategic points" or places where students gathered that were especially advantageous for reaching them. In a November 26, 1905, note, Sedgwick reported that a family's monthly open house for students was such a location: "I rather fancy that to a Mott this house is a strategic point." She joined student groups, like the Libertas (a temperance club), a study group, and attended lectures.

On February 13, 1906, in Switzerland, Sedgwick worked with an existing group of eight students and one professor, where she labeled herself the lone "feminist."

Sedgwick's ministry at what was later called the Brasserie Meeting was one of the most important examples of how she, as a subterraneous pioneer, joined groups of students. The gathering got its name because it was held at the Café Brasserie, a local pub well known as a gathering place for socialist agitation.

The Brasserie Meeting was held on January 30, 1906, and was the result of the efforts by a small Christian group composed of Sedgwick and a group of men. Planners hoped the meeting would permit them to preach the Gospel or, at least, become acquainted with more students. According to Rouse, Sedgwick and the men were shocked at the size of the crowd. From estimates, one-third of the university packed the café with an even mixture of foreign and Swiss students. The audience consisted of "long-haired men and short-haired women; faces stamped with sin, suspicion, hatred, sorrow and despair."[15]

During the meeting, Sedgwick and three men each spoke for about ten minutes, giving a simple, direct account of what Jesus Christ meant to them. The audience greeted each speaker with rounds of applause, and mocking laughter. However, one older woman, identified by Rouse as "a well-known feminist," told the crowd that she was bothered by the tone of the audience. The Christians had spoken honestly and were quite fair and serious. Yet the crowd had made violent, mostly unfair attacks and had derided the speakers. In the end, according to Rouse, the older woman made the audience listen politely.[16]

The meeting triggered a variety of responses. Sedgwick observed that the general opinion of the university community was that the Chris-

---

15. Wilmina M. Rowland, "The Contribution of Ruth Rouse to the World's Student Christian Federation" (MA thesis, Yale University, 1937), 210–11.

16. Ibid., 211.

tians had made fools of themselves. Her public stance also changed her relationships with other women. On February 13, 1906, she noted that some women viewed her now as an "object of curiosity, a little mild surprise." Some former acquaintances ceased to relate to her, while others became new friends.

Most important, contact work at the Brasserie Meeting paid off because it launched a series of meetings in which Sedgwick played an important role. She helped plan the first gathering that followed the Brasserie Meeting but chose not to give a speech as she had at the earlier one. On February 13, 1906, she wrote, "The very thought of it [giving a speech] makes me shiver—one gets so sick of controversy! But it is obviously the right thing to do and if only as a result of it small groups may be formed for study, won't it be worthwhile." The meeting was attended by two to three hundred students, and afterward most of the crowd remained to discuss future plans.

The group decided to hold regular meetings on announced topics directed by an oversight committee with representatives from the Christian and free-thought groups. When it was suggested that a woman be placed on this committee, Sedgwick was the logical person. Her enthusiasm was palatable in her February 28, 1906, note:

> The first committee is to meet tomorrow and I am to be there to represent feminine Christianity. . . . Isn't it thrilling? Or isn't it simply splendid? I could dance a jig of joy—I don't believe you would find such a society anywhere else—and if only it works and if only we can keep up this "entente cordiale" and meet each other fairly regularly just think of the possibilities of it. The audience seemed to think it was quite a good idea. Of course, we can't say a bit how it will actually work, but as a net result of our experiment, it is simply astonishing. It has been worthwhile.

LONG-TERM PIONEERS

The second type of basic pioneer was the *long-term organizer*. As opposed to the short-term worker, who was usually a recent college graduate, a long-term pioneer could be either a recent graduate or an older adult with or without a college education.

While short-term pioneers emphasized contacts with individuals and groups, long-term workers focused their attention on establishing permanent ministries through which they could serve during their lengthy tenure. The long-term worker's ministry could last just a year or extend to an entire lifetime. For women, commitment to long-term pioneering effort meant deviating from the domestic life expected of them. Choosing a long-term pioneering ministry deferred marriage and children. Instead, a woman could have an independent self-supporting position. She could establish a reputation based on her own efforts, not on those of a significant man in her life. Like other SCM women leaders, these pioneers worked with men and women.

In this section, the ministries of one long-term pioneer will be examined: Olga Kuleshova, a recent college graduate ministering in Russia.

RECENT COLLEGE GRADUATE, LONG-TERM PIONEER: OLGA KULESHOVA

Soon after law school, Olga Kuleshova (sometimes spelled Kulishova) began a ministry to students in Kiev which lasted from 1911 to at least 1921.[17]

Rouse wrote that Kuleshova went to Kiev to advance the work she had begun in 1911:

> My work in Kiev owes a great deal to Miss Kuleshova, and most of the responsibility in Kiev is now on her shoulders. . . . The work of conserving these hard-won results is being effectively carried on by a St. Petersburg woman student, sent down especially for the purpose. Her presence during the next few months will be invaluable to the newly found leaders.[18]

She also noted that Kuleshova had a "peculiar gift for student work. . . . The Kiev girls took to her at once." Rouse never wrote about Kuleshova's ministry with men. Although the movement only acknowledged her work with women, Kuleshova actually worked with both genders.[19]

Little is known about Kuleshova. Even her birth and death dates are unknown. She was active in a Christian Union in St. Petersburg while a law student there, although Rouse says Kuleshova first became interested in the SCM in Moscow. When the Russian SCM was officially

---

17.   For details on Kuleshova's life and ministry, see Archives of the WSCF, Record Group No. 46 (Box 100, Folders 809, 813, 814, 815, and Box 103, Folder 848), Special Collections, Yale Divinity School Library; and Greta Langenskjold, *Baron Paul Nicolay: Christian Statesman and Student Leader in Northern and Slavic Europe* (New York: George H. Doran, 1924). The history of the Russian SCM from its founding in 1912 through the Revolution and afterward is a story waiting to be told.

18.   Rouse visited Kiev from October 30 to November 25, 1911. Rouse, *Russia III*, 5; and *Miss Rouse's Tour in Russia*, 2, Archives of the WSCF, Record Group No. 46 (Box 44, Folder 363), Special Collections, Yale Divinity School.

19.   Rouse, *Russia III*, 5.

launched on November 3, 1912, with its headquarters in St. Petersburg, Kuleshova was appointed a special secretary with voting power when present at executive committee meetings. Her ministry lasted until at least 1921 because she is referred to in the letters of other SCM workers dated from that time. The Bolshevik destruction of Christianity in the 1920s, including the SCM, effectively ended the ministry of the Russian SCM inside Russia, and Kuleshova disappeared from the historical records. Like huge numbers of Russian Christians was she murdered by the Bolsheviks or did she escape to the West? No one ever knew.

As with short-term pioneers, long-term pioneers, like Kuleshova, had to understand the local culture. This determined how they would pursue their work. Kuleshova knew that Kiev was a very old civil and religious city. Eastern Orthodox Christianity was the largest and most dominant religious group among its diverse religious population. Local Orthodox leaders were generally inhospitable to the Protestants, Roman Catholics, and Jews present in the city. For the 20,000 students in Kiev, life was more cosmopolitan than in Moscow or St. Petersburg, and students were better dressed and richer. According to Rouse, though poor moral conditions existed among students, "religious societies were in vogue; there is a real desire for better things and for God, and the deepest interest in religious questions." Of these students, 7,000 to 8,000 were women. At the time of Kuleshova's arrival, women students had just been allowed to return to school. They had earlier been expelled en masse because it was generally believed that "women corrupted men morally and men corrupted women politically."[20]

To carry out her tasks, Kuleshova developed relationships with a variety of individuals. Like Sedgwick, she had to mix her apparent natural friendliness with a strong faith and fearless spirit.

Kuleshova met regularly with other SCM leaders, such as George Martin Day who served with the YMCA from 1909 to 1917. He later recalled that when he arrived in Kiev to work with the student YMCA in 1911, Kuleshova greeted him warmly and made him feel that God had prepared the way for him. This warm relationship continued for many years.[21]

---

20. Ruth Rouse, "Kiev," *Russia III (October 31–November 25, 1911)*, 2, Archives of the WSCF Record Group No. 46 (Box 44, Folder 363), Special Collections, Yale Divinity School.

21. George Martin Day (1882–1958), 6 foot 7 inches tall, hailed from American Fork, Utah, where his parents were missionaries to Mormons. He received his AB (1905) and MA (1908) from Hamilton College and earned his Phi Beta Kappa key there. In 1908, Day graduated from San Francisco Theological Seminary and was ordained a Presbyterian minister. He went to Russia in 1909 in YMCA service and became the first secretary sent by the YMCA International Committee to that country. He ministered

Kuelshova had a close but confrontational relationship with the senior women's SCM leader in Kiev, Princess Natalie Orgewsky, which did not appear to affect Kuleshova's ministry. Orgewsky argued with Kuleshova about when and how she should open a student hostel for women.[22]

Most likely the most controversial part of Kuleshova's Kiev ministry was her outreach to Orthodox theological students. This was quite extraordinary for the time, given that the church's leaders were all male, mostly celibate, and generally inhospitable to Protestants. Her dealings with these students involved making pastoral calls on sick students, handling challenges from individuals over theological issues, and visiting theological institutions incognito.

During her SCM Bible study for SCM leaders, an Orthodox theological student questioned one of her interpretations of a Bible verse. In doing so, he sought to challenge her intellectual credibility. However, the student was forced to respect and admire Kuleshova because she quoted extensively from "several weighty Russian commentaries" to support her case.[23]

---

in St. Petersburg and Kiev where he worked with college students and businessmen. In 1913, Day attended the WSCF Lake Mohonk Conference (see chapter 13). During World War I, he helped out in Allied hospitals in Kiev and in France. For his heroism, Day was awarded the Third Degree of the Order of St. Stanislas by the Russian Empire. After the Russian Revolutions, he taught economics and sociology at Occidental College (1923–1950). Day earned a PhD from the University of California in 1930.

22.   Nathalie (or Natalie?) Orgewsky (1860?–?) was a member of the Russian nobility, a devout member of the Russian Orthodox Church and a Red Cross worker. On a passenger manifest for May 15, 1913, her record said that she was born in "tserokoje sielo." This was possibly a misspelling of Tsarkoe Selo, a small town about fifteen miles from the imperial capital St. Petersburg. Tsarkoe Selo contained residences of the imperial family and visiting nobility. On this passenger list, she noted that her nearest relative was Prince Dmitry Tschachovsky (?), who lived in Moscow. Orgewsky also listed Novaja Chartoria in the Ukraine as her permanent residence.

Widely traveled and a hard worker for international WSCF, Rouse wrote that Orgewsky loved and understood the WSCF in a "remarkable way." Her first exposure to the SCM came in 1909 in Paris during a visit by Mott. She and Marguerite Carlovna (the Countess Toll), the wife of Alexander Petrovich Izvolskey (or Iswolsky), the Russian ambassador to France from 1910 to 1917, found a house in the Latin Quarter. There a student hostel for fifteen students was established. Orgewsky worked with Jeanne Pannier, one of the early women leaders of the SCM in France. In 1913, her brief biographical information for the WSCF Conference held in Lake Mohonk, New York, included membership on the National Central Committee of the Russian SCM and interests in the government, church, and the student movement. Eventually she returned to Russia after the 1917 Revolution. In a 1921 letter to John Mott, Orgewsky noted that she and a young niece had spent six months in a Bolshevik concentration camp. Living in poverty, she supported herself by teaching and working with students. She died about 1930.

For more information on Orgewsky, see Archives of the WSCF, Record Group No. 46 (Box 100, Folder 815), Special Collections, Yale Divinity School.

23.   George M. Day, "Extracts from a Letter of George M. Day of Kiev, Russia," (1912-1914), Archives of the WSCF, Record Group 46 (Box 100, Folder 813), 2, Special Collections, Yale Divinity School Library.

George Day recalled that he and Kuleshova visited a local theological school at the invitation of a student, where they met with several students:

You may be sure that we accepted with alacrity. So the next afternoon at 5:30 found us there (I had invited the secretary of the men students, Rindaloff, to join us) within the very citadel of our friend's enemy. If the metropolitan knew that the leaders of "that hated sectarian SM" were taking tea and incidentally spreading propaganda within the precincts of the Orthodox Theological Academy, oh what wrath and anathemas would descend upon us![24]

The most significant aspect of the long-term pioneer's ministry was the attempt to organize a local movement, since any long-term worker needs a well-organized permanent infrastructure to back him or her up. Without this, the pioneer would have been left alone to carry out the burdensome tasks of continuing student outreach. This might lead to burnout, which might make the long-term pioneer leave the field earlier than planned.

Kuleshova's organizational efforts were manifold. During a bedside visit with a sick theological student, she offered him her apartment to lead a men's Bible study. This group was established and soon sponsored by the YMCA. By December 1912, Kuleshova helped start seven men's and seven women's Bible studies. She led three of these groups. Kuleshova also worked with group leaders. Leaders' meetings of men and women were held every other week, with separate men's and women's meetings held in the intervening weeks. In somewhat broken English, Kuleshova wrote about her work with these leaders:

We frequently organize meetings of the leaders. . . . I prepare the material for these meetings, I praise and direct them and always I fear only to mistake, but I believe God is my helper.[25]

---

24. Ibid.

25. Olga Kuleshova, Extract from a Letter of Miss O. Kuleshova, Kieff (May 28, 1912), 1, Archives of the WSCF, Record Group No. 46 (Box 100, Folder 813), Special Collections, Yale Divinity School Library.

8

Pioneers of Targeted Student Groups

Naples is certainly the most satisfactory association of the
Italian Federation, at least from the masculine standpoint. From
the feminine point of view, there are hardly more than six or
seven women students. . . . The women students have always
been very much less drawn to Miss Leavitt than the men.[1]

---

1. Suzanne Bidgrain, "Report of Italy Visit, November 20–December 4, 1920."
Archives of the WSCF, Record Group No. 46 (Box 42A, Folder 327), Special Collections,
Yale Divinity School Library.

Suzanne Helene Bidgrain (1879–1961) was considered one of the most intelligent,
versatile, and international of the SCM's women leaders. She had an analytical and critical mind, a philosophical bent, a vigorous interest in theology, and was an able evangelist
and Christian apologist. Bidgrain could write and speak French, German, and English
and had a thorough knowledge of student life and SCM work in Great Britain, France,
Germany, and North America.

Bidgrain was born in Caen, in northwest France near the English Channel. She
was raised in a non-Christian home. Her parents tried to keep her from contacts with
Christianity. Bidgrain read the New Testament for the first time at age twenty-four. After
further study, she became a convinced Christian and joined the French Reformed Church.
Bidgrain held a MA from Glasgow University (1915) with advanced theological study at
the Universities of Marburg and Heidelberg in Germany.

Prior to World War I, she represented the World's YWCA at its 1911 Biennial
Meeting in Indianapolis and traveled for the YWCA in the United States.

During the war, Bidgrain served as the secretary for women for the French SCM.
She guided Ruth Rouse's extensive travels to French universities during the 1917–1918
school year.

After World War I, Bidgrain joined the World Student Christian Federation (WSCF)
staff in 1920 as part of its general secretary team (1920–1924) and served as a traveling
secretary.

In a 1921 sailing record, she listed her permanent address as her mother's home in
La Brousse, in southwestern France. In another 1921 record, she is listed as a spinster. She
never married. Her 1922 sailing record has her coming from Kyoto, Japan, to the United
States after visiting Annie Caroline Macdonald. Macdonald is featured in chapter 15.

In 1924, Bidgrain compiled the WSCF's first multilingual hymnal, *Cantate Domino:
World's Student Christian Federation Hymnal* (Geneva: WSCF, 1924). It contains sixty-
four hymns. One of these, "Thine Be the Glory, Risen Conquering Son," became in effect
the anthem of the WSCF.

110

This quotation from Suzanne Bidgrain, a leader in the Student Christian Movement (SCM), refers to the ministry of just one woman targeted pioneer, Almira Fay Leavitt. After the basic pioneers, these specialized pioneers targeted specific groups for outreach, such as students in teacher training colleges, schoolboys and schoolgirls, blacks, international students, refugees, and women. On one hand, this development was a return to the earliest years of SCM history when the movement had one specialized focus: potential student missionaries. On the other hand, specialized pioneering was part of the SCM's maturing process in pioneering efforts. As the SCM carried out basic pioneering, it discovered untouched groups that needed focused outreach. This increasing specialization was demonstrated in 1894 when the British movement reorganized itself by creating three departments, each with a different focus—missionary volunteers, theological students, and undergraduate students. The growth of targeted outreach was also due to the increasing financial resources of the SCM. This gave the movement the wealth to provide increasingly larger pioneering staffs to serve its widening variety of student communities.

To understand the work of specialized pioneers, this section investigates three examples: Elizabeth Morris Clark's creation of the "foyer" method, Leavitt's ministry to men in Naples, Italy, and Lilian Stevenson's outreach to fine arts students. Typical of targeting pioneers, these women worked extensively with men as well as women. One, Almira Fay Leavitt, worked exclusively with men.

ELIZABETH MORRIS CLARK (1869–?)

Elizabeth Morris Clark had a lengthy "complicated" career with the SCM from college through at least her mid-fifties. Clark was an independent woman, someone who might be called a "lone ranger."[2] She once wrote to John R. Mott that her own plans "would be naturally to some extent guided and modified by yours."[3] Her use of "some extent" spoke volumes.

Clark was especially gifted with the ability to create new ways to reach college students. Ruth Rouse reserved her highest praise for her, saying that she was one of the greatest contributions to the federation of any woman. But more important here, she claimed that Clark developed

---

2. Elizabeth Morris Clark spelled her last name without the "e" ending, despite the fact that some of her compatriots and records spelled her last name Clarke.

3. Elizabeth Morris Clark to John R. Mott, August 1910, Archives of the World Student Christian Federation, Record Group No. 46 (Box 164, Folder 1171), Special Collections, Yale Divinity School Library.

the idea of foyer ministry, which later spread throughout the SCM world community in Russia, France, Great Britain, and Switzerland.[4]

Foyers were the latest version of the salon. Starting in the French Enlightenment, men and women would gather in salons to discuss new ideas and philosophies under the direction of a leader.

The term *foyer* was derived from the Latin word *focus*, which meant fireplace or hearth, hence home. Foyers were turn-of-the-century coffee-houses or drop-in centers designed with a homelike atmosphere. Foyers were usually established for either men or women with many mixed activities. They were established to meet the social, physical, moral, and spiritual needs of students. At a foyer, students found subsidized meals and tea, free or low cost entertainment, classes, discussion groups, assistance in living needs (housing, employment, referrals to medical facilities) and spiritual activities. Most important, foyers provided opportunities for lively conversation and a friendly ear for the lonely student.

Clark was one of three daughters of Reverend William Walton (1846–1932) and Elizabeth Wyckoff (1844–1933) Clark of Brooklyn, New York. A member of the Wyckoff family, a prominent Dutch New York clan, her mother was educated at the Brooklyn Female Seminary (now Packer Institute) and was vice president of the Woman's Missionary Union Society of America, a group that advocated for women's foreign missions. Clark's grandmother helped found the society, and her grandfather, Rufus Clark, was a famous minister. Clark had an uncle serving as a missionary in China and a cousin in Japan. She was a member of the Congregational Church. Clark probably never married, but the records say nothing about this either way. Although in her childhood, she lived wherever her father pastored churches, the family lived most consistently for several generations with some members of her extended family at 532 Clinton Avenue, Brooklyn, New York.[5]

Clark studied at Wells College (1889–1890) and then focused on French and German at Bryn Mawr College (1890–1891). She left Bryn Mawr prior to graduation and studied at the Universities of Zurich (1892–1893) and Leipzig (1893–1894). She was a graduate of the University of Zurich. From 1894 to 1898, Clark was a Salvation Army worker.

Clark set out to be a teacher and sometimes did that job. She is listed as a teacher and religious worker in the 1914 *Woman's Who's Who of America*.[6]

---

4. For more details on the SCM's foyer ministry, see Elizabeth Clark, "At a Swiss University," *Association Monthly* 4, no. 8 (September 1910): 314–17.

5. In 2009, the house was listed for sale at $3.5 million. A big "W" still hangs over the front door (2012). For more details on 532 Clinton Avenue plus pictures, see http://www.brownstoner.com.

6. John William Leonard, *Woman's Who's Who of America: A Biographical*

After serving as an English and German teacher (1898–1899) and educational director at the Harlem YWCA (1899–1900), Clark became a professor of English at the Huguenot College, Stellenbosch, South Africa (1900–1906). She believed that she had a call to this teaching ministry: "Having received a call to work under Andrew Murray, in Wellington, South Africa, I have—after long and prayerful consideration—decided to accept."[7]

John and Leila Mott and Ruth Rouse recruited Clark for World Student Christian Federation (WSCF) work during their 1906 visit to South Africa. Leila Mott and Rouse decided immediately that Clark was suited to lead the Swiss outreach to foreign students. After all, she had studied there, and her French, German, and Italian were very good.

Clark was a traveling secretary for the YWCA in 1908 and 1909. She began working in Geneva in 1909 with no official recognition from the WSCF or Swiss SCM. She worked there until 1911. In 1914, she was offered the job as general secretary of the World's YWCA, which she did not take. In 1916, Clark made it clear that she needed an official position: "I was merely a vague nobody; and one cannot continue to be. . . . One is either an accredited representative of some organization, or one is a private person."[8]

During World War I, prior to the entrance of the United States, she joined several other WSCF-related secretaries from neutral countries in visiting student communities of the nations at war. This ceased when the United States entered the war on April 6, 1917.

Due to increasingly bad health and signs of an impending nervous breakdown, Clark resigned on December 26, 1918. She had had a "difficult" relationship with the SCM due to her independence, complicated ministry environments, intermittent poor health, and financial strains. Clark commented in 1912 that she was experiencing great mental and spiritual pressures. In 1914, in a letter to Mott, she expressed her fear of

---

Dictionary of Contemporary Women of the United States and Canada, 1914–1915 (New York: American Commonwealth, 1915), 180.

7. Elizabeth Morris Clark, *Confidential Personal Blank* (New York: SVMFM, June 5, 1900), 2, Archives of the Student Volunteer Movement for Foreign Missions, Record Group No. 42 (Box 42, Folder 267), Special Collections, Yale Divinity School Library.

Andrew Murray (1828–1917) was a South African pastor, writer, educator, public speaker, and missionary. He was ordained by the Dutch Reformed Church in the Netherlands. He had extensive SCM connections through his writings, links with the Keswick Higher Life Movement, and missions. Murray was a forerunner of the Pentecostal Movement with his support for divine healing and the continuation of the apostolic gifts.

8. Elizabeth Morris Clark to John R. Mott, December 15, 1916, Archives of the WSCF, Record Group No. 46 (Box 164, Folder 1172), Special Collections, Yale Divinity School Library.

a nervous breakdown.[9] Her work had been very difficult, perhaps more difficult than any other SCM woman's ministry. This was particularly true during World War I. Women students came from several nationalities, and many came as refugees. They spoke different languages. Many branches of Christianity were represented, including Eastern Christianity. Clark had difficulties working with the male leaders of the Swiss SCM, and her funding from outside American sources was resented. She was arrested for being a spy in Innsbruck while visiting students.

However, Clark may have inherited problems from her family. In 1928, her sister, Alice, who had just come home from the hospital after suffering a nervous breakdown, jumped or fell from the third floor of her parents' Brooklyn home.

Clark returned to WSCF work for one year after the war (1919), traveling in England, Belgium, Czechoslovakia, and Switzerland.

In the 1920 United States Census, Clark is listed as a YMCA welfare worker. In the 1925 State of New York Census, she is listed as doing housework. In the 1930 Census, she is listed as a college teacher. In all cases she is living in the family home on Clinton Avenue with her elderly parents and sister(s).

ALMIRA FAY LEAVITT (1849–1937)

Using Elizabeth Morris Clark's foyer method, Leavitt established and then directed Il Salotto, an all-male foyer in Naples, Italy (1904?–21).[10] The term *Salotto* meant "reception room." Because of extensive records, the ministry of Leavitt presents a clear picture of the ministry of a specialized pioneer.

Leavitt's efforts were pioneering because she worked in Roman Catholic Italy but was Protestant. It was also pioneering because she worked with men almost exclusively. In fact, it could be argued that of all the SCM's women leaders, she worked the most with male students.

---

9. Elizabeth Morris Clark to John R. Mott, October 31, 1914, Archives of the WSCF, Record Group No. 46 (Box 164, Folder 1171), Special Collections, Yale Divinity School.

10. For more details on the SCM's foyer ministry, see Clark, "At a Swiss University"; Fritz de Rougemont, "The Work among Foreign Students in Switzerland," *Student World* (July 1914): 81–92; Ruth Rouse, *The World's Student Christian Federation: A History of the First Thirty Years* (London: SCM Press, 1948); Wilmina M. Rowland, "The Contribution of Ruth Rouse to the World's Student Christian Federation" (MA thesis, Yale University, 1937); and Johanna M. Selles, *The World Student Christian Federation, 1895–1925: Motives, Methods, and Influential Women* (Eugene, OR: Pickwick, 2011). For more information on Leavitt's ministry, see the *Student World* (April 22, 1906; March 7, 1909; July 30–August 4, 1914; and November 25, 1918).

Leavitt was born in Lowell, Massachusetts, to Erasmus Darwin (1808?–88) and Almira Fay (1812–1895) Leavitt. According to the 1870 United States Census, her father was a retired merchant. He was also a business manager. Leavitt had five brothers and two sisters. Her distinguished family included her brother, Erasmus Darwin Leavitt Jr. (1836–1916), a noted engineer, and her niece Henrietta Swann Leavitt (1868–1921), a world-renowned Harvard University astronomer. Leavitt was physically short (about five feet tall, according to various sources) with brown hair and eyes. The 1880 United States Census notes she had a spinal problem. Leavitt never married. Leavitt died in Pelham, Massachusetts, in 1937 at the age of eighty-seven years, and she was buried with many of her Leavitt relatives in the Cambridge Cemetery, Cambridge, Massachusetts.

In 1910, Leavitt gave a speech at the Battle Creek Sanitarium about her Il Salotto ministry.[11] She was there to visit a nephew who was receiving treatment after his lengthy stint as a YMCA secretary in Japan.

The sanitarium's *Battle Creek News* on September 16, 1910, reported on her presentation which was "a most interesting and instructive address." In very broad strokes, Leavitt talked about why she came to Naples, Italy, and what ministries she led.

Leavitt said that her ministry in Europe occurred because she had been sick. She reported that she had taken tours of Europe, Africa, and Asia to restore her health. Since Italy had had the most restorative effects, Leavitt dedicated her life to help that country. Rouse noted the same fact. She said Leavitt had come from New England to recover from illness.

Once she came to Italy, Leavitt's burden for college students became immediately evident. She quickly sized up their living conditions and noted that students did not have any campus organizations or clubs. Leavitt remarked that students had few interactions with instructors outside of classwork. Because of all these things, they wandered the streets and were exposed to bad influences. Leavitt thought that most

---

11. Opened in 1866, the Battle Creek Sanitarium, Battle Creek, Michigan, was a place for the rich and famous to rejuvenate, listen to lectures, mostly on healthy living, and to learn practices of a healthy lifestyle. It was established on principles taught by the Seventh-day Adventist Church. The sanitarium's early years were closely associated with John Harvey Kellogg and his brother W. K. Kellogg, the founder of Kellogg Company, a maker of breakfast foods. The number of patients at the hospital grew quickly with 106 in 1866 and 7,006 in 1906. Some of the institution's treatments included hydrotherapy, phototherapy, thermotherapy, electrotherapy, dietetics, physical exercise, and cold air exposure. The sanitarium closed its doors in the late 1970s. Famous patients included Mary Lincoln, Sojourner Truth, Warren Harding, William Post (founder of Post Cereals), Amelia Earhart, Henry Ford, James Cash Penney, and Johnny Weissmuller.

students were not religious or believers in God. To her, they were intemperate and corrupt.

According to Leavitt, she began her ministry "in spite of many difficulties and single-handed." Soon she had a large number of University of Rome students in her home. After a brief period, Leavitt moved to Naples because she felt it had greater need. Despite criticism from friends and the challenge of a new location, Leavitt eventually established Il Salotto ministry "with a class of men who became much attached to her." Her work increased so quickly that it garnered worldwide attention.

The large evangelistic meetings she organized formed the foundation of Leavitt's work. For example, in 1909, Leavitt made arrangements for a series of evangelistic meetings to be given by Italian SCM president Dr. Giovanni Luzzi. She got permission from the Neapolitan civil authorities to use the Prince of Naples Gallery. According to Luzzi, the meeting hall was packed each night with a wide assortment of individuals, ranging from students to professors, pastors to friars, and Christian Democrats to modernists. Rouse corrected Luzzi's lack of reference to Leavitt's significant role in planning these meetings in her report to the WSCF: "Besides to Prof. Luzzi, merited praise was given to the gentle, Signorina Leavitt, who, with manifest wisdom and a master hand, prepared this stupendous welcome."[12]

Leavitt and her Il Salotto also arranged Mott's entire 1911 visit. He spoke for two nights before crowds of six hundred, containing some of the most influential students. Later, Mott noted that the second night bore the fruit that Il Salotto desired: "The second night was one of great

---

12. Professor Luzzi's Conference at Naples, Archives of the WSCF, Record Group No. 42 (Box 174, Folder 1230), 1, Special Collections, Yale Divinity School Library. Giovanni Luzzi, DD (1856–1948), a Protestant pastor and theologian, was one of the most important Italian Reformed theologians of the twentieth century. Born in Switzerland, but raised in Italy, he was the son of a businessman and his wife. Except for his graduate studies at the University of Edinburgh and his numerous trips outside Italy, Luzzi spent most of his time in Florence, Italy. There, Luzzi studied at the Waldensian Seminary of Theology, Florence, Italy (1877–?). Then he was appointed a faculty member, and later he was chair of systematic theology and president. Between 1877 and 1902, Luzzi was also pastor of the Waldensian Community of Florence, Italy. He was very involved in many social initiatives, such as a school, a clinic, and a counseling center. In 1904, he helped launch the Italian Federation of the Religious Culture Students, the Italian branch of the WSCF. In addition, in April 1905, he was awarded an honorary degree in theology by the University of Edinburgh. From 1923 onward, Luzzi continued to serve as a pastor while he worked on his own Italian translation of the Bible. He had begun this project in 1906 and completed it in 1931. He was the author of *The Struggle for Christian Truth in Italy* (New York: Fleming H. Revell, 1913), and *The Waldensian Church: Her Work, Her Difficulties, Her Hopes* (New York: Dodd, Mead, 1914).

solemnity. One was conscious that the living God was striking home His own truth and moving with convicting power on the consciences and hearts of the students. At the close, they came around me in large numbers. Interviews with students revealed a genuine hunger and responsiveness."[13]

Leavitt's organizational work centered on the establishment and direction of Il Salotto. An important aspect of her ministry was selecting a location for it. The foyer moved to Palazzo Lemme Parco Antonio Vomero which had a beautiful view overlooking the city.

According to her, Il Salotto's "sole . . . objective [comprises the] solution of the problems of conduct, the building up of character, and the best employment of the energies of the young men who are desirous of using their facilities for the general good."[14]

The most important aspect of this was the leading of each student to faith in Jesus Christ as Savior and Lord. Leavitt made it clear that she was not attempting to make the men Protestant or Roman Catholic, but simply children of God. In a 1909 presentation to the WSCF executive committee, Leavitt stated, "They use neither the term Protestant nor Roman Catholic, but Christian. At least two loyal Roman Catholics are earnest members of the Salotto."[15]

She also wanted to create a "home away from home." In a 1909 pamphlet, Leavitt wrote that she hoped to create "an agreeable and home-like atmosphere."[16] The word "home" appeared in most of Il Salotto's literature. In a 1907 letter to Mott, Leavitt wrote, "Will you give a little time to the story of the Woman's Home—Rooms for University Students in Naples. The title is long, but it seems needed to define the work. More and more it is this home quality which wins the young men."[17]

From all reports, Leavitt was quite successful in establishing a home-like atmosphere. In the 1909 pamphlet, she wrote, "Great Cordiality and real family feeling reign among them."[18] As one Salotta participant,

---

13. John R. Mott, *Addresses and Papers of John R. Mott: The World's Student Christian Federation* 2 (New York: Association Press, 1947), 412–13.

14. Almira Fay Leavitt, *Italian Student Federation for Religious Culture, Branch of the WSCF, The Salotto* (June 1909): 7–8, Archives of the WSCF, Record Group No. 46 (Box 174, Folder 1228), Special Collections, Yale Divinity School Library.

15. Minutes of the Meeting of the General Committee of the WSCF, held in Oxford, England, July 13–17, 1909, 20, Archives of the WCSF, Record Group No. 42 (Box 36, Folder 284), Special Collections, Yale Divinity School Library.

16. Leavitt, *Italian Student Federation*, 7.

17. Almira Fay Leavitt to John R. Mott, August 15, 1907, Archives of the (John R.) Mott Papers, Record Group No. 45 (Box 17, Folder 1241), 1, Special Collections, Yale Divinity School Library.

18. Leavitt, *Italian Student Federation*, 10.

an atheist prior to his contact with the foyer, observed, "None of us can find in our own houses what we find here."[19]

To carry out these goals, Leavitt served also as Il Salotto's publicist, fundraiser, and director. She publicized Il Salotto's ministry through *Il Salotto*, the group's official magazine, pamphlets, articles, and letters. Examples of her work include a 1909 pamphlet, "The Salotto," and a 1915 *Student World* article, "A Successful Experiment in Naples." In each case, the history, ministry, and organization of the group was thoroughly discussed. Il Salotto's main focus on men was highlighted, and Leavitt's role was downplayed.

Leavitt was also Il Salotto's main fund raiser. Leavitt funded Il Salotto herself until her money ran out and then sought assistance from the WSCF.[20]

Leavitt's letters to Mott demonstrate the evolution she went through concerning finances. Early on, she was so confident that financial needs would be met, that she never asked for money directly: "I have never asked financial aid from them—nor from anyone. My needs have been wonderfully met. Nearly all visiting tourists volunteer to help. Mrs. Blagden of New York—proposed unsolicited by me—to assume the main part of the necessary cost."[21]

Later, she was still confident despite the fact that support was lagging: "God does not intend I shall walk by sight, as regards finances. Mrs. Blagden is again behind, and at least two other remittances promised for January have not been heard from."[22]

Finally, Leavitt asked for money directly and said that she was willing to give up her vacations and endanger her health to raise the necessary funds.[23] Mott came to Leavitt's rescue with money from Vanderbilt University's Dr. Willis Weatherford.[24]

---

19. Leavitt to Mott, August 15, 1907, 3.

20. Almira Fay Leavitt to Reverend Andersen, June 22, 1911, 1, Archives of the WSCF, Record Group No. 46 (Box 177, Folder 1242), Special Collections, Yale Divinity School.

21. Leavitt to Mott, August 15, 1907, 7.

22. Almira Fay Leavitt to John R. Mott, February 2, 1910, 1, Archives of the WSCF, Record Group No. 45 (Box 177, Folder 1241), Special Collections, Yale Divinity School.

23. Leavitt to Andersen, July 22, 1911, 1.

24. Dr. Willis Duke Weatherford (1875–1970) graduated from Weatherford College (BS, 1895) and Vanderbilt University (BA, 1899; MA, 1900; PhD, 1907). He served as the YMCA's international secretary (1901–1919). Later, he became president of the YMCA Graduate School, Nashville (1919–1936); a faculty member at Fisk University (1936–1946); a trustee of Berea College, Berea, Kentucky; and President of Blue Ridge College (1906–1944).

Mott used the correspondence to encourage Leavitt to link her Salotto officially with the WSCF through the Italian SCM.[25]

Leavitt's most important organizational task was as Il Salotto's director. She held a firm if not dictatorial grip on the group's leadership. In a 1907 note to Mott, she stated: "Those who fully understand my aim, and heartily sympathize with it, become members of my council—my body guard—my helpers in each and every way."[26] In a 1911 letter, Leavitt called Il Salotto her "private work."[27] She also dominated committee meetings. At a 1907 meeting, when a student leader moved that all atheists be excluded from Il Salotto, Leavitt responded with commanding authority: "'Excuse me gentlemen' . . . Please remember that a few months ago you were *all* atheists.'"[28]

Finally, Leavitt controlled Il Salotto's Bible studies by dictating their topics and aspects of student preparation. She also selected which topics she felt best qualified to handle. Leavitt wrote, "Certain topics—the more spiritual—it seemed necessary for me to handle.[29] As I finished a paper on the temptations of Christ, one of the most gifted of the circle—a very fine Calabrese medical student started up—his face all aglow and exclaimed, 'Signorina I am surprised. I did not suppose.'"

After a lengthy ministry, Leavitt ended her SCM-related career. The *Intercollegian* announced that she returned to the United States permanently in 1921, thus ending her Naples ministry. The periodical praised her ministry, saying she had left an "enduring work in the Naples branch of the Italian Movement which is by far the strongest in Italy." Her Il Salotto was a "pioneer in various forms of social work in Naples." And it concluded with hagiographic overtones, "As she spends her eveningtide years in her own land, she is surrounded by the love and gratitude of hundreds of Italian students and of the Federation workers in Italy and other lands who have had the privilege of knowing her, working with her and learning from her."[30]

Leavitt's ministry had garnered quite a reputation among Protestants and Roman Catholics. Dr. Giovanni Luzzi wrote, "At Naples, we

---

25. John R. Mott to Almira Fay Leavitt, November 19, 1910. Archives of the WSCF, Record Group No. 45 (Box 177, Folder 1241), 1, Special Collections, Yale Divinity School Library.

26. Leavitt to Mott, August 15, 1907, 2.

27. Leavitt to Andersen, July 22, 1911, 2.

28. Leavitt to Mott, August 15, 1907, 2.

29. Ibid., 4.

30. See "Students of the World," *Intercollegian* 39, no. 3 (December, 1921): 11.

have a group of students which, from the point of view of our work of conquest, is without doubt the most interesting and the most important in our field."[31] In her 1913 report, Rouse wrote that Roman Catholics had copied Leavitt's method: "Imitation is the sincerest tribute to success and Il Salotto has found imitators. Before it began no one cared about the soul of the Neapolitan student; recently a large student club on a definitely Roman Catholic basis has been started, with a program clearly and closely modeled on that of Il Salotto—even the Bible classes on the 'Social Teachings of Jesus' reappears as a series of lectures on the 'Social Teachings of St. Paul.'"[32]

LILIAN SINCLAIR STEVENSON (1870–1960)

Lilian Sinclair Stevenson was another prominent example of an SCM specialized pioneer. By her "indefatigable work," she successfully established a special Christian association for fine arts students called the Art Students' Christian Union (ASCU). It was another example of a targeted outreach to one student subculture.[33] She worked with the ASCU for at least eleven years (1897–1908).[34] Stevenson was a leader of men and women.

---

31.   See Giovanni Luzzi, "Religious Interest in Italy." In "Needs and Encouragement in Work among Students in Roman Catholic Lands," in Report of the Conference of the WSCF, held at Oxford England (July 13–17, 1909), 12–17.

32.   Rouse, *Italy* (March 1–10, 1913), 2–3, Archives of the WSCF, Record Group No. 46 (Box 44, Folder 361), Special Collections, Yale Divinity School Library.

33.   Tissington Tatlow, *The Story of the Student Christian Movement of Great Britain and Ireland* (London: SCM Press, 1933), 286.

34.   Lilian Sinclair Stevenson wrote *A Child's Bookshelf: Suggestions on Children's Reading with an Annotated List of Books on Heroism, Service, Patriotism, Friendliness, Joy, and Beauty* (London: SCM Press, 1917); *Amor Vincit Omnia: Thoughts on the War, Together with Notes on What to Read and Helps to Intercession* (London: SCM Press, 1917); and *Towards a Christian International: The Story of the International Fellowship of Reconciliation* (Paris: International Fellowship of Reconciliation, 1936). She also authored a verse for the hymn "Fairest Lord Jesus."

For more information on Stevenson, see Vera Brittain, *The Rebel Passion: A Short History of Some Pioneer Peacemakers* (Nyack, NY: Fellowship Publishers, 1964); Mary L. Hammack, "Lilian Stevenson Sinclair," in *A Dictionary of Women in Church History* (Chicago: Moody Press, 1984), 138–39; John Ferguson, "Stevenson, Lilian Sinclair," in *Biographical Dictionary of Modern Peace Leaders*, ed. Harold Josephson (Westport, CT: Greenwood Press, 1985), 902.

For more information on the ASCU, see *The ASCU Record Book* (1897–1920), *Arts Student Christian Unions* (SCM/A4, Records of the Student Christian Movement) and *Arts Student Christian Union* (SCM/A5, Records of the Student Christian Movement), Cadbury Research Library, Special Collections, University of Birmingham, and the Archives of the WSCF, Record Group No. 46 (Box 207, Folders 1552, 1553, 1554, 1555), Special Collections, Yale Divinity School Library.

Lilian Sinclair Stevenson (3rd from left, middle row)
at the International Fellowship of Reconciliation
Conference, Bilthoven, The Netherlands, October 4-11, 1919.
(Courtesy Swarthmore Peace Collection)

Considered "a lady of leisure" because of her great wealth and armed with a natural dignity and grace, Stevenson was the daughter of the Reverend William Fleming (1832–1886) and Elizabeth Montgomery Sinclair (1838–1916) Stevenson. She had two brothers and two sisters.

Her father earned an MA from the University of Glasgow (1848–1951), did graduate work at the University of Edinburgh (1854), and was a Presbyterian pastor, writer, author, missionary leader, and educator. In his career, he was a pastor from 1860 to 1886 of the Rathgar Presbyterian Church, which served a newly established congregation outside Dublin, Ireland. By 1862, a new church built largely through Stevenson's exertions was opened. His ministry was so popular that the church was soon filled, and was twice enlarged. In 1877, Stevenson's father and mother made a journey round the world, visiting mission stations, especially in China and India, at the request of the General Assembly of the Presbyterian Church of Ireland. In 1879, the Crown appointed Stevenson as one of the first senators of the newly established Royal

University of Ireland. In 1879–1880 he held the chair of Evangelistic Theology in New College, Edinburgh. In 1881, he was elected moderator of the General Assembly of the Presbyterian Church of Ireland. From 1882 until 1886 he was Duff Lecturer on Foreign Missions at New College, Edinburgh. In 1886, he was appointed the first Presbyterian chaplain to the Lord Lieutenant of Ireland. After his death, the Fleming Stevenson Missionary Training College was established in Ahmedabad in 1892. His library was named the Stevenson Memorial Library and given to the Assembly's College (now Union Theological College) in Belfast.

Lilian Stevenson's rather simple faith was revealed in her translation of "Fairest Lord Jesus," verse 4: "All fairest beauty, heavenly and earthly, Wondrously Jesus, is found in Thee; none can be nearer, fairer or dearer, Than Thou, my Savior, art to me." This short verse summed up her commitment to Jesus Christ. In a very unassuming fashion, she wrote that nothing compared to her Savior.

With her parents' enthusiastic support, Stevenson attended Cheltenham Ladies' College and the Slade School of Art (1892–1893 and 1895–1896). She never married. Listed as a spinster at the time of her death, Stevenson's will stated that she left an estate of £58,000 in 1960. In 2016, this would have been worth £1,218,000.

Stevenson's involvement with the SCM began in college and lasted for many years. In 1933, Tatlow wrote, "This gifted Irishwoman threw herself heart and soul into whatever she had in hand, and her influence lives on in the movement today."[35] She was a secretary of Slade College of Arts Women's Christian Union (1896–1897), editor of the *Student Volunteer* (1896–1898) and the *Student Movement* (1898–1900, 1902–1904?), and editorial secretary for the British SCM (1899–1900). Stevenson also served as secretary of the Student Volunteer Missionary Union (SVMU) Register and Hindered SV Committee (1905–1907).[36] She was also a member of the senior advisory committee (1906–1909). As part of her work, Stevenson revised the register of student volunteers by creating a new system which made it possible to know at a glance exactly how many volunteers had joined and what had happened to each after joining.

With the assistance of Temple Gairdner and the Women's Christian Union at the Slade School of Art, Stevenson launched the ASCU.[37] At

---

35. Tatlow, *Story*, 287.

36. The Hindered SV Committee was for those called to missionary work but who were unable or "hindered" from going overseas.

37. For more information on Temple Gairdner, see chapter 9. For more information on the Slade School of Art, see chapter 4.

the 1896 summer conference of the British movement, she and Gairdner decided to hold an organizational meeting for this new group. On November 27, 1897, sixty men and women from the Royal Academy, Slade, Herkomer, South Kensington, South Bloomsbury, Lambuth Blackheath, and Crystal Palace met to organize.[38] Men and women fine arts students came from South Kensington and the Royal Academy, while women only came from all the other institutions. The Reverend Evan Hopkins, vicar of St. Luke's, Redcliffe Square, served as the meeting's chair. He introduced Gairdner, who gave the opening speech on the British SCM.

Without any introduction, from her vantage point as an art student, Stevenson spoke next about why a ministry to fine arts students was necessary. She argued that art students had a deep-rooted need that would not be met even with the perfection of their artistic skills. Art students were also isolated because the pursuit of their talents demanded it. This separation caused even the most spiritually interested students to "shut out Christ also, and so miss the presence of the only One, who can perfectly sympathise with every longing of our artist-soul."[39] It also created an intense loneliness and what Stevenson called a "wasted life" that withered away and fell short of using one's artistic gift to glorify God. To overcome this isolation, Stevenson said rather bluntly, "We must bring Christ to him and to him as an art student."[40] Her speech convinced the members of her audience of the need for a Christian association for fine arts students.

Thanks to Stevenson's appeal, the ASCU was launched in March 1898. In London, unions were quickly established at the Royal Academy, the Royal College of Art, the Slade School of Art, the Central School of Arts and Crafts, the Royal College of Music and Alexandra Hall, Trinity College of Music, the Royal Academy of Music, and the Guildhall School of Music. Outside London, groups were established in Edinburgh, Glasgow, Dublin, Manchester, Liverpool, Nottingham, Sheffield, Leeds, Birmingham, and Bristol.

The ASCU's goals reflected Stevenson's concerns. As a subgroup of the British SCM, the ASCU had three aims: (1) to be a bond of union

---

38. Tatlow, *Story*, 284.

39. Lilian Stevenson, "Art Students and the Christian Movement in British Colleges," speech delivered to a meeting of students from the London Schools of Art, held by the invitation of Blanche, Countess of Rosslyn, at 8, Seamore Place, Park Lane, on Saturday, November 27, 1897, during which the need for an Art Students' Christian Union was addressed. The ASCU was formed in March 1898 as an outcome of this meeting. (London: British College Christian Union, 1902), 14, Archives of the WSCF Record Group 46 (Box 207, Folder 1552), Special Collections, Yale Divinity School.

40. Stevenson, Speech, 13, and Tatlow, *Story*, 285.

between all art and music students who desire to follow Christ, (2) to emphasize the claims of Christ upon both the life and the work of art students, and (3) to help in establishing Christian unions in art and music schools. Any male or female student could join by assenting to the group's basic statement: "I desire, in joining this Union, to state my belief in Jesus Christ as my Savior, my Lord and my God."

As with other groups within the SCM, the ASCU had an executive committee and two general secretaries, one for men and one for women. The ASCU held its own separate meetings during British College Christian Union summer conferences, where they elected these officers. The group had its own supplement to the British movement's periodical, the *Student Movement*, called the *Art Students' Christian Union Supplement*. The union had a circulating library with a catalogue divided into Art and Religion, Apologetics, Missions, and Devotional Books. Besides Bible studies, the ASCU sponsored lectures on connections between religion and art. It also provided opportunities for members to use their skills. For example, ASCU members provided charts and diagrams needed for SCM activities, decorated movement facilities, and created illustrations for missionary stories.

Stevenson played a significant role in the expansion of the ASCU. She corresponded regularly with local leaders and individual members, gave public speeches on the union's behalf, and held many positions within the fledgling organization. She was the ASCU's traveling secretary from 1897 to 1898, women's secretary in 1898, and treasurer and secretary in 1899. Stevenson chaired several annual meetings held in conjunction with the summer British conferences. In 1902, Stevenson presided over a meeting with twenty women and six men, where she asked Gairdner to pray, reports were read, and elections were held for the group's traveling secretaries. Again in 1904, she chaired the ASCU's annual meeting. At this time, she heard reports on the activities of men and women's groups and on budgetary concerns, held discussions on revisions of the ASCU's constitution, and ran elections of new officers. In 1908, Stevenson spoke to forty women students at the annual meeting of the South Kensington Union on behalf of the ASCU.

Though Zoe Fairfield was a student at the Slade School of Art at this time, no official connection can be established between her and Stevenson. However, it is possible that Stevenson served as a role model of a woman leader in mixed groups for Fairfield.

After her SCM ministries settled down, Stevenson went on to have ministries outside the movement. Of particular interest to her was Christian pacifism. In 1914, Stevenson participated in the founding of the Cambridge Fellowship of Reconciliation. She served on its first executive committee along with Marian Ellis, Agnes Maude Royden, Constance Todd, and Emmeline Pethwick-Lawrence. In October 1919, Stevenson used her skills as a specialized pioneer to launch the movement toward a Christian International at Bilthoven, Holland, which in 1922 joined with the International Fellowship of Reconciliation. From then on, as the "Grande Dame of Christian Pacifism," she devoted all her energies to this organization through extensive travel, writing, and conferences. Her home in Buckinghamshire became its own league of nations, a place where all nationalities found a home.

9

"Warp and Woof" Pioneers

Ministering in what Ruth Rouse called the "warp and woof" of growth in the Student Christian Movement (SCM), another type of woman pioneer was the conference leader.[1] This variety of pioneer helped the SCM employ its newly developed conference method to reach out to the student world.

The conference method was basically the use of gatherings of SCM participants to promote the SCM cause. Looking back in 1948, Rouse observed that the conference "proved itself at once the most effective pioneering agency, the strongest evangelistic force, the best recruiting and training ground for leaders, and the focusing point of new ideas and fresh movements of the Spirit amongst students in generation after generation."[2]

These meetings were extremely popular, and excitement over conference participation abounds in SCM literature and the personal stories of those in attendance. Besides joining a large collection of like-minded people, these meetings brought students face to face with God and with their lifetime goals. As Rouse observed:

> Some students went willingly, eager for light, seeking God and His way for them. Some were dragged by friends sorely against their own inclination, but they too found a way. . . . Northfield! Blue Ridge! Aislomar! Counchiching! Swanwick! Ligotka! Woudschoten! Bievres! Wernigerode! Gotemba! Piriapolis! And

---

1. Ruth Rouse, *The World's Student Christian Federation: A History of the First Thirty Years* (London: SCM Press, 1948), 68. "Warp and woof" are names for sections of yarn or thread in weaving. The warp runs lengthwise and the woof runs across to make fabric. These terms are used metaphorically to denote the essential foundation or basis of any structure or organization, such as the United States Constitution is the "warp and woof" of the United States. Rouse's creative use of this term highlights the foundational function of SCM conferences.

2. Ibid., 65.

a hundred other names: refrains of sacred music in student ears on five continents! "That's where God found me. That's when I found my life's work."[3]

CONFERENCE HISTORY

Originating in the fertile mind of Luther Wishard and made concrete by D. L. Moody's advocacy and planning, the SCM conference first took shape.[4] On an organizational level, the conferences played a strategic role in overall SCM development. About their regular use in the Federation, Rouse wrote:

> The history of the Federation is to no small extent the history of its Conferences. . . . From Vadstena, 1895, to Peking, 1922, is the eleven-rung Federation conference ladder. Each rung marks an ascent, an advance into some new area of the world or into some new region of thought, or the initiation of some new phase of policy or activity. . . . Each conference or meeting was held in some place chosen with imagination as strategic in Federation history or strategic for the next development indicated in the Federation campaign. . . . To a remarkable extent, successive developments of interest in new regions or the world, or in new areas of life or thought have found their focusing point at Federation conferences.[5]

Of all the conferences the SCM ever held, the 1886 Mt. Hermon Conference was arguably the most important because of its place in the mythology of the SVMFM. And yet it was ironic that the role of the 1886 conference itself in developing the conference method has also been ignored. In 1948, Rouse noted this issue. She wrote, "So great and far-reaching were the results of the launching of the SVM in 1886 that they have obscured the fact that the Mt. Hermon Conference gave birth to an idea as significant in modern religious history as the volunteer movement itself—the Student Summer Conference or School."[6]

Even though a few student conferences had occurred previously, Mt. Hermon 1886 triggered the establishment of the American SVMFM. This

---

3. Ibid., 66–67.

4. Clarence Prouty Shedd, *Two Centuries of Student Christian Movements: Their Origin and Intercollegiate Life* (New York: Association Press, 1934), 252.

5. Rouse, *World's Student Christian Federation*, 68–69.

6. Ibid., 65.

was followed quickly by what Rouse later called "a swarm" of conferences in SCM circles around the globe. Some of the conferences that developed out of this meeting included regional conferences, committee retreats, pre-session or setting-up meetings, training schools for leaders (especially secretaries), conferences for Bible study and social service ministries, schoolboys' and schoolgirls' camps, conferences for theological, medical, journalism, and education students, and meetings for foreign students. Arguably the most important were the quadrennial student conferences hosted by the British, American, and German movements.[7]

CHARACTERISTICS OF CONFERENCES

Conferences were mostly composed of students with a smattering of university administrators and faculty, postgraduates, YMCA and YWCA officers, mission board and denominational recruiters, the press, and special guests.

These gatherings varied in size and numbers. In the year the World Student Christian Federation (WSCF) was founded (1895), the worldwide SCM held 10 conferences attended by 2,600 students. By 1919, these numbers had jumped to 123 conferences with 19,700 students in attendance.[8] Although conferences were held throughout the year, the Christmas break and the summer were most popular. One unique pioneering aspect of these SCM conferences was that there was a mix of men and women—as delegates, special guests, and directors.

CONFERENCE ACTIVITIES

Conferences had a combination of small and large group meetings, both of a devotional and informational nature. At these meetings, students listened to a variety of speakers dealing with Christ, living the Christian life, and missions. During free time, they could view exhibits or enjoy fellowship with others in attendance.

At these SCM-sponsored gatherings, business decisions were made (e.g., ratify major decisions of executive committees, elect new committee members, change SCM constitutions, discuss budgets, and receive annual reports), and hitherto hostile or ambivalent dons and clergy were appeased. However, the most important feature of a conference was how it was used as a vehicle to transmit the SCM's vision. This was to bring

---

7. Ibid., 67.

8. John R. Mott, *Addresses and Papers of John R. Mott: The World's Student Christian Federation* (New York: Association Press, 1947), 2:173.

students to Christ and to transform the world through them.

Whether they were conference visionaries and advocates, planners and directors of actual meetings, career recruiters, or informational, evangelistic, or inspirational speakers, women played a vital role in this facet of SCM life.

CONFERENCE VISIONARIES AND ADVOCATES

Endless reruns of the popular 1970s TV show *Little House on the Prairie* flash the name Wilder across the consciousness of every American consumer. This adaptation of Laura Ingalls Wilder's *Little House on the Prairie* or *Little House* series tells the partially fictional account of the Ingalls family living in Walnut Grove, Minnesota, in the 1870s and 1880s. And that is what the world knows about the Wilder family.

This focus on the popular TV show and books behind it obscures the possibly more influential story of the conference visionary and advocate Grace Evelyn Wilder and her brother Robert. Grace Wilder was a first cousin of Almanzo Wilder who in real life was married to Laura Ingalls Wilder, the author of the *Little House* series.

GRACE EVELYN WILDER (1861–1911)

If any SCM woman served as a conference visionary and advocate it was Wilder. Individuals like Wilder "pushed" the use of the conference method in SCM circles. They could be male or female, leader or regular member, and could be found throughout the SCM. They may have not even used the expression "conference method."

Wilder was born in Saratoga Springs, New York, to the Reverend Royal Gould (1816–1887) and Eliza Jane Smith (1842–1910) Wilder. She had three brothers and one sister. From 1846 to 1875, the Wilders were New School Presbyterian missionaries in Kolhapur, India, about two hundred miles southeast of Mumbai. Her uncle and cousins were missionaries among the Zulus in South Africa.

The senior Wilders postponed furloughs from mission work on several occasions. But finally because Royal Wilder developed cholera, they decided to come to the United States. They left India just prior to the start of the Indian Rebellion of 1857. One source says the rebellion broke out one day after they left the country.[9] Their departure might have spared the life of Wilder's parents, given the violence and high death toll. If they had been killed, she would never have been born.

---

9. http://www.thetravelingteam.org/articles/grace-wilder.

Grace Evelyn Wilder
(Mount Holyoke College Archives and Special Collections)

Eventually, the Wilders retired and settled in Princeton, New Jersey, where Grace Wilder's father became the editor of the *Missionary Review of the World*.

During this time, Wilder attended Mt. Holyoke Seminary (after 1893, Mount Holyoke College), graduating in 1883. After graduation, she taught dance and music and assisted her father in his work with his periodical.

After Royal Wilder's death in 1887, Grace and her mother went back to India. At first, Grace was associated with the Western India Mission of the Presbyterian Board of Foreign Missions (Presbyterian Board).

In 1897, she struck out on her own and established the Village Settlement, a semi-independent ministry at Islampur in Kodali. It was loosely connected to the Presbyterian Board. The Village Settlement was located in an isolated area where no Christians lived. On her own, Wilder selected workers and erected facilities in her own name. After her death, the Village Settlement came under the direct supervision of the Presbyterian Board.

Remaining in India until her sudden death in 1911, Wilder was buried at the Wilder Memorial Church (formerly the American Mission Presbyterian Church) in Kolhapur, India.

Wilder's role as visionary and advocate for SCM conferences was based on her own call to missionary work. This was revealed in her short poem, "The Secret of God's Will." In it, she wrote:

I sought the secret of Thy will; But, Lord, I did not know
Thy lowly life—Thy heavy cross—Life's plan and purpose show.

I sought some special path and plan, Bearing my name, I'd see;
Instead, I found in Jesus' life, Footprints for such as me.

To save the lost His aim, so mine, Poor, hungry ones to feed;
Weak, sightless eyes to turn to light; Save, erring feet to lead.

Since Jesus' life reveals God's will, Surely I'm in His way
When choosing rough, dark mountain paths to find the sheep
     who stray.

To be like Him, I ask to hold, My light where it is dark,
To carry bread to those passed by; Let this, Lord, be my part.

Thus preaching Christ where yet unknown, God's world-wide
     love I show;
And since for this, Christ lived and died, God's will for me I know.[10]

Wilder believed that instead of a "special path and plan" designed specifically for her, she should choose to be like Jesus. This meant that she would "save the lost," feed the poor and hungry, provide sight to the blind, and show God's love for the whole world. Wilder would preach Christ wherever he was not known.

Armed with this personal vision and seeking those with a similar call, Wilder helped organize and lead the Mt. Holyoke Missionary Association in 1878. Wilder helped craft a missionary pledge similar to the Volunteer Pledge later used by the SVMFM and other SCM groups. The Holyoke group's signed promise said, "We hold ourselves willing and desirous to go wherever the Lord may call us, even if it be in the foreign land." Thirty-four members of the group signed this pledge.

However, Wilder's biggest role in SCM circles was as a conference visionary and advocate. She helped develop what became the "conference method." This was especially seen with her role in the 1886 Mt. Hermon Conference.

---

10.   Grace E. Wilder, "The Secret of God's Will," http://www.findagrave.com.

Wilder's role in advocating for the Mt. Hermon conference had two aspects. First, as one contemporary ministry with a vision similar to the SVMFM suggests, she worked "behind the scenes" as "one of those most precious of the Lord's gems, whose only contentment was to be hidden that He might receive more praise."[11]

As a "behind the scenes" visionary and advocate, Wilder was a woman of prayer. While living in Princeton with her parents, her brother, Robert, then a student at Princeton, launched a men's missionary society. While they met in his parents' home, she would pray regularly in the next room that these men would become missionaries. The two Wilders also prayed nightly for a widespread missionary movement in the colleges asking God for 1,000 volunteers for the foreign mission field. After her death, one of her pastors observed, "Others are receiving the praise for this movement. We should not forget that God redeemed His promise of answering prayer, and this was the faithful and effectual prayer of Miss Wilder and her brother, which, humanly speaking, began this work."[12]

Wilder was also a very visible advocate for the conference. John R. Mott said, "Someone had the vision enough to see that there might be God's opportunity. Among the very first to see this with a clear eye was a young woman who went to her reward a few months ago, Miss Grace Wilder. She discerned that conditions were going to be furnished at Mount Hermon that might make possible the generation of a great movement."[13]

As an activist, Wilder had a great influence on her brother, Robert, and his friends.[14] Wilder may have implanted her vision for missions

---

11.   http://www.thetravelingteam.org/articles/grace-wilder.

12.   Ibid.

13.   John R. Mott, *Addresses and Papers* (New York: Association Press, 1946), 1:277.

14.   Reverend Robert Parmelee Wilder (1863–1938) was totally committed to the missionary cause, for which he served as a visionary, an advocate, and in actual missionary service. Wilder was born in Kolhapur, India. He married Helen Sophie Olssön (1859–1903) in 1892 and had four daughters. At age ten, he pledged himself to serve as a foreign missionary. Wilder attended Princeton Preparatory School, Williston Seminary, Princeton University (1886), and Union Seminary (1891). At Princeton, he met with several students to study the Bible and to pray for missions. When he was a junior, Wilder attended a conference of the Inter-Seminary Alliance. Afterward he helped found the Princeton Foreign Missionary Society. In the summer of 1886, Wilder attended a month-long Bible conference at Mt. Hermon. The topic of foreign missions was not on the agenda of the conference. However, Wilder recruited a group of men there to pray daily for missions, and each one of them signed the Volunteer Pledge. Wilder organized an entire night of the conference, where students were presented with the spiritual needs of ten nations. By the end of the conference, 100 volunteers had pledged to go to the mission field. During the next school year, Wilder and John Forman traveled to 162 campuses and recruited 2,106 more volunteers, including 500 women. After a five-year ministry with the Student Volunteer Movement for Foreign Missions (SVMFM) both in North America

and the 1886 conference in his soul. This inspiration flowed through him and the entire early SCM. In 1945, Sherwood Eddy, an SCM leader, observed that the SVMFM was the "result of Wilder's vision, Moody's spiritual drive and Mott's organizing genius."[15]

Wilder also challenged her brother and his friends to go to Mt. Hermon. "Were it not for the urging of his sister who saw clearly that Mt. Hermon might be God's answer to their prayers for laborers, Robert may have missed his opportunity to be His instrument."[16] And as they headed to the Mt. Hermon conference, Wilder "charged them before God to persevere in prayer and effort that this Mount Hermon gathering might not close without the inauguration of a missionary movement that in some sense would be worthy of the wonderful situation then confronting the Church on the foreign field."[17] When her brother left for the 1886 conference, Grace Wilder said to him, "I believe there our prayers will be answered."[18]

CONFERENCE PLANNERS

Conference pioneering involved planning and managing the meeting. It was an elaborate enterprise that was carried out under Mott's watchful paternal eye. Executive committees had to plan the

---

and Europe, Wilder was appointed a missionary for the Presbyterian Board of Foreign Missions. He and his wife left for India in 1893, where they worked with students in Calcutta and Poona. In 1897, Mott asked him to come back to the United States to serve as a traveling secretary for the SVMFM. Between 1899 and 1902, Wilder served as the traveling secretary for the Indian YMCA. From 1905 to 191(5?) Wilder served as a traveling secretary for the British SCM. During World War I, he briefly served as the British SCM's foreign secretary. In 1916, at Mott's request, Wilder came back to the United States to serve as secretary of the Religious Work Committee of the International YMCA. Between 1919 and 1927, Wilder served as the general secretary of the SVMFM. Between 1927 and 1933, Wilder served as executive secretary of the Christian Council of Western Asia and Northern Africa (renamed Near East Christian Council). Poor health caused him to retire at age seventy. He and his wife moved to Norway, her home country. There he promoted the cause of missions in Scandinavia. Beginning in 1935, his campus tours came under the authority of the British Inter-Varsity Fellowship of Evangelical Students. Wilder died from pneumonia in 1939 and was buried in Oslo, Norway. For more information on Wilder, see Ruth E. Braisted, *In This Generation: The Story of Robert P. Wilder* (New York: Association Press, 1941); and James Patterson, "The Legacy of Robert P. Wilder," *International Bulletin of Missionary Research* 15, no. 1 (January 1991) (New Haven, CT: Overseas Missions Study Center): 26–32.

15.   Sherwood Eddy, *Pathfinders of the World Missionary Crusade* (New York/Nashville: Abingdon-Cokesbury Press, 1945), 41.

16.   http://www.thetravelingteam.org/articles/grace-wilder.

17.   Mott, *Addresses and Papers* 1:277–78.

18.   Rouse, *World's Student Christian Federation*, 35.

actual meeting's time and place, budget, program, and follow-up activities, which included publication of conference reports. When they helped organize conferences, women took on a variety of tasks in different national movements. They worked as leaders of men and women.

AMERICAN SVMFM CONFERENCE PLANNERS

In the American SVMFM between 1886 and 1920, women usually performed duties that were traditionally ascribed to women or that directly affected them. Their limited role was somewhat surprising given that men and women served as co-equal leaders of the SVMFM. No woman was ever chair or vice-chair of the meetings as a whole, although they sat on conference executive committees. Instead, they served on committees for women delegates and hospitality, and also led women's sectional meetings. In addition to these visible activities, women worked in invisible ways to assure the success of a conference. They served as conference stenographers, assisted men with the exhibits, and prayed for the meeting's success.

BRITISH SCM CONFERENCE PLANNERS

British women had broader roles in conference planning than their American counterparts. They helped organize and direct these gatherings. For example, women selected meeting locations and provided music. E. F. Fox chose the small town of Baslow for the 1908 British summer conference. According to the *Protestant Standard*, "a musical program of a refined and charming nature was carried out by three lady violinists, two gentlemen violinists, and a gentlemen pianist."[19]

Dr. Emmeline Marie Stuart was a notable example of a British conference planner.

EMMELINE MARIE STUART (1866–1946)

Dr. Emmeline Marie Stuart was born to Robert Laidlaw (1832–1899) and Maria Campbell Hill (?–?) Stuart of Edinburgh, Scotland. Her father was a member of the highly regarded Society of Writers to Her Majesty's Signet, then a private society of Scottish solicitors. Emmeline had four brothers and three sisters. Her uncle was a well-known and well-regarded Anglican missionary bishop, the Right Reverend

---

19. *Protestant Standard* 24 (January 4, 1896), 1241:2.

Emmeline Marie Stuart
(From Gulnar Francis-Dehqani, Religious
Feminism in an Age of Empire; *used by permission.)*

Edward Craig Stuart. Because her uncle is listed in the Peerage Book, he married someone in the peerage, or the Stuart family was a member of the peerage.[20]

Stuart was a Low Church Evangelical Anglican. She was one of the earliest women to train as a doctor in a British university, and she graduated from Queen Margaret College, Glasgow, with a BM and MS (1895).

In his excellent studies, Gulnar Francis-Dehqani identifies some of the traits that Stuart possessed. He uses words such as strong, confident, stubborn, and capable. She was "unafraid of voicing opinions and acting accordingly even if this placed her in a disparate position." Francis-Dehqani goes on to say that Stuart was a skilled doctor with a "persuasive and powerful personality."[21]

---

20. See Lundy, *The Peerage*, Person Page, 29967.

21. Gulnar Francis-Dehqani, "Medical Missions and the History of Feminism: Emmeline Stuart of the CMS Persia Mission, 1897–1934," *Currents in World Christianity Position Paper* 103, 15. For an expanded version, see Gulnar Francis-Dehqani, "Religious Feminism in an Age of Empire, CMS Women Missionaries in Iran, 1869–1934" (PhD diss., University of Bristol, 1999), 180–219.

In 1896, Stuart was appointed a missionary to Persia for the Church Missionary Society (CMS). She went there because resident missionaries in Persia asked for "medically-trained women workers."[22]

In 1897, Stuart came to Persia at an important moment in Persian mission history. Her professional role and her confidence, strength, and single-mindedness were problems for those who had different ideas about the proper role for women. By merely doing her missionary work, Stuart conquered any objections and served as an example for future women doctors who would come to Persia after her.

The CMS paid Stuart a salary. But there are several references in CMS records to her paying her own traveling expenses and financially assisting other missionaries. Stuart even said she would reduce her income if the CMS could use the money to send added missionaries.

Stuart started her medical work by assuming the leadership of the hospital started by Mary Bird. In 1897, the CMS Women's Medical Mission was set up. Other medical personnel joined these efforts, including fifteen women doctors by 1934. Stuart remained in Persia for thirty-seven years. She first served in Julfa with its majority Armenian population, and then Ishafan and Shiraz, southeast of Tehran.

To Stuart, evangelism was always first. But improving medical care and the lives of women were also important. She went to many outlying villages and gave medical care. The Bakhtiari Tribe even invited her to give them medical care. The Bakhtiari were a long-distance nomadic group migrating from summer to winter quarters and living in central Persia.

The dangers of World War I touched Stuart and other CMS missionaries. In June 1916, the magazine of St. John's Parish included a report from an unnamed missionary, which may have been Stuart. It was titled, "Missionaries Told, 'Not a Hair on Your Head Shall Be Injured!'"[23]

Early in World War I, Stuart and other non-German missionaries had been forced to flee Ispahan (Isfahan) when German occupiers took the city. As a result, she and another woman went to India. When Russian forces regained control in March 1916, they were invited back. The article quoted one of the missionaries about this return:

---

22. Mary Bird (1859–1914), the CMS missionary in Persia at the time, who pioneered Christian ministry to Iranian women and women's medical missions in the CMS, had argued that medically trained women were needed. In 1893, another Persian missionary, William St. Clair Tisdall, wrote, "A medical mission lady, fully qualified, would be invaluable, and would enable us to reach women of all classes most widely." In Francis-Deqani, "Medical Missions," 13. The cousin of Mary Bird's father was Isabella Bird Bishop, who is featured in chapter 10.

23. *St. John Parish Magazine, June 1916 (D/P172/28A/24);* https://berkshirevoic-eswwi.wordpress.com.

The people of Yezd need us very badly and are prepared to give us a great welcome we have heard from various sources. Only last week, among numerous letters from Yezd was one from a large landowner, in which he said how very badly the people needed their hospital and doctor. He went on to say, "If you will only come back I will guarantee your safety; in fact, not a hair on your head shall be injured!" Another Yezd grandee who has been living in Teheran and has just been appointed to a high office in Yezd came to see me before he left and pressed me to go back with him, and said, "As soon as I arrive in Yezd I shall begin an agitation to bring you all back again."

Stuart retired in 1934 at age sixty, but because she was asked to extend her tour, she stayed a bit longer. She died in 1946 in Surrey, England, at seventy-nine years of age. Her funeral occurred at Christ Church, Richmond, and her body was cremated, a rare occurrence at the time. Stuart's will stated she left £7,193, which would have been worth £280,527 in 2016.

Stuart wrote several articles and reports on her work in Iran, including "The Woman's Hospital Isfahan" and "The Social Conditions of Women in Muslim Lands."[24]

Stuart was in contact with the SCM as a traveling secretary for the British Student Volunteer Missionary Union (SVMU) (1895–1896), as a member of the SVMU executive committee, and as a leader of the International Student's Missionary Conference held in Liverpool on January 1–6, 1896.

Stuart's work with the British planners came when she, Rouse and de Selincourt, all members of the SVMU executive committee, served as co-planners and co-directors of the International Students' Missionary Conference. Rouse, de Selincourt, and Stuart had visible, influential, roles, despite the fact that Wilmina Rowland believed Rouse's main contribution was "behind the scenes."[25] They participated in planning meetings, joined male traveling secretaries in recruiting delegates at local campuses, advertised the upcoming affair in the *Student Volunteer*, helped secure speakers, and gave speeches themselves.

Typical of speeches at the conference, Stuart gave an impassioned plea to her audience of men and women to come to Persia:

---

24. Emmeline Stuart, "The Woman's Hospital Isfahan," in *Mercy and Truth* (London: CMS, 1906), 368–70; and "The Social Conditions of Women in Muslim Lands," *Church Missionary Review* (August 1909): 458–64.

25. Wilmina M. Rowland, "The Contribution of Ruth Rouse to the World's Student Christian Federation" (MA thesis, Yale University, 1937), 68.

Can none of you come to help us? Are none of you nearly ready? In face of the great need out here will you decide to stay at home, where the professional ranks are already over full? Here there is abundant room and scope for your energies. We are so few and so scattered, and the work is so immense. Where, I ask you to ask yourselves, will your lives most count for Christ? Where will you best serve your generation?[26]

A few women who were not on the SVMU executive played key roles in the conference's organization. May F. Hodges, a noncollegiate traveling secretary for the collegiate department (1894–96), recruited delegates, and J. W. Carr, of the London School of Medicine for Women, helped locate speakers and handle speakers' needs at the conference.

CONFERENCE MISSIONARY RECRUITERS

In the final conference role (besides the speakers discussed in chapter 10), SCM women leaders recruited future SCM leaders and missionaries. Rouse's skill in this area became legendary. A close friend and fellow SCM leader, Frederick William Scott O'Neill believed that her ability to recruit was one of her most outstanding qualities.[27] SCM leader Annie Beatrice Glass Fraser felt that Rouse was skilled at "picking out people to follow up her work."[28] Rouse recruited leaders outside of conferences

---

26. "Students and the Missionary Problem," in *Addresses Delivered at the International Student Missionary Conference, London, January 2–6, 1900* (London: SVMU, 1900), 513.

27. Frederick William Scott O'Neill (1870–1946), an Irish Presbyterian, was a member of the SVMU, who served on the British executive committee and helped draft a document which was used to adopt the Watchword in 1897. O'Neill served as a missionary to Fakumen (Faku), China, in Manchuria. His book, *The Quest for God in China* (London: George Allen & Unwin, 1925) and his relatively open view of other religions put him under a cloud of suspicion from his more conservative compatriots. O'Neill retired in 1945 and died in Ireland.

28. Rowland, "Contribution of Ruth Rouse," 73. Annie Beatrice Glass Fraser (1873–1970) was from Whickham, Durham, a small prosperous town in northeast England near the North Sea coast. Her parents were Robert (1839–?) and Anne Burlinson (1838–?) Glass. Her father was listed as a "brewer's traveler" (1871 British Census) and a "brewers agent" (1881 British Census).

Fraser attended Newnham College, Cambridge, England (1894–1896). She only went there for two instead of three years and did not take the Tripos Exams for her BA. After college, Fraser was traveling secretary for the British College Christian Union and the SVMU from 1897 to 1899 until she was appointed as CMS missionary to Uganda in 1900.

In 1901, Fraser married Alexander Garden Fraser in Uganda. The couple had two sons and two daughters. Her husband's father was Sir Andrew Henderson Leath Fraser.

as well. She discovered Tissington Tatlow at an 1897 Irish SCM conference. Rouse discovered Bertha Condé at the Christadora Settlement House in 1898 and an unnamed principal for the Scottish Missionary Training School at Girton College.

ANNIE VAN SOMMER (1854–1937)

Annie Van Sommer was another conference recruiter. She used speeches and one-on-one ministry to enlist suitable missionary candidates. Van Sommer recalled how she recruited Temple Gairdner, later a missionary to Egypt, while a speaker at the 1897 British Summer Conference:

> Gairdner came up to me and said, "I was wanting to speak to you. Will you please come outside with me?" We went out on the lawn and sat down on a plank. He said, "I heard you speak for Egypt the other evening. If you remember, I came in just as you began to speak. It was just as though a voice said to me, 'Why not you?' I have been thinking a great deal lately about the Nile Valley."[29]

He had been born in Bombay, India, and served as a British Indian civil servant and lieutenant governor of Bengal (1903–1908). Sir Andrew Fraser was subject to at least one assassination attempt by Indian nationalists.

Because of her ill health, the Frasers had to leave Uganda in 1903. After Alexander Fraser spent a year in England doing theological study, the Frasers moved to Ceylon. There he became principal of Trinity College, Kandy, a Church Missionary Society grammar school. Annie Beatrice Glass Fraser lived in Kandy from 1904 to 1924.

In 1924, Fraser lived in Accra, Ghana, until 1935 because her husband was appointed head of a government college project. He developed and directed Achimota College.

After 1935, the Frasers lived in Scotland, Jamaica, Wales, and Sussex, England. In these places he worked in education and pastoral care.

On an April 22, 1957, incoming United Kingdom sailing list, both Frasers are listed as "retired educationalists."

Annie Beatrice Glass Fraser became a widow in 1962, when her husband died after a lengthy illness. She died in Newcastle on the Tyne in 1970 at ninety-seven years of age.

For more information on Annie Beatrice Glass Fraser, see her notebook containing the journal she kept as a Church Missionary Society worker. It can be found at the University of Birmingham Archives, Birmingham, England. CMS/ACC915. http://calmview.bham.ac.uk.

29. Constance E. Padwick, *Temple Gairdner of Cairo* (London: Society for Promoting Christian Knowledge, 1929), 67. Later in life, Canon W. H. Temple Gairdner (1873–1928) served as missionary to Muslims in Cairo and authored many books on missions. For more information, see *Temple Gairdner*.

The parents of Van Sommer were James (1822–1901) and Mary Maria Arnott (1818–1892) Van Sommer. The Van Sommers had six children. Annie Van Sommer's father was a solicitor and editor of the *Missionary Reporter* (which became the *Missionary Echo* in 1872, *Echoes of Service* in 1885). This was a magazine for the Open Brethren branch of the Plymouth Brethren. The family was quite comfortable. Annie's father came from a prosperous business family, and in 1870, he was given a law practice by a family friend.

Annie Van Sommer served as a missionary with the London Missionary Society with a special interest in Egypt and Moslems. A sister, Elizabeth Van Sommer, worked as a missionary as well. Van Sommer edited the quarterly *Blessed Be Egypt* in connection with the Prayer Union for Egypt from approximately 1903 to 1908. She was a member of the continuation committee of the General Conference on Missions to Moslems, held at Lucknow, India, in 1911. There she presented a paper in the section *Social and Educational Developments among Muslim Women* titled "In Egypt, Turkey, and Persia."[30]

With Samuel M. Zwemer, she edited *Daylight in the Harem: A New Era for Moslem Women: Papers Presented on Present-day Reform Movements, Conditions and Methods of Work among Moslem Women, read at the Lucknow Conference, 1911*, and together they wrote *Our Moslem Sisters: A Cry for Need from Lands of Darkness Interpreted by Those Who Heard It.*[31]

Van Sommer died in 1937 in London. She was labeled a spinster and left an estate worth £10,370, which would have been approximately £660,569 in 2016.

---

30. See Annie Van Sommer, "In Egypt, Turkey and Persia," in *Social and Educational Developments among Muslim Women*, Friday, January 27, 1911. In C. G. Mylrea, E. M. Wherry, and S. M. Zwemer, eds., *Lucknow, 1911: Papers Read and Discussions on the Training of Missionaries and Literature for Muslims at the General Conference on Missions to Muslims, Held at Lucknow, January 23–28, 1911* (London, Madras, and Columbo: Christian Literature Society for India, 1911), 27.

31. Annie Van Sommer and Samuel M. Zwemer, eds., *Daylight in the Harem: A New Era for Moslem Women: Papers Presented on Present-day Reform Movements, Conditions and Methods of Work among Moslem Women, Read at the Lucknow Conference, 1911* (Edinburgh: Oliphant, Anderson and Ferrier, 1911); and Annie Van Sommer and Samuel M. Zwemer, *Our Moslem Sisters: A Cry for Need from Lands of Darkness Interpreted by Those Who Heard It* (New York: Fleming H. Revell, 1907).

10

Conference Speakers

A speaker electrified an audience at the United Brethren in Christ Church located in Union City, Indiana, on October 3, 1899. Surrounded by three male pastors, this woman was Barbara Ellen Groenendyke, and this was her farewell service just prior to her departure for the denomination's missionary work in Sierra Leone. After hearing her speak, her good friend and fellow missionary Frankie Williams said, "Miss Groenendyke's first public sentence, so strong, representing so much character, went like a thunderbolt through the audience, captivating every interested heart."[1]

Groenendyke was just one example of a group of women speakers in Student Christian Movement (SCM) circles. Although these women gave speeches in a variety of settings, the most significant settings were movement conferences. Conferences gave women who had the passion, intellect, and oratorical skills an opportunity to speak publicly. This public speaking was pioneering in many ways. Those who spoke educated their audiences about world needs, brought listeners to Christ for the first time, and challenged believers to have a deeper Christian faith. Through their presentations, speakers also helped establish a sense of corporate unity. Finally, during these talks, women assumed an air of spiritual authority over their audiences of men and women that was usually ascribed to men.

INFORMATIONAL CONFERENCE SPEAKERS

Although there are too many informational speeches to recount, two stand out as notable examples. World explorer and travel writer Isabella Bird Bishop gave several speeches on missionary work and her travel

---

1. Rev. Job Smith Mills, *Mission Work in Sierra Leone, West Africa* (Dayton, OH: United Brethren Publishing House, 1898), 190.

141

experiences for the British SCM, and the Reverend Ellen Groenendyke spoke on medical missions for the American Student Volunteer Movement for Foreign Missions (SVMFM).

ISABELLA LUCY BIRD BISHOP (1831–1904)

Isabella Lucy Bird Bishop was an explorer, naturalist, photographer, and one of the most prominent travel writers of the Victorian era. Because she was a household name, she was arguably the most famous of the SCM women.

Bishop was outspoken and independent even from childhood. Though she usually wore trousers under her dress, in other ways she had the manners of an educated, upper-class woman of the Victorian Age.

She had many admirers. One said that Bishop had "unusual courage and energy," and another said, "There never was anybody who had adventures as well as Miss Bird."[2] Another said she possessed "right intelligence, [and] an extreme curiosity as to the world outside."[3]

Yet Bishop was frail, suffering from a spinal complaint, nervous headaches, and insomnia. Early on her doctors recommended she travel to healthier climates. As a result, Bishop traveled extensively throughout the world and even had planned a fresh trip to China just before her death.

Her trips were highly unusual. She climbed a volcanic crater and spent months in snowbound cabins (once with two young men). She was attacked as a foreign devil in China. One time when men battered down the door to her lodging, she shot a revolver at them. After this experience, she always carried a gun with her. Bishop took a 1,000-mile horseback ride at age seventy.

Travel in the Rockies in 1873 brought Bishop a budding romance with Jim Nugent, "Rocky Mountain Jim," an outlaw who lived on the edge of society. After she left him, she said, that this violent man with a love for poetry was "a man any woman might love but no sane woman would marry." Nugent seemed to like her independent spirit.[4] In Switzerland in 1874, Bishop had a vision of Nugent standing by her bedside with sorrow in his eyes saying, "I have come as I promised." Soon after she found out that Nugent had been shot and was dead.

---

2. B. E. Schneller, "Isabella Bird Bishop," in *Dictionary of British Women Writers,* ed. Jan Todd (London: Routledge, 1989), 64–66.

3. "The Life of Isabella Bird," *Spectator,* January 1907, 6.

4. See Kari August, *Reaching Rocky Mountain Jim: A Novel Based on the True Life Stories of James Nugent and Isabella Bird* (Denver: Mountain Track Publishing, 2014).

Bishop was born in Edinburgh, Scotland, to the Reverend Edward (1794–1858) and Dora Lawson (1803–66) Bird. She came from a distinguished family line, which included bishops, an Archbishop of Canterbury, and abolitionist William Wilberforce. Bishop was a committed Low Church Anglican and a Sunday school teacher in one of her father's churches in 1848.

As her life moved forward, Bishop worshipped with the Scottish Presbyterians. She said, "The church of my fathers has cast me out by means of inanities, puerilities, music, and squabblings, and I go regularly to a Presbyterian church, where there is earnest praying, vigorous preaching, and an air of reality."[5] Because she admired the missionary zeal of some Baptist friends, she was baptized by immersion by Charles Spurgeon.

Bishop's only education came through the nineteenth-century version of home-schooling. She had no formal education; her parents taught her a wide range of subjects. Bishop was an avid reader.

In 1881, at age fifty, Isabella Lucy Bird married Dr. John Bishop (1842?–1886), an eminent surgeon. With her husband, Bishop planned to establish hospitals on the mission field.

Her husband's early death in 1886 did not deter her. Armed with his ample wealth, she decided to become a missionary. Bishop felt that her earlier travels had been for her own self-centered pleasure. She studied nursing, joined the Church Missionary Society, got involved in YWCA work, and funded the John Bishop Memorial Mission Hospital in the Diocese of Amritsar, Kashmir.

In 1892, Bishop was the first woman Fellow of the Royal Geographic Society, and in 1897, she was made a member of the Royal Photographic Society. She addressed the British House of Commons on Armenian and Syrian immigration problems and had an audience with Queen Victoria in 1893.

Bishop became a popular and widely read writer. Her first publication was at the age of sixteen, a pamphlet addressing Free Trade and Protectionism. Her book *The Englishwoman in America*[6] was an immediate best seller and began her writing career. She wrote for travel, inspirational, and literature magazines. Bishop's writing were characterized by a natural curiosity, detail, and unprejudiced reporting.[7]

---

5. "Life of Isabella Bird," 6.

6. Isabella Bishop, *The Englishwoman in America* (London: John Murray, 1856).

7. Some of Bishop's other writing include *The Hawaiian Archipelago: Six Months among the Palm Groves, Coral Reefs and Volcanoes of the Sandwich Islands* (London: John Murray, 1875); *A Lady's Life in the Rocky Mountains* (New York: G. P. Putman, 1879–1880); *Unbeaten Tracks in Japan: An Account of the Travels on Horseback on the Interior including Visits to the Aborigines of Yezo and the Shrines of Nikko and Ise* (New

In 1893, Bishop gave a lecture to men and women titled "The Importance and Value of Missions" at the annual Student Volunteer Missionary Union (SVMU) conference held at Keswick.[8] In this talk, she informed her audience about the magnitude of world problems, emphasizing the needs of women. Bishop said that the conditions women had to endure were intolerable, especially in polygamous marriages. She told her audience that if the status of women were improved, the status of men would also rise. To encourage her listeners to get more involved in the missionary cause, Bishop said she had met seekers after God on every continent who were ready to meet God if only someone would lead them to him. She asked Westerners to give more money to missions and challenged her audience to think about a missionary career by telling them to have no other ambitions other than serving Jesus Christ.

At the same conference, Bishop joined a panel of men to discuss "Missionary Preparation and the Care of the Body on the Mission Field."[9] She began by telling her listeners that she did not expect to say anything. But going on and ignoring the men in her audience, she spoke directly to the women about staying healthy on the mission field. Bishop said that women had a harder time with this because they did not have the same freedom as men. A woman could not take a walk or ride a horse alone for an outlet as a man could do. So Bishop suggested that women have chaperoned, regular morning exercises, meals, and rest.

Then in direct opposition to what she had just said about women's proper behavior, Bishop described the "unwomanly" life she led: "I carry my own camp-bed, which lifts me two feet above the ground. I carry also a pocket filter and boil the water, adding a little Condy's fluid. My underclothing is always of wool. I protect my head most carefully from the sun; and though I have traveled from morning to night, with the sun sometimes at 157 F., I have never had a feeling of faintness. It is a good rule never to drink when one is hot."[10]

York: G. P. Putnam, 1881); *The Golden Chersonese and the Way Thither* (New York: G. P. Putnam, 1883); *Journeys in Persia and Kurdistan, including a Summer in the Upper Karun Region and a Visit to the Nestorian Rayahs*, 2 vols. (London: J. Murray, 1891); *Korea and Her Neighbors: A Narrative of Travel with an Account of the Recent Vicissitudes and the Present Position of the Country* (New York: Fleming H. Revell, 1898); *The Yangtze Valley and Beyond: An Account of Journeys in China, Chiefly in the Province of Sze Chuan and among the Man-tse of Somo Territory* (New York: G. P. Putnam, 1900); and *Among the Tibetans* (London: Religious Tract Society, 1904).

8. *Report of the First Conference of the SVMU, Held at Keswick, July 19th–24th, 1893* (Glasgow: James Frazer, 1893), 32–37, Archives of the World Student Christian Federation Record Group 46 (Box 204, Folder 1521), Special Collections, Yale Divinity School.

9. Ibid., 43–44.

10. Ibid., 44.

THE REVEREND BARBARA ELLEN GROENENDYKE
(1859–1947)

The headlines "Go Ye and Preach the Gospel—Five Devout Americans in Remote Ecuador Follow This Precept and Are Killed" and "Martyrdom in Ecuador" grabbed readers of *Life Magazine* in its January 30, 1956, edition.[11] Accompanied with pictures, the article told the story of Operation Auca. Five men had gone deep into the rain forest to bring the Gospel to a remote Ecuadorian tribe, the Huaorani, and they had been murdered by those they came to reach.

This story grabbed America's attention in 1956–1957. It created a groundswell of support of missionary efforts in the United States that had not been seen since the Mt. Hermon 1886 Missionary Conference and the creation of the Student Volunteer Movement. In 1957, Elisabeth Elliot, the widow of one of the slain men, published the best-selling book on the story, *Through Gates of Splendor*.[12] These deaths have been frequently remembered in film and evangelical publications. In 2006, the tragedy was the subject of a new film by Steve Saint (the son of Nate Saint, one of the missionaries killed) and Mincayani, one of the tribesman who took part in the attack.

A few years after the deaths of the men, two women, Rachel Saint, the sister of Nate Saint, and Elisabeth Elliot, the wife of Jim Elliot, went as missionaries to the tribe that had killed the men. The evangelization of the tribe began in earnest. Many were converted to Christ, including some of the killers. The Gospel of Mark was published in the Auca language. And amazingly, Kimo, the pastor of the tribe and one of the killers, baptized Steve and Kathy Saint, Nate's children.

Though the American public was fixated on this story in book and film, another similar story happened 118 years previously. It was one among many similar stories because missionary work was dangerous in the late nineteenth century.

In 1889, the Reverend Barbara Ellen Groenendyke had traveled to Sierra Leone with other United Brethren in Christ missionaries. Then in 1898, after she had left the mission to return to the United States to speak about it and raise money for the mission, Ellen Groenendyke's friends were swept up in the Hut Tax War of 1898. This revolt was an African-led war against a new, severe tax on individual huts, a form

---

11. "Go Ye and Preach the Gospel—Five Devout Americans in Remote Ecuador Follow This Precept and Are Killed," *Life Magazine* 40, no. 6 (January 30, 1956): 10–19. The five men were Jim Elliot, Nate Saint, Peter Fleming, Ed McCully, and Roger Youderian.

12. Elisabeth Elliot, *Through Gates of Splendor*, 1st ed. (New York: Harper and Brothers, 1957).

of a property tax, which had been imposed by the British government. In the resulting bloodshed, many Europeans, Americans, educated Africans, and indigenous pastors were murdered. Five missionaries were killed on May 4, 1898, in Rotofunk, Sierra Leone, and two more were killed close by in Taiama on May 9. The violence was so intense that one missionary couple, the Reverend L. A. and Clara McGrew, were beheaded. If Groenendyke had remained in Sierra Leone just a bit longer she would have probably perished herself.

Just like Rachel Saint and Elisabeth Elliot later on, Groenendyke returned a few years later to do missionary work in the same place and to the same people who killed her colleagues. One can only imagine the range of emotions that Groenendyke felt, or those felt by Saint and Elliot. She probably had anger at the unnecessary deaths, fear for her own life, and excitement about fulfilling her missionary call to Sierra Leone again. In an article about missionary work in Sierra Leone in 2009, the *Standard Times Press* noted that the returning missionaries went through "gates of splendor" when they returned to reconstruct what had been destroyed.[13]

Barbara Ellen Groenendyke was born to the Reverend Monroe (1830–1890) and Elizabeth Pressel (1833–1927) Groenendyke. She was named after her grandmother Barbara Groenendyke, but went by her middle name, Ellen. Groenendyke had four brothers. Some of the early Groenendykes were Dutch immigrants who settled in Long Island, New York, in the 1600s. Ellen's family moved to Indiana.

Groenendyke studied at Hartsville College, Hartsville, Indiana. In the 1906 program for the Nashville, Tennessee, SVMFM Quadrennial Conference, she was listed as having earned a BA in music at Hartsville College.

Hartsville College no longer exists except for a historical marker and Hartsville College Cemetery. Hartsville College was established in 1847 as one of the first coeducational institutions in the United States. It came under the control of the Church of the United Brethren in Christ in 1850. The college eventually was integrated into Huntington College, Huntington, Indiana, a present-day university.

One of the most notable names associated with Hartsville College was Wright. Bishop Milton Wright (1828–1917), the father of Wilbur (1867–1912) and Orville (1871–1948) Wright, the inventors, builders, and flyers of the first airplane, met his wife, Susan, there in 1853 while they were students. Depending on which record one chooses, between 1868 and 1869, Bishop Wright was either the supervisor of the prepa-

---

13. "Spotlight on the United Methodist Church in Sierra Leone," *Standard Times Press*, February 13, 2009. http://www.standardtimespress.org.

ratory department or a professor of theology at Hartsville College. At the same time he may have been a pastor in Hartsville, Indiana. Wilbur Wright spent a brief period in Hartsville as an infant. Though the Wright brothers were ten years younger than Groenendyke, in a small denomination like United Brethren in Christ, it is not difficult to assume that they crossed paths many times. At the least, Groenendyke would have known a denominational celebrity such as Bishop Wright.

Groenendyke was a missionary teacher in Africa under the auspices of the Women's Missionary Association of the United Brethren in Christ. The ministry was established in the 1850s. By 1898, it had over 6,000 converts, and several hundred young people had been educated in its schools.[14]

In November 1889, Groenendyke and her fellow missionary Frankie Williams joined this ministry. Records indicate that she served there from 1889 to 1893 and from 1900 to 1902. In an 1899 article her speech to that year's annual meeting of the Women's Missionary Association of the United Brethren in Christ Church, Groenendyke was identified as having five years of missionary service.

At her first meeting with Groenendyke in 1889 in the United States, described on the opening page of this chapter, Frankie Williams described her as "God's anointed."[15] While on shipboard for the crossing across the Atlantic, Groenendyke wrote, "We are afloat at last. I was never happier in my whole life. The Ninety-first Psalm comes to me o'er and o'er again."[16] Her transatlantic journey was marked by a lot of seasickness and good fellowship on board with some fellow Christians. She said, "Spent the time in reading, talking, walking, music, eating, sleeping in larger and smaller quantities."[17]

On January 25, 1891, Groenendyke and Williams were ordained to pastoral ministry in Sierra Leone.[18] The United Brethren in Christ allowed for women's ordination. One report on this ordination service noted that after the service, Frankie Williams baptized and administered communion. Since this was an article on Williams, there is no way of knowing if Groenendyke did the same at this meeting. However, it does clearly suggest that Groenendyke was now ordained and would be able to do these things officially.

In her missionary work, Pastor Groenendyke visited different villages, preached, baptized, administered communion, and provided

---

14. For more information, see Mills, *Mission Work*.
15. Ibid., 190.
16. Ibid., 191.
17. Ibid., 192.
18. Ibid., 197.

other pastoral care. Besides missionary work, Groenendyke served as a trustee or officer (unclear) for the United Brethren in Christ Women's Missionary Association from 1893 to 1897 and then from 1905 to 1907. As a strong supporter of temperance her entire life, Groenendyke was a charter member of the Decatur (Alabama) Woman's Christian Temperance Union (WCTU) in 1884 and leader of the Band of Hope, a children's organization connected to the WCTU. In 1889, she was elected president of the New Decatur WCTU. She was involved in the state convention of that organization when it was held in Decatur on October 12–13, 1930. At that meeting, Groenendyke donated a coin given to her by Africans to support temperance to the Willard Fund for Alcohol Education.[19]

Groenendyke died in 1947 and is buried in Roselawn Gardens of Memory, Decatur, Alabama, with some members of her family.

At the 1906 American SVMFM Conference held in Nashville, the storm of protest surrounding the seating of blacks and whites on the floor of Ryman Auditorium overwhelmed another significant development. For the first and only time in SVMFM history between 1866 and 1920, an *ordained* woman gave a public speech, and no one questioned its propriety. The Reverend Barbara Ellen Groenendyke gave an informational lecture titled "Medical Work among Women."[20]

Groenendyke began her speech by announcing the great need for women medical workers. To substantiate her point, Groenendyke gave a lengthy presentation on the specific social and medical problems women faced, such as child marriage and low status in society.

Then, to encourage women to become medical missionaries, Groenendyke cited two examples which demonstrated their impact. In one story, she spoke about a family that all converted to Christianity after a woman doctor had treated a female family member. As a result, three family members were rescued from sin and one woman has a home of "culture and refinement, letting her light beautifully shine."[21] In a second example, Groenendyke spoke about the "power of doctor as preacher." Armed with Western medical knowledge and a deep spiritual life, the woman doctor preached a powerful and clear message. Groenendyke noted:

---

19.   For more information on the Alabama WCTU, see Mrs. J. Simpson Hamilton, *The Story of the Alabama Woman's Christian Temperance Union* (1959).

20.   Rev. Ellen Groenendyke, "Medical Work among Women," in "Medical Missions," in *Students and the Modern Missionary Crusade: Addresses Delivered before the Fifth International Convention of the SVMFM, Nashville, Tennessee, February 28–March 4, 1906* (New York: SVMFM, 1906), 506–09.

21.   Ibid., 508.

I saw a remarkable demonstration of the power of the doctor as preacher at a postmortem examination. At the request of the relatives, we were searching for the witch which had killed the man. We found it in the hob-nailed liver; and the doctor, with the object lesson before her, preached to the large company looking on such a sermon on personal purity, total abstinence, and God as judge of those who defile the body, that had not been forgotten eleven years afterward.[22]

EVANGELISTIC SPEAKER: CLARA RUTH ROUSE

Women also served as evangelists at conferences. According to Clara Ruth Rouse, this type of speaker fulfilled the goal at the heart of the federation—to lead students to Jesus Christ. She believed that no federation pioneer would have considered an SCM engagement complete without the opportunity to witness to students that Jesus Christ was savior and God.[23]

Although the SCM had several women evangelists, Rouse had the most influential and longest evangelistic ministry of any woman. She served as an SCM evangelist longer than most men, with the exception of John Mott. Because of this, transcripts of some of her speeches are available.[24]

Although Rouse's ministry was rejected by some university authorities and students, she was a popular and effective evangelist for the

---

22. Ibid., 509. Given Groenendyke's support of temperance, the phrase "to be in a hob-nailed liver," most likely suggested that the witch abused alcohol. A hob-nailed liver was a slang term for cirrhosis of the liver, which had protruding scars on its surface that looked like hobnobs. Hobnobs were nails with large heads and short pins which were used to protect the shoe leather of shoes and boots. The term was used by temperance workers like Groenendyke to demonstrate the negative effects of alcohol.

23. Ruth Rouse, *The World's Student Christian Federation: A History of the First Thirty Years* (London: SCM Press, 1948), 62, 81.

24. Some of these transcripts include "The Missionary Settlement for the University Women," given at the International Students' Missionary Conference, January 1–5, 1896, in *Make Jesus King: Report of the International Students' Missionary Conference, Liverpool, January 1–5, 1896* (London: SVMU, 1896), 242–43; "The Blessedness of Purpose," given at the International Convention of the SVMFM, Cleveland, Ohio, February 23–27, 1898, in *The Student Missionary Appeal: Addresses at the International Convention of the SVMFM, Cleveland, Ohio, February 23–27, 1898* (New York: SVMFM, 1898), 268–70; "The Training of Students for World Leadership," given at the Fourth Biennial Convention of the YWCA, April 9–15, 1913, in *The Fourth Biennial Convention, Richmond, Virginia, April 9–15, 1913* (New York: National Board of the YWCA of the USA, 1913), 113–17; and "The Meaning of Vocation," given at the British Quadrennial Conference, Birmingham, England, January 1–7, 1937, in *God Speaks to This Generation: Report of the British SCM Quadrennial Conference, Birmingham, England, January 1–7, 1937* (London: SCM Press, 1937), 107–09.

most part. Typical of the former was a Finnish professor of theology who mistakenly refused to hear her "on the grounds that he was not interested in hearing an American lady speak on philosophy" during her 1897 ministry there.[25]

However, for the most part, reviews of Rouse's ministry as an evangelist were positive. Frederick Scott O'Neill later recalled that Rouse had the "power of public speech, characterized by thought, facts, conviction, and inherent appeal."[26] According to an unknown Finnish woman, "Miss Rouse had a great power of making clear the message of Jesus Christ so that students could understand and draw near."[27] Another woman said, "When she spoke to students she touched their sphere of interest so that they were really taken by her message. She used very good illustrations."[28]

Even nonstudents made similar comments about Rouse's abilities. After a visit to Finland, a student, Helmi Forsman, wrote that Rouse had impressed university and church authorities.[29] Wilmina Rowland described Rouse's influence over these individuals: "Such impressions of Miss Rouse were held not only by students and younger persons, but by such persons as Mr. de Szilassy and some of the Protestant bishops and theological professors. Such men were wont to say that they had never met or heard a woman of such commanding personality, power and force in presenting the great issues of Christianity for the growing mind."[30] Szilassy was one of the presidents of the Supreme Court of Hungary, chief curator of the Reformed Church of Budapest, and president of the local and national Hungarian YMCAs.

How did Rouse describe her evangelistic talks? The answer to this question can be found in her description of her and Mott's 1906 evangelistic meetings at the Presbyterian mission in Lovedale, South Africa, then one of the centers of Presbyterian work in that country. She spoke seven times, and Mott spoke fifteen. Overall, Rouse called these speeches "a wonderful experience." She said it was a time of "apostolic revival" in which "the Spirit was poured out." Rouse noted that this occurred after several weeks of prayer by students and missionaries. This revival included after-meetings for the confession of sins, "making restitution,"

---

25. Wilmina M. Rowland, "The Contribution of Ruth Rouse to the World's Student Christian Federation" (MA thesis, Yale University, 1937), 78.

26. Very Reverend William Scott O'Neill letter to Wilmina Rowland, December 12, 1926, in Rowland, "Contribution of Ruth Rouse," 273.

27. Rowland, "Contribution of Ruth Rouse," 178.

28. Ibid., 89.

29. Ibid.

30. Ibid., 175.

and a call to service, with many volunteering for missions work. The meetings created a continuing revival after their departure.[31] Slipping in a bit of Anglo smugness, Rouse observed, crowds were touched "without any of the emotional excitement so easy and so dangerous with the Native."[32]

Reports abound of Rouse's evangelistic ministries. Typical of her work were her campaigns in Scandinavia between 1897 and 1915. During an 1897 visit to Denmark, she preached to three hundred women and a gallery of men in a large hall.

Rouse gave evangelistic sermons in Finland in 1897, 1903, 1907, and 1915.

In 1897, she gave speeches in girls' schools, training schools, the YWCA and the YMCA. Rouse called her 1903 visit "principally evangelistic." Of eleven sermons preached, five were evangelistic, of which three had men and women present. On her third visit (1907), within eight days, Rouse spoke at four evangelistic meetings (two for women only and two for men and women).[33]

Rouse later claimed that her April 8–15, 1915, ministry at the University of Finland was the "most satisfactory" she had ever had. Even though the term had just begun, her evangelistic meetings were packed with "instant response to very simple and direct speaking." The visit included two large evangelistic meetings, one for men and women and the other for women only, and two YWCA meetings.[34]

Rouse's Russian evangelistic campaigns of 1903, 1907, and 1911 were especially intriguing. Given the oppressive and xenophobic atmosphere of late tsarist Russia, and the patriarchal and anti-Protestant nature of Russian Orthodoxy, Rouse's evangelism with men was nevertheless quite successful. During a 1907 evangelistic mission to St. Petersburg, Rouse spoke to over one thousand men and women on "The Meaning of Life." She later wrote that she felt that the majority of the group had no religious faith but were curious or had come to heckle.

---

31. Ruth Rouse, *The Problem of the Relation of the Native Schools to Movement*, in "South Africa Report III (June 24, 1906)," 1, in "Program of South Africa Tour, 1906, Archives of the WSCF, Group No. 46 (Box 45, Folder 365), Special Collections, Yale Divinity School Library. For more information on the Lovedale Mission, see R. H. W. Shepard, *Lovedale, South Africa, 1824–1955* (Cape Town: Lovedale Press, 1955).

32. Rouse, *Problem*, 1.

33. For Rouse's reports on her ministries in Finland, see *Scandinavia II: Finland*, "Reports of Ruth Rouse, Reports A–E" (October–November 1903, November 1907, October,1911, April 1915 and Private Report, 1915), Archives of the WSCF, Record Group No. 46 (Box 45, Folder 364), Special Collections, Yale Divinity School.

34. Ruth Rouse, "Finland (April 8–14, 1915)," 1–2, Archives of the WSCF, Record Group 46 (Box 45, Folder 364), Special Collections, Yale Divinity School.

Though Rouse had agreed afterward to answer questions from the audience, this plan was interrupted by a man who stood up and attacked Christianity. He and his companions had planned to turn this gathering of students into a revolutionary meeting.

After the man had spoken for over two minutes, a policemen stood up and said only Rouse and Baron Paul Nicolay (the head of the Russian SCM) had permission to speak. Rouse wrote, "For once, I rejoiced in the autocratic policeman, for we were utterly helpless to check the flood of revolutionary speeches. It was pretty plucky of him, for the students were widely angry, and shouted and hissed, and they did not stick at such trifles as assaulting a policeman."[35] The crowd calmed down and handed their written questions to Rouse, who spent over two hours providing answers. Rouse wrote, "A good many contained pointed remarks on the fanaticism, the naiveté, the impertinence and the folly of attempting to preach the antiquated doctrines of Christianity to modern, scientific, twentieth-century students."[36]

INSPIRATIONAL SPEAKER:
MARY "MINNIE" GERALDINE GUINNESS TAYLOR

In addition to informational and evangelistic sermons, conferences also employed inspirational speakers, who encouraged Christians to follow Jesus Christ more closely.

The SCM had many inspirational women speakers, but one of the most popular and effective was Mary Geraldine Guinness Taylor. She believed that she had the power to stir her listeners, and she yielded that power to the Lord to be used by the Holy Spirit.[37] Taylor's biography and traveling secretary work were featured in chapter 6. Here her inspirational speaking ministry will be detailed.

Taylor's inspirational talks inspired many lives. For example, one individual attested to being moved by Taylor's speech in New Zealand:

> The first time I saw Mrs. Howard Taylor was at an evening service at the Devonport Presbyterian Church, Auckland, New Zealand, during the summer [i.e., January] of 1900. Dr. and Mrs. Howard Taylor were both in the pulpit, and Mrs. Taylor gave the address. Her text was: "I am not ashamed of the

---

35.   Rowland, "Contribution of Ruth Rouse," 161.

36.   Ibid.

37.   Joy Guinness, *Mrs. Howard Taylor: Her Web of Time* (London: SCM Press, 1949), 175.

Gospel of Christ: for it is the power of God, unto salvation to everyone that believeth." It was a heart-searching, unforgettable address, bringing home to us the power, the present power of Christ to save. Mrs. Taylor gave vivid instances from their own experiences in China of the Lord's saving power. As I write I can see the whole scene again—the well-filled church, the people listening intently, Dr. Taylor seated beside Mrs. Taylor as she stood in the pulpit. It was a night to be much remembered.[38]

Two of Taylor's addresses given at the 1894 SVMFM conference most represent the typical inspirational sermon delivered by women in the SCM. In both cases, Taylor spoke to large crowds of men and women. In her first sermon on Chinese missions, Taylor displayed an uncanny ability to challenge her audience to have a deeper, personal relationship with Christ. After talking about how the Chinese were dying without Christ, she got to her two main points. First, Taylor asked her audience, "What are you going to do about the needs and claims of China?" Second and more important, Taylor asked if her audience had experienced the full presence and power of the Holy Spirit:

Do you know the Holy Spirit as a person, a personal reality, just as real as Jesus Christ, just as real as God the Father, one with whom you have to do in your daily life? Do you know what communion of the Holy Ghost is? If not, seek him now, oh, seek him now. Ask Him to reveal himself to you. . . . Will you, oh, will you seek Him more and more fully as you go on, and pray for us that we may know Him more? And let us commit our lives utterly to Him, because he can make us sufficient wherever we are to show forth the living Christ in all his gracious saving power.[39]

On March 10, 1894, *The Michigan Christian Advocate* rated this sermon higher than the one given by missionary icon J. Hudson Taylor: "No other two persons in attendance at the convention were the center of so much interest, or so eagerly listened to, as the veteran apostle of the China Inland Mission . . . the talented, consecrated historian of the movement, Miss Guinness, who has herself been six years on the field.

---

38. Ibid., 166.

39. Max Wood Moorhead, ed., *The Student Missionary Enterprise: Addresses and Discussions of the Second International Convention of the Student Volunteer Movement for Foreign Missions held at Detroit, Michigan, February 28 and March 1, 2, 3, and 4, 1894* (Boston: T. O. Metcalf, 1894), 61.

The address of each was full of interest, that of Miss Guinness being especially thrilling and soul-inspiring."[40]

Taylor's second sermon was delivered at a Sunday morning consecration service to over one thousand men and women. She was a last-minute substitute for a man who was unable to deliver his address due to illness. Afterward, the *Intercollegian* reported that Taylor "led the Sunday morning consecration service, perhaps the meeting of all the convention most distinguished for its manifestation of spiritual power."[41]

In this speech, Taylor challenged her audience to receive the fullness of the Holy Spirit. To do this, she cited personal experience. While witnessing to sailors onboard a British man-of-war, she saw her need for the Holy Spirit: "I longed to these men brought to Christ, but God didn't use me. . . . After about three hours that Sunday afternoon I was with those two men, pointing them to Jesus, and I saw in everything I said to them something for myself. . . . I saw that what I needed to do was just to take the Holy Spirit as I urged these men to take Jesus Christ."[42] Taylor then said that the two men gave their lives to Christ and she gave her life to the Holy Spirit.

Likewise, she challenged her audience to turn their lives over to the Holy Spirit: "Are you satisfied? . . . There is no reason why anyone of us should go away from this city until the Holy Spirit of God has taken real, full, deep possession of our whole being, and transformed our Lives. . . . Don't go away without having some definite transaction with Jesus Christ."[43]

At this pivotal movement, Taylor stepped back, and a period of prayer and brief petitions for a greater outpouring of the Holy Spirit on the audience followed. Then Mott, not Taylor, issued an invitation. Visibly touched, everyone stood up.

The SCM's women speakers touched the heart and soul of their audiences. They fearlessly addressed the intellectual, physical, and spiritual needs of their listeners. These speakers broke convention by talking to large groups of men and women and were respected for their platform skills, courage, insights, and spiritual authority.

---

40. *Michigan Christian Advocate* (March 10, 1894), 4, Archives of the SVMFM, Record Group No. 46 (Box 72, Folder 586), Special Collections, Yale Divinity School Library.

41. "The Missionary Campaign of Dr. and Mrs. Howard Taylor," *Intercollegian* 23, no. 8 (May 1901): 180.

42. Moorhead, *Student Missionary Enterprise*, 134–36.

43. Ibid., 132–33, 137.

11

Ecumenical Pioneers

In her June 1919 World Student Christian Federation (WSCF) report on her ministry in the Balkans, Grace Helena Saunders wrote, "It is important that the YMCA and YWCA leaders should keep clearly in mind that 'Christian' is not synonymous with Protestant. . . . Our associations will assuredly be enriched in their turn, by learning the points of view of these men and women."[1] Saunders's attitude is typical of the ecumenical pioneers of the Student Christian Movement (SCM) as they learned to navigate the waters of relationships between different Christian groups. Given that ecumenical relationships are so commonplace today, it is hard to imagine just how novel these pioneering attempts of inter-Christian partnerships were at the turn of the twentieth century.

This ecumenical ministry has been the most celebrated contribution of the SCM to the twentieth century and has been the subject of most of the many scholarly projects that have dealt with the SCM. These projects have generally been limited to the activities and individuals who helped establish the World Council of Churches. This limited interest has missed huge swaths of ecumenical Christians.[2]

What is also intriguing about this investigation is the fact that women played a leading role in the SCM's ecumenical work, a contribution

---

1. Grace Saunders, "Miss Saunders' Report on the Balkans" (March to June 1919), 7, Archives of the WSCF, Record Group No. 46 (Box 284, Folder 2496), Special Collections, Yale Divinity School Library.

2. For links between the SCM and the ecumenical movement, see Herbert Reece Coston Jr., "The World's Student Christian Federation as an Ecumenical Training Ground" (PhD diss., Northwestern University, 1963); Suzanne de Dietrich, *Fifty Years of History: The WSCF, 1895–1945* (Geneva: WSCF, 1993); William Richey Hogg, *Ecumenical Foundations; A History of the International Missionary Council and Its Nineteenth-Century Background* (New York: Harper and Brothers, 1952); Lee Rosenthal, "Christian Statesmanship in the First Missionary Ecumenical Generation" (PhD diss., University of Chicago, 1989); Ruth Rouse and Stephen Charles Neill, eds., *The History of the Ecumenical Movement,* (London: SPCK, 1954); and Hans-Ruedi Weber, *Asia and the Ecumenical Movement, 1895–1961* (London: SCM Press, 1966).

155

largely unexplored in accounts of the development of the ecumenical movement.[3]

The SCM's interest in ecumenical questions had to do with the nature of the movement itself. In its earliest years, it was primarily a Protestant group with an emphasis on missions sponsored by many different denominations. Wherever the SCM organized, it sought out Protestant students of all denominations with that understanding. In 1893, A. T. Pohill-Turner, secretary of the British Student Volunteer Missionary Union (SVMU), wrote about his group:

> Feeling the pulse of Christian students where I have visited, I have found that they seem just ripe for such a movement, welding into one Union our students—Episcopalian, Presbyterian, Wesleyan, Baptist and Methodist alike—united into one brotherhood hitherto thought impossible, all one in Christ Jesus.[4]

Similarly, Ruth Rouse wrote that the founders of the SCM were evangelical men and women who had no personal difficulty associating with a variety of Christians and schools of Christian thought if they had an interest in missions. They forged relationships in Britain with Anglo-Catholics, radical Free Churchmen, and with scholars and students holding a variety of views on the inspiration of Scripture. The close working relationship of the women studied in this book demonstrates the interdenominationalism of the SCM. These women were Anglican/

---

3. The term "the ecumenical movement" is usually applied to modern attempts to develop associations between groups of Protestants first, then between these Protestants and Eastern Christians second, and then finally between these Protestants and Eastern Christians and Roman Catholics. This movement was particularly influential until the late 1960s.

However, the term has much broader application. It was originally and is still used with terms such as "ecumenical council" or "ecumenical patriarch." And the term can be used to cover all attempts to work together either structurally or on specific activities and agendas. Since the late twentieth century, the international charismatic movement has forged relationships between Protestants and Roman Catholicism. Particularly noted here is the ministry of South African Pentecostal Johannes du Plessis (1905–1987). Du Plessis was a Pentecostal "observer" at the 1954 and 1961 World Council of Churches meetings and served as Pentecostal representative at the Second Vatican Council. Recent rapprochements include meetings between bishops of the Charismatic Episcopal Church and Roman Catholicism in the Vatican.

Examples of these ecumenical movements are on the student level, the International Fellowship of Evangelical Students and the World Student Christian Federation and beyond the student community, the World Pentecostal Fellowship, the World Evangelical Alliance, and the World Council of Churches. The SCM's founders and earliest generations spawned these movements.

4. Rouse and Neill, *History*, 329.

Episcopalian (Rouse, Sedgwick, Fairfield, Pym); Presbyterian (Condé, Stevenson); Congregationalist (Root, Wiley); Independents (Taylor); Quakers (Stuart); and United Brethren in Christ (Groenendyke).

As the SCM expanded into non-Protestant lands, the movement had to decide if it would remain a Protestant group and thus assure its minority status in non-Protestant lands or whether it should expand to include Christians who were not Protestants. The SCM chose to enlarge its membership to include Eastern Orthodox and Roman Catholic Christians. This ideal was spearheaded on the local, national, and international level. One of the earliest examples was featured previously in this book. In her Salotto ministry, Almira Leavitt made it clear that she wanted men in Naples to become Christians, not Protestant Christians.

These ecumenical pioneers left their comfortable denominational settings and expanded themselves, the SCM, and Christianity as a whole. They were not satisfied to limit themselves to one branch of Christianity. Instead, they were successful ecumenical workers because they knew about religious differences and had the sensitivity and diplomatic skill to negotiate between groups.

Out of several SCM women, four stood out as ecumenical workers: Grace Helena Saunders, Zoe Fairfield, Michi Kawai, and Ruth Rouse. In each case, these women served as leaders of men in this ministry.

GRACE HELENA SAUNDERS (1874–1970)

As a budding ecumenicist, Grace Helena Saunders served in Bulgaria, Serbia, Romania, and Hungary. She was a "kind of area secretary" in Bulgaria from 1912 to 1916 and again in 1919.[5] She had official funding, but there appeared to be a lack of clarity about her position. In different periodicals and reports, Saunders was the organizing secretary for the Women Students' Christian Association, the YWCA women's secretary at Sophia University, Sophia, Bulgaria, a WSCF representative, and a nurse.[6] Though sent to work with women, she worked with both men and women.

---

5. For more information on the Bulgarian movement, see Kenneth Scott Latourette, *World Service: A History of the Foreign Work and World Service of the Young Men's Christian Association of the United States and Canada* (New York: Association Press, 1957), 387–89; and Anna Rice, *A History of the World's YWCA* (New York: Woman's Press, 1947), 167–68.

6. Saunders was identified as the organizing secretary for the Women Students' Christian Association, Sofia University, Bulgaria, in the byline for her article "Red Cross Work in the Balkans," *North American Student* 2, no. 1 (New York: Council of North American Student Movements, October 1913): 15–19.

Whether or not Saunders knew and was influenced by her famous neighbor, Beatrix Potter, may never be proven.[7] These two were close neighbors in Bolton Gardens, London. Potter lived at Two Bolton Gardens and Saunders lived at Three Bolton Gardens (and at least one report at One Bolton Gardens), an exclusive, wealthy, and well-connected neighborhood in West London. Saunders and Potter were born eight years apart (Potter in 1866 and Saunders in 1874). They had siblings around the same age as well. Despite holding very different views on many things, they were similar in how they faced life as independent, well-educated, well-placed women. Like her neighbor, Saunders traveled widely.

Saunders was born to Herbert Clifford (1834–1893) and Octavia Grimston (1845–1926) Saunders in London. Her father graduated from Oxford University (BA, 1856, and MA, 1860). Herbert Saunders was an English barrister of the Middle Temple (1871) and a Queen's Counsel (1881).[8]

In a serendipitous event, in November 1865, while in Lexington, Kentucky, Herbert Saunders had a lengthy conversation about the Civil War with former Confederate General Robert E. Lee.[9] Afterward, Saunders asked if he could publish their conversation in England, and Lee politely refused permission.

Grace Saunders had one brother and seven sisters. One of her sisters, Una Josephine Saunders, was involved in the SCM.

The position and wealth of the Saunders family were demonstrated in many ways. The Saunders family was found in the *Plantagenet Roll of the Blood Royal Being a Complete Table of All Descendants Now Living of Edward III, King of England*.[10] Grace Saunders had royal blood.

---

7. Known internationally for her children's books, such as *The Tale of Peter Rabbit* (London: Frederick Warne, 1902), Beatrix Potter (1866–1943) was not only an author but also an illustrator, natural scientist, conservationist, and farmer. Her father was a barrister, and her mother's family were cotton brokers and ship builders. She was a Unitarian.

8. The Middle Temple is one of the four Inns of Court exclusively entitled to call their members to the English Bar as barristers. Queen's Counsel barristers are particularly eminent lawyers, mostly barristers, appointed by letters patent to be one of "Her Majesty's Counsel learned in the law." Because members wear silk gowns of a particular design, the award of Queen's Counsel is known informally as taking silk, and hence QCs are often colloquially called "silks."

9. Douglas Southall Freeman, *R. E. Lee: A Biography* (New York: Charles Scribner's Sons, 1934), 4:237–40.

10. The Marquis of Ruvigny and Raineval, *The Plantagenet Roll of the Blood Royal: Being a Complete Table of All the Descendants Now Living of Edward III, King of England* (London: T. C. & E. C. Jack, 1905–1911), 195–96.

Moreover, in 1881, their household had a governess, a kitchen maid, a nurse, a lady's maid, a housemaid, an undermaid, a footman, a cook, and a nursemaid. In 1901, after Herbert Saunders death, Octavia Saunders had a cook, a lady's maid, a parlor maid, a housemaid, a second housemaid, a kitchen maid, and a houseboy. At his death, Herbert Saunders's estate was worth £32,450, which in 2016 would have been worth £3,731,750.00.

Like Potter, in her early years Saunders was educated at home. Later while Potter studied at the National Training School in London, Saunders attended Kensington High School. Saunders never married and died at ninety-five years of age in Marylebone, London, not far from where she grew up.

Rouse wrote that Saunders brought many qualities to bear on her pioneering efforts. Her description of Saunders's "highly unusual" ocean voyage pointed to these:

> She has developed greatly in powers of leadership and in general adaptability in Canada. To give you an example of the kind of things she is up to now—She came home steerage from America, just by way of a social experiment and on board ship indulged in public controversy with an anarchist, who was attacking Christianity and amongst all things marriage, in his address on deck. Grace ascended the tub to answer him in public. Various lines of thought that have been brought into her life have prepared her curiously well, I think, for dealing with some of the moral questions which are bound to come up.[11]

Showing her ecumenical motivations, Saunders developed her student ministry along distinctly Orthodox lines in terms of membership (i.e., more Orthodox than Protestant members), and atmosphere (i.e., there were icons hanging in the meeting rooms). The group encouraged its members to participate in their local Orthodox church.

Saunders fostered cordial relationships with Orthodox, Roman Catholic, and Protestant leaders. In 1919, she received the endorsement of Orthodox Bishop Miron Christea of Karansehes, Romania.[12] In a

---

11. Ruth Rouse to Winifred Sedgwick, August 10, 1910, Archives of the WSCF, Record Group No. 46 (Box 210, Folder 1600), Special Collections, Yale Divinity School Library.

12. Miron Christea (1868–1939), a bishop of Transylvania, became the metropolitan-primate of the Orthodox Church in Romania in 1919. In 1925, he was enthroned as its first patriarch. In 1938, Cristea became the prime minister of Romania. His term was quite short because he died within a year.

formal letter to other Orthodox bishops, he wrote that he was pleased with her explanation of the aims and methods of SCM work. He also officially welcomed other SCM workers and hoped that other bishops would also. During the same period, Saunders met with Sister Augustine, a well-known nun of the St. Vincent de Paul Convent and Mr. Bates of the British YMCA, Mr. Masterson and Mrs. Williams of the American YMCA, and Dr. McElroy of the Scottish Women's Hospital for Serbians, who was most likely Presbyterian.

Saunders advocated that Orthodox Christians reach out to other Orthodox Christians. She felt that earlier efforts to minister to these Christians had been hindered because they were overly Protestant:

> American and Congregational and Episcopal Methodist missions have been doing educational work in the country for fifty years, but the fact of their having formed Protestant communities, has been deeply resented by the nation as a whole. The Bulgarian YMCA (it is really a Young People's CA, as it includes girls) has grown up around these mission churches, and uses Protestant hymns and extemporary prayer, which are regarded as foreign practices. . . . It is owing to the Protestant associations of the name that it seems unlikely that the Bulgarian Student Association will be willing to affiliate, at least for a considerable time, to the YMCA or YWCA.[13]

In 1919, Saunders requested that Vasilka Dimitrieva, an Orthodox Bulgarian student, be sent under the auspices of the World's YWCA, not a national YWCA. Dimitrieva had earned her MA in philosophy at King's College, most likely London, and had been working for the British SCM. She was appointed secretary of the YWCA and WSCF in Bulgaria. Dimitrieva edited the Bulgarian supplement of the *Near East*.

ZOE BARBARA FAIRFIELD

In addition to her ministries discussed in chapter 4, Zoe Fairfield convinced the British SCM to establish interdenominational fellowships. These groups discussed denominational differences, the possibilities of joint ministries between churches, and Christian unity. During the 1918–1919 school year, thanks to Fairfield's efforts, over fifty new mixed

---

13. Saunders, "Miss Saunders' Report," 4.

groups of college-age and older men and women of different denominations and points of view sprung up.[14]

Because of her emerging interest in Eastern Christianity and ecumenism, in the 1920s Fairfield joined efforts to mix the SCM Western Christians with Eastern Christianity. An example of this was her ministry with the Russian émigré Fellowship of St. Alban and St. Sergius. Under the auspices of the British SCM, the Anglo-Russian student conferences of 1927 and 1928 forged fresh relationships between these two groups. Despite the fact that there was some interest from evangelicals, Methodists, and Scottish Presbyterians, SCM participants like Fairfield generally came from the Anglo-Catholic wing of the Church of England.[15]

MICHI KAWAI (1877–1953)

Ecumenical historian Hans-Ruedi Weber called Michi Kawai one of Christ's Asian ambassadors between World War I and II.[16] She was an educator, Christian activist, "speaker against the tide," advocate for peace, proponent of good Japanese-American relations, world traveler, and ecumenical pioneer. Kawai held several positions within the SCM or SCM-related circles. Like the other women in this book, she worked extensively with men and women even though her felt call and official work was with women.

Observers noted that Kawai was a friendly and helpful person. "The way she cocked her head when talking conveyed the impression that she was truly interested in what others had to say," wrote an American woman who knew her.[17] Another observed that Kawai joined her when she was washing the school floors because the janitor was not there. Kawai said, "Two hands are better than one" and went to work.[18]

---

14. Tissington Tatlow, *The Story of the Student Christian Movement of Great Britain and Ireland* (London: SCM Press, 1933), 737.

15. See Zoe Fairfield, "Nicholas Zernov," *Sobornost*, n.s. 2, no. 10 (June 1937): 38. For more on the Fellowship of St. Alban and St. Sergius, see Nicolas and Militza Zernov, *The History of the Fellowship of St. Alban & St. Sergius: A Historical Memoir* (1979). http://www.sobornost.org.

16. Weber, *Asia and the Ecumenical Movement*, 257. For more information on Kawai, see Michi Kawai, *My Lantern*, 2nd ed. (Tokyo: Kyo Bun Kwan, 1940); Johanna M. Selles, *The World Student Christian Federation: Motives, Methods, and Influential Women* (Eugene, OR: Pickwick, 2011), 199–203, 209–11, 213–15; and Archives of the WSCF, Record Group No. 46 (Box 228, Folders 1784–85), Special Collections, Yale Divinity School.

17. Marlene Ritchie, "Michi Kawai: An Inspiring Woman with a Mission," *New Directions* (Tokyo: Child Research Net, May 21, 2010), n.p. See http://www.childresearch.net.

18. Ibid.

Kawai was born in Yamada City, in the province of Ise, to Kawai Noriyasu, a Shinto priest, and Shimosato Kikue, the daughter of the village master of Makkido. The dates of their births and deaths are unknown. She was descended from families of community and religious leaders. Kawai's maternal grandfather, Yujiro Shimosato, was born a samurai and was known for being a reputable village leader when he collected taxes and with his creation of a water system that benefited the surrounding paddy fields. Kawai's paternal grandfather came from a long line of hereditary Shinto priests reaching back over 2,000 years, according to Kawai. His interests involved the business side of the Ise Shrine, one of the most spiritual and politically significant sacred centers of Shintoism in the Japanese islands.

Kawai was one of the first seven girls to graduate from Hokusei Joggako, which was directed by Presbyterian missionaries. She converted to Christianity because of the witness of her uncle who was a Protestant minister. Kawai was a devout Christian most of her entire life, and her faith motivated her actions. Her call to serve Japan's girls came at the 1902 YWCA Conference in Silver Bay, New York. Remembering this event later, Kawai wrote, "I sat one day in the boat house, watching the girls swimming and boating, and my heart was lifted up in a prayer to God that he would use me for the girls of my country, to bring them together for mutual helpfulness."[19]

Kawai took her first trip to the United States to attend college. She graduated from Bryn Mawr College (BA, 1904) and the YWCA Secretary Training School (1916). Kawai attended Union Theological Seminary in New York for a few months, but had to stop to return to Japan to tend her ill mother in 1921.

Despite worsening relations between Japan and the United States, Kawai came to the United States to promote Japanese-American relations in 1934. On the eve of the violent Japanese invasion of China in 1937, she went to China.

Kawai was in Japan during World War II. Her school maintained its Christian focus in spite of governmental disapproval.

On a 1941 trip to the United States just prior to the outbreak of World War II, Kawai was awarded a Doctor of Humane Science from Mills College, Oakland, California. When she received this award, Kawai said, "'This is a gesture of American goodwill to Japan at this critical moment,' said my soul to me, 'therefore accept the honor, not for

---

19. Kihm Winship, "Michi Kawai at Silver Bay, May, 1902," *Silver Bay Blog* (May 13, 2013), n.p. See https://kihm4.wordpress.com.

yourself, but for your country, and pledge yourself to stand for the cause of peace and friendship in this hour of tribulation.'"[20]

Though she traveled regularly around the world, Kawai mainly worked in Japan. Confident in the value of education, she taught at Tsuda Juku and other schools, founded Keisen Jogakuen as a secondary school for girls (1929) and served as its first principal. Keisen Jogakuen became one of Japan's most influential high schools and junior colleges for women. Kawai was also one of the founders of the Japanese International Christian University at Mitaka.

Within SCM circles, she attended the 1902 YWCA Conference in Silver Bay where she was inspired to develop a woman's YWCA in Japan. As an ecumenical leader, Kawai addressed the international WSCF conference held in Tokyo (1907), which was attended by many different nationalities, representing a variety of Christian groups under the movement's motto, "One in Christ." Kawai was also vice-chair of the women's subcommittee of the WSCF executive committee (1911–1920) and vice-chair of the executive committee (1920–1922). She traveled for the WSCF and YWCA in Europe in 1911 and attended the 1911 WSCF Constantinople conference. She was one of the founders of the Japanese YWCA in 1912 and was the YWCA's first full-time secretary (1916–1925). She was the first Asian vice president of the World's YWCA.

Kawai was active in circles outside the SCM. Kawai attended a lecture by Carrie Chapman Catt, the leader of the National American Suffrage Association, given at an International Suffrage League meeting in Geneva in 1920. She promoted the Church of Christ in Japan (Kyodan), which was formally organized in 1941. Kawai was active in the worldwide peace movement. Under her tenure as president of the Japanese Women's Peace Society (1931–1933), she led the society to collect signatures endorsing the 1932 Geneva Disarmament Conference and took these to the Japanese prime minister. She was also a member of the Japanese branch of the Fellowship of Reconciliation. In 1941, Kawai promoted peace in the United States as a member of the Riverside Group, which sought to clarify Japanese positions on problems with the United States. During World War II, Kawai was often interrogated by the Japanese police for her international peace and Christian school work.

During two European tours (1910–1911 and 1920), she had private meetings with a variety of denominational leaders, ranging from German Methodists to Dutch Reformed Church personnel. During the first

---

20. Michi Kawai, *Sliding Doors* (Tokyo: Kasai, 1950), 11.

tour of Europe, Kawai gave a speech to an audience composed almost entirely of men in Delft, The Netherlands. She thought to herself, "I was grateful of my brazen facedness. There was no time to feel awkward or timid. . . . Just imagine, an Eastern woman to talk to Western men-students!" She overcame her hesitancy by saying, "I had some things to say to the sons of Adam as well as to the daughters of Eve."[21]

Kawai never married and took the unheard-of step for a woman of establishing her own home and alternative family. She was the head of this all-female nonsexual family. Kawai died at seventy-six years of age.

CLARA RUTH ROUSE

Clara Ruth Rouse defined ecumenism as "the experience of 'fellowship in faith with all those who worshipped the Lord to whom her life was dedicated.'"[22] Due to her position as an SCM traveling secretary, as featured in chapter 5 and 6, Rouse was the most significant woman ecumenical worker the movement had on the international level. She acknowledged that her own ecumenical vision had evolved alongside the SCM's vision from "those of a narrow young thing" to a leader who helped make the WSCF an "experimental laboratory for ecumenism."[23]

Rouse's broadening perspectives could be seen in her changing choice of churches. Her childhood church, Spurgeon's Metropolitan Tabernacle, had been involved in evangelical ecumenism among dissenters and evangelical Anglicans prior to Rouse's involvement. In college, she became a member of the established church, the Church of England. Ecumenism in that environment included a wider range of Christian groups, such as High Church followers and Eastern Christians.

Yet in retrospect Rouse was not as ecumenical as she appeared. During the fundamentalist-modernist controversy, she took what can be considered a decidedly nonecumenical stance. Siding with the modernists, Rouse argued that fundamentalists were too narrow, even though they could fit under her definition of ecumenism. As evidenced by her attendance at Student Volunteer Missionary Union (SVMU) meetings at Keswick, she had been a conservative Christian and had worked with conservative Christians earlier in her life. But as time passed, Rouse had strained relationships with them and they with her.[24]

---

21.   Michi Kawai, "Report," March 21, 1910, Archives of the WSCF, Record Group No. 46 (Box 228, Folder 1783), Special Collections, Yale Divinity School Library.

22.   Herbert Reece Coston Jr., "The World's Student Christian Federation as an Ecumenical Training Ground." (PhD diss., Northwestern University, 1963), 72.

23.   Ruth Rouse, *The World's Student Christian Federation: A History of the First Thirty Years* (London: SCM Press, 1948), 20.

24.   For Rouse's views of fundamentalists, see Rouse and Neill, *History*, 380–82.

An example of Rouse's ecumenical undertakings can be seen in her efforts to gain acceptance for the 1911 WSCF Constantinople Conference, which she later called "sheer pioneering."[25] Despite political unrest and a cholera epidemic, the WSCF had chosen to hold the meeting in Turkey to signify the group's broadened ecumenical spirit.

Rouse believed that conferences like the one in Constantinople were ecumenical laboratories because students and speakers from a variety of churches and nations came together for a short, intense series of meetings. Those in attendance found themselves in the midst of an ecumenical fellowship already in actual operation. They learned about Christian traditions other than their own; they used a variety of worship forms; and above all, those in attendance established lasting friendships with men and women of other churches.

To prepare for the conference, Rouse set out to educate herself and her fellow Western Christians about Eastern Christendom. In his biography of John R. Mott, Charles Hopkins credited much of the local acceptance of the conference to Rouse, who had spent several months learning about local religious beliefs and practices.[26]

Because of these endeavors, Rouse saved the WSCF a potential embarrassment. She discovered that the meeting had been scheduled for the Orthodox Easter by those who were unaware that Eastern Christians had a different religious calendar. When she cabled Mott about it, he had the WSCF executive immediately change the date.[27]

Rouse also met with theological students, archimandrites, bishops, and patriarchs.[28] "I, too, have learned how to kiss an ecclesiastical hand as the years have gone by," she observed.[29]

In Bucharest, Rouse met with Vasile Ispir, then a student at the local Orthodox seminary. He was president of several student societies at the time. When she explained the WSCF and its conference to him, Rouse reported that "he jumped at the idea of the Federation as something that might help the students of his country."[30] He ended

---

25. Rouse, *World's Student Christian Federation*, 153.

26. Charles Howard Hopkins, *John R. Mott, 1865–1955: A Biography* (Grand Rapids, MI: William B. Eerdmans, 1979), 371.

27. Wilmina Rowland, "The Contribution of Ruth Rouse to the World's Student Christian Federation" (MA thesis, Yale University, 1937), 270.

28. An archimandrite is either a title for a superior abbot appointed by a bishop to supervise several lesser abbots and monasteries or it is a title of honor with no link to an actual monastery. As an honorary title, it is given to a priest as mark of respect and thanksgiving for service to the church.

29. Tatlow, *Story*, 421.

30. Coston, "World's Student Christian Federation," 120. Vasile Ispir (1886–1947) was a theologian, ecumenist, and missionary. He studied in Berlin (1910–1911), Oxford (1911–1914), and the Orthodox Theological Seminary in Bucharest (1919). He taught

up attending the 1911 Conference as the only Romanian delegate.

In Romania, Rouse recorded that an archimandrite said that he knew all about her and the WSCF. She wrote that he "cheerfully greeted me. . . . One felt at once in the completest sympathy with him."[31] Perhaps in reference to him or another archimandrite in Romania, Tissington Tatlow mentioned that Rouse spoke with an eager archimandrite and with the bishop of Starvopolis. About the latter, Tatlow noted:

> Miss Rouse relates how she went to see him and attempted to explain the Federation with no results until she produced a pamphlet descriptive of the Movement she had written for us, and known as "The Green Rouse." As soon as he saw it he said, "Oh! Now I know what you are talking about."[32]

The bishop went on to endorse the conference.

Rouse had a letter of introduction to the metropolitan of the Serbian Church from a Serbian student she had met in Geneva. This opened the door in Serbia.[33] There, Rouse had a surprising experience:

> The Synod of the Serbian Church was in session in Belgrade to elect a new bishop, and the Metropolitan invited Mr. Mott to address the bishops assembled in the Cathedral! This did not come off, owing to the illness of two bishops. It was I who addressed the bishops finally, not by invitation, however, except in so far as the bishops invited themselves to a meeting at which I was speaking![34]

What a scene this must have been when a non-ordained English Protestant woman gave a religious address to a mostly male audience that included Orthodox bishops. Even Rouse could not contain herself!

---

at the last school as a professor of theology. He became one of the leading supporters of ecumenism in the Balkans.

31.   Ruth Rouse, "Roumania" (January 25–February 2, 1911), 4, Archives of the WSCF, Record Group No. 46 (Box 44, Folder 356) Special Collections, Yale Divinity School Library.

32.   Tatlow, *Story*, 421.

33.   See Ruth Rouse, "Confidential Report" (February 3–7, 1911), 3–4, Archives of the WSCF, Record Group 46 (Box 44, Folder 356), Special Collection, Yale Divinity School Library. Coston also mentions other unspecified letters that Rouse and Mott had. Coston, "World's Student Christian Federation," 118.

34.   Ruth Rouse, "Serbia II" (May 1–4 and May 13–15, 1911), 2, Archives of the WSCF, Record Group No. 46 (Box 44, Folder 356), Special Collections, Yale Divinity School Library. A metropolitan is the head of an ecclesiastical province.

Rouse's most important ecumenical work came in her meetings with the ecumenical patriarch and his Armenian counterpart.[35] Rouse wrote, "Introductions from the Archbishop of Canterbury, complete with official seals, worked wonders" in getting audiences.[36] The archbishop of Canterbury had asked the archbishop of Gibraltar to write letters to these men.[37]

When Rouse went to see Joachim III, the ecumenical patriarch, she "boldly asked for permission" to address the Greek Girls' School in Constantinople about the WSCF and the conference.[38] Not only did he give his permission, but he also gave his blessing on the gathering: "I consider such a conference to draw Christians into fellowship and cooperation as one of the most sacred causes, and I will help it in any way in my power."[39] Tatlow later noted that Joachim III had been "very kind to Miss Rouse."[40]

So successful was all this ecumenical outreach that the ecumenical patriarch did more than support the 1911 Constantinople meeting. But also with approval of his Holy Synod, he sent a delegate to the 1913 WSCF Conference. A copy of the appointment letter was included in the conference report. The letter stated, "The aim of the Federation is indeed worthy of sympathy and attention," and it calls the organization a "beneficial Federation."[41]

---

35. If this reference to the Armenian patriarch refers to the head leader of the Armenian Apostolic Church, the Catholicos of All Armenians, then Rouse met with either Matthew II Izmirlian (1908–1910) or George V of Armenia (1910–1930).

Joachim III (1834–1912) was seen as one of the most prominent and important patriarchs of the twentieth century. He was the patriarch of Constantinople twice (1878–1884 and 1901–1912). In 1864, Joachim III was elected bishop of Varna and in 1874, bishop of Thessalonika. He served as the protosyngellos for Patriarch Joachim II and prior to his election as patriarch was the metropolitan of Thessalonika. Joachim III improved the financial status of the patriarchy, founded the magazine *"Truth,"* and did many charitable acts. He was a Mason. A protosyngellos or "first cellmate" (in monastic orders as first cellmate of a bishop) was an honorary title given by a bishop for either a high-ranking or most senior cleric in a diocese. It might also have been a job title, such as chancellor.

36. Coston, "World's Student Christian Federation," 118.

37. This was most likely William Edward Collins (1867–1911) who was there from 1904 to 1911. Because he was a sub-prelate of the Order of St. John of Jerusalem, he had close ties with Eastern Christian leaders. He died in Constantinople and is interred at St. John the Evangelist's Anglican Church in Izmir, Turkey.

38. Ruth Rouse, "Constantinople II" (December 24, 1910, to January 24, 1911), 2, Archives of the WSCF, Record Group No. 46 (Box 44, Folder 362), Special Collections, Yale Divinity School Library.

39. Rouse, *World's Student Christian Federation,* 154.

40. Tatlow, *Story,* 421.

41. "Letter from the Patriarch of Constantinople to the Rev. C. H. Demetry, D. D.,"

As a result of her successful meeting with the Armenian patriarch, Rouse persuaded him to endorse the WSCF because his young people needed a spiritual movement like the SCM.

Report of the Tenth Conference of the World's Student Christian Federation, Lake Mohonk, New York, June 2–8, 1913 (New York: World's Student Christian Federation, 1913), 464.

12

Intellectual Pioneers

I have felt increasingly during my contact with students that one of
the greatest responsibilities of the SCM is to help its members and
others to face with candor and courage whatever in modern thought
seems to mitigate against the Christian position, quietly confident
that religion, far from being endangered, can only be enriched by the
fearless assimilation of whatever truth our age has to offer.[1]

This 1909 statement by Marie Luise (or Louise) Christlieb sums up
clearly and directly what many of the intellectual pioneers of the Student
Christian Movement (SCM) thought. Instead of being purely pietisti-
cally focused, she was a committed Christian who was very interested in
dealing with the burning intellectual questions of her day.

After the successes of basic and specialized pioneering, theoretical
pioneers who worked in the realm of ideas emerged, whether these were
intellectual, social gospel, or women's movement pioneers. Typical of
other SCM leaders, these women worked with men and women. The last
two will be discussed in the following chapters.

WHAT WAS AN INTELLECTUAL PIONEER?

Christlieb and other intellectually gifted and interested college-
educated women were intellectual pioneers in the SCM and fulfilled
an important part of the SCM's mandate. As Ruth Rouse stated, in its
desire to minister to students and the world, it was assumed that the
federation advance was not only geographic and targeted, but also in
"successive regions of thought and activity, social and ecumenical."[2]

---

1. M. L. Christlieb, Report, Nottingham, February 2–5, 1909, SCM, Records of the
Student Christian Movement) Cadbury Research Library, Special Collections, University
of Birmingham.

2. Ruth Rouse, *The World's Student Christian Federation: A History of the First
Thirty Years* (London: SCM Press, 1948), 165.

169

The intellectual pioneer challenged the premise held by secularists that an individual could not be an intellectual and a Christian at the same time.[3] They recognized that Christianity had to respond to those who challenged commonly held assumptions about the Bible, Christian faith, and human relations.

Typical for an intellectual pioneer, Bertha Condé contended that intellectual questioning was an important and appropriate aspect of a person's faith. Christians should anticipate that they would be led by God to use their God-given intellect. Therefore, they should never be afraid of any honest question or new thought. Believers could also maintain an active spiritual life even if intellectual doubt existed, because all knowledge is only partial.

British women were in the forefront of intellectual questioning. About them Zoe Fairfield wrote, "It is certainly true in the student movement of this country that there is more theological questioning among the women students than among men."[4] Tissington Tatlow added, "Intellectual questioning about Christianity was rife among women students at the Oxford and Cambridge Colleges. . . . The women students were the first among the undergraduates to be concerned with intellectual questions."[5]

British intellectual pioneers took two approaches. Some used a roundabout, indirect method. At several universities, women gave the substance of their apologetics discussions to local male leaders, who brought these to the attention of the local association as a whole. According to Tatlow, quotations from these inquisitive women even appeared in the British executives' annual reports.[6]

A second group of women pioneers took intellectual issues straight on. Long before men students, the London Arts Students' Christian Union and the London Women's Committee asked Tatlow in 1905 to meet weekly with them to discuss apologetics. They wanted a lecture followed by a discussion. Supposedly limited to thirty students, the meeting was seldom that small. Tatlow later recalled that the group met for one and one-half hours, dealt with doctrinal more than apologetic questions, and members were "eager and live-minded."[7] Regular meetings were held in the dining room of the Reverend Alexander Connell of the Regent Square Presbyterian Church.

---

3. See Tissington Tatlow, *The Story of the Student Christian Movement in Great Britain and Ireland* (London: SCM Press, 1933), 424–25.

4. Zoe Fairfield, "Some Aspects of the Woman's Movement," *North American Student* 3, no. 1 (October 1914): 63.

5. Tatlow, *Story*, 214n1, 427.

6. Ibid., 427.

7. Ibid., 260.

Because they were excited about their meetings with Tatlow, these London groups asked him to give several lectures on "Christian Evidences" at the 1906 summer conference. According to Tatlow, "These meetings were crammed and the Bible readings parallel to them were deserted."[8] At Bible reading sessions, individuals read from the Bible without commentary. As a result, the British executive decided that intellectual meetings should be a part of every summer conference from then on.

As another result of Tatlow's London meetings, the city's women's committee sponsored a conference on Bible study in 1907. Topics included "How To Face Difficulties in the Bible?" and "The Use and Abuse of Textbooks."

The British SCM also formed an apologetics subcommittee, which held conferences and lectures and published books on a variety of intellectual issues. A November 13, 1912, report listed topics of interest for the group: comparative religions and the uniqueness or finality of Christianity, modern thought (i.e., materialism), the problems of evil and pain, the validity of experience, Christian ethics, and theosophy.[9]

LILY DOUGALL (1858–1923)

While Canadian author and feminist Lily Dougall resided in Cumnor near Oxford, she had an extensive ministry as an intellectual pioneer with the British SCM. She had great intellectual skills and interests and contributed to intellectual discussion and debate within SCM circles along modernism lines. Dougall also had a great sense of humor and a simple and childlike faith. Once she said, "Religion can never safely lose touch with the simple things of life."

The youngest of nine children, she was born to John (1808–1886) and Elizabeth Redpath (1819–1883) Dougall. She was baptized in a Congregational church in Montreal, Canada, in 1858. Her father was a merchant, journalist, and publisher, and her mother's family was composed of successful contractors and industrialists. At first Dougall's family was Presbyterian, but later it became Congregationalist. The family was actively involved in church, missions, religious publications, temperance, and the YMCA.

After receiving her early education in private schools, she began taking courses at the University of Edinburgh Center for the Education of Women in 1881 to prepare for a writing career. In 1885, she began

---

8. Ibid.
9. Ibid., 435.

studies at the University of St. Andrews in Scotland, and in 1887, she earned an LLA, the equivalent of the MA awarded to male students.

Dougall's varied interests included the psychological parts of religious experience, connections between religion and science, the arts, and social issues. Over time, she particularly became interested in the links between physical, psychological, and spiritual health. Dougall was ecumenical in spirit with connections to a variety of Protestant churches, Unitarianism, Christian Science, and Mormonism. She joined the Society of Psychical Research in 1895 because of her lifetime interests in mental telepathy, spiritualism, and faith healing.

Between 1885 and 1900, Dougall split her time between Great Britain and Canada. After 1900, she decided to make her home in England, largely due to her asthma. She eventually settled in Cumnor near Oxford in 1911 with her lesbian partner Sophie Earp. Dougall died suddenly of heart failure at the age of seventy-five and left an estate of £3,248 to Earp. This amount would have been worth £166,620.40 in 2016.

Dougall's Cunmore home became a center for intellectual conversation, particularly with discussions about religious issues in groups of men and women. Some of these conversations resulted in three books: *Concerning Prayer: Its Nature, Its Difficulties and Its Face Value*; *Immortality: An Essay in Discovery*; and *The Spirit: God and His Relation to Man Considered from the Standpoint of Philosophy, Psychology and Art*.[10]

Some of Dougall's internationally read articles and books include ten novels starting with *Lovereen: A Canadian Novel* under a male pseudonym, *Beggars All*, *Pro Christo et Ecclesia*, and eight books on religious philosophy. Dougall's female characters are typically independent women drawn to egalitarian marriage.[11]

Pro Christo et Ecclesia argued that Christianity could be renewed by love and joy. Dougall criticized secularism and challenged Christianity to adapt to new lines of thought.

Dougall's extensive and regular interactions with SCM personnel were shaped by her intellectual skills and interests. In turn, the SCM

---

10.   Lily Dougall, *Concerning Prayer: Its Nature, Its Difficulties and Its Face Value* (New York: Macmillan, 1917); Burnett Hillman Streeter, A. Clutton-Brock, Cyril W. Emmet, J. A. Hadfield, and L. Dougall, *Immortality: An Essay in Discovery* (New York: Macmillan, 1917); and Burnett Hillman Streeter, A. Seth Pringle-Pattison, L. Dougall, James Arthur Hadfield, Charles Archibald Anderson Scott, Cyril William Emmet, and A. Clutton-Brock, *The Spirit: God and His Relation to Man Considered from the Standpoint of Philosophy, Psychology, and Art* (London: Macmillan, 1920).

11.   Lily Dougall, *Lovereen: A Canadian Novel*; *Beggars All* (New York: Longmans, Green, 1891); and *Pro Christo et Ecclesia* (London: Macmillan, 1900).

reflected these things. Reminiscing about his contact with Dougall, Tatlow said that she had published more than one book with the SCM.[12] He said that she

> became our friend and benefactor. . . . She was a woman of learning, with an original and sympathetic mind. She found herself thoroughly at home in the atmosphere of the Student Movement summer conferences and might invariably be seen with a group of students round her, discussing all kinds of theological questions. A memory cherished by Student Movement secretaries in office at the time was a secretaries' meeting lasting for several days at her beautiful home in Cunmor.[13]

Three of the most important concerns of intellectual pioneers will be dealt with here. These were the new disciplines of the social sciences, the sociology of religion, and biblical criticism.

THE SOCIAL SCIENCES

Some SCM intellectual pioneers tackled Christian connections with the newly emerging field of the social sciences. Subfields included anthropology, economics, psychology, and sociology. The social sciences attempted to understand all phenomena on the human level. By seeking to explain things in this way, most social scientists downplayed or simply ignored the role of God or transcendence in the origin and development of human interactions, in particular, in religious belief and practice.

The SCM's social science pioneers took two approaches. One approach was to use the new social sciences to understand Christianity first and foremost in human terms. A second approach was to challenge the social sciences by arguing that Christianity had to be understood as more than merely a human phenomenon.

Taking the first approach in *The Human Element in the Making of a Christian: Studies in Personal Evangelism*, Bertha Condé used a psychological rather than a spiritual approach to explain conversion.[14] She laid

---

12. An example is Lily Dougall, *God's Way with Man: An Exploration of the Method of Divine Working Suggested by the Facts of History and Science* (London: SCM Press, 1924).

13. Tatlow, *Story*, 435–36. For more information on Dougall, see Joanna Dean, *Religious Experience and the New Woman: The Life of Lily Dougall* (Bloomington: Indiana University Press, 2007).

14. See Bertha Condé, *The Human Element in the Making of a Christian: Studies in Personal Evangelism* (New York: Charles Scribner's Sons, 1917).

out elementary psychological principles that aided in one's efforts to help others know God. In practical terms, she suggested that the temperament of the individual dictated the evangelistic method needed to reach that person. This meant that the evangelist had to understand human temperaments. Condé's book included Bible studies for each chapter that helped the reader focus on the psychological side of evangelism. Condé gave a suggested reading list for further study on the subject. A majority of these focused on psychological explanations of religious experience and represented some of the leading figures in the new social sciences.[15]

Taking the second approach, Ruth Rouse and Hugh Crichton-Miller in *Christian Experience and Psychological Processes* defended the Christian faith against those who used psychology and sociology to explain religious experience in purely human terms.[16]

Hugh Crichton-Miller was a prominent psychiatrist and the founder of the Tavistock Clinic in London. He served as vice president of the International General Medical Society for Psychotherapy. He was the son of a Scottish Presbyterian minister. Hugh Crichton-Miller pioneered the treatment of those with "functional nervous disorders," and he helped establish the professional field of modern psychology. One of his closest friends was Carl Jung.[17]

In the book's preface, Rouse wrote that she and Crichton-Miller wrote the book because of the current popularity of the social sciences: "[They were] much to the fore in the colleges and elsewhere just now and in urgent need of treatment."[18]

Rouse argued that although psychology and sociology could explain the surface experience of Christianity, they could not disclose what caused this experience at its most fundamental level. Rouse believed that religious experience had divine, supernatural origin. To make this case,

---

15. Condé's bibliography included William James, *Talks to Teachers on Psychology and to Students on Some of Life's Ideals* (New York: H. Holt, 1914), and *The Varieties of Religious Experience* (New York: Longmans Green, 1902); George Albert Coe, *The Psychology of Religion* (Chicago: University of Chicago Press, 1916); George Steven, *The Psychology of the Christian Soul* (London: Hodder and Stoughton, 1911); Herman H. Horne, *Psychological Principles of Education* (New York: Macmillan, 1906); Samuel McComb, *The Power of Self-Suggestion* (New York: Moffat, Yard, 1909); and Hugo Munsterberg, *Psychotherapy* (New York: Moffat, Yard, 1909).

16. Ruth Rouse and Hugh Crichton Miller, *Christian Experience and Psychological Processes: With Special Reference to the Phenomenon of Autosuggestion* (London: SCM Press, 1918).

17. For more information on Hugh Crichton-Miller, see *Hugh Crichton-Miller, 1877–1959: A Personal Memoir by His Friends and Family* (Dorchester: Longmans, 1961).

18. Rouse and Crichton-Miller, *Christian Experience*, preface, v.

she argued that psychology portrayed religion in a limited fashion as a human phenomenon based on self-hypnotism or a crowd mentality. Then Rouse presented the case for the divine origin of Christian experience. To state this case, Rouse used Christ's own religious experience and the experiences of Christians in history to show that God acted in individual lives. In the end, Rouse asked her readers to choose between the surface explanations of religion based on the new social sciences or deeper understandings of religious life based on a supernatural God.

MARIE LUISE CHRISTLIEB (1868–1946)

Thanks to nineteenth-century theorists such as Emile Durkheim (1858–1917), Karl Marx (1818–1883), and Max Weber (1864–1920), the use of sociological methods to understand religious beliefs, practices, and organizations became quite popular. As opposed to a theological and pietistic approach, these methods were secular and exterior to Christianity. Some of them were quantitative, such as the use of surveys, polls, demography, and census analysis, and some were qualitative, such as interviewing, participant observation, and the use of archival, historical, and documentary materials.

Marie Luise (or Louise) Christlieb can be described in many ways. At one time or another, she was an evangelist, pastor, missionary, missionary strategist, and author. Christlieb used a primitive form of the newly emerging field of the sociology of religion. It does not appear that she actually used the term, however.

Christlieb was a German citizen born in Bonn, but she also lived in England and India. Her family was steeped in the intellectual side of the Christian life and in missions. Christlieb's parents were Theodor, DD (1833–1889) and Emily Weitbrecht (?–?) Christlieb. She was the granddaughter of Dr. John James Weitbrecht, a noted missionary to India who belonged to the London Missionary Society. That the biography of him written by his wife had a preface written by Henry Venn suggests the family's evangelical Anglican tone.[19] This would be reflected in Marie Luise Christlieb's faith commitments.

Christlieb's father, Theodor, was a German professor of theology and pastor. After serving two German curacies, he moved to London

___

19. Mary Edwards Weitbrecht, *A Memoir of the Reverend John James Weitbrecht, Late Missionary of the Church Missionary Society at Brudwan, in Bengal: Comphrending a History of the Burdwan Mission* (London: James Nisbet, 1854). Henry Venn (1796–1873) has been recognized as one of the most famous evangelical Protestant missionary strategists of the nineteenth century. He was the honorary secretary of the London Missionary Society (1841–1873) and a supporter of abolitionism.

from 1858 to 1865 to serve the German population there. In 1865, he became pastor at Friedrichshafen, where his ministry involved the German royal family. From 1868 to 1889, Theodor Christlieb was chair of the Department of Pastoral Theology in Bonn. There he had a large influence on the future kaiser, Wilhelm II (1859–1941). James Edwin Orr calls Theodor Christlieb, "one of Germany's greatest evangelistic forces," in his book on the worldwide impact of the 1858 Awakening. He said that Christlieb served as a "revival worker" in the German part of that awakening.[20] In that role, he also supported missionary work.

Because she grew up amid significant theological debates, Marie Luise Christlieb learned different sides of many debates. Her father held conservative views in opposition to such German biblical critics as Friedrich Schleiermacher (1768–1834), David Friedrich Strauss (1808–1874), and Ludwig Feuerbach (1804–1872).

At age seventeen, Marie Luise Christlieb first considered missionary work as a career. She settled this issue with the conviction, "I have no reason not to go." In the 1892 London Missionary Report, Christlieb was linked with the multidenominational East London Institute as a deaconess at Doric Lodge. This was part of the East London Training Institute for Home and Foreign Missions established by Reverend Henry and Fanny Guinness, parents of Geraldine Guinness Taylor. Wearing a uniform like her fellow deaconesses, Christlieb was heavily involved in evangelism, work with the poor, and personal counseling in East London. Eventually she joined over one-thousand overseas missionaries who had been students at the lodge and institute between 1873 and 1903.

She is listed in a 1901 British Census as living with close family just east of London in Essex.

After college, Christlieb became a missionary with the London Missionary Society in Anantapur, India. She attended the India National Conference at Calcutta, December 18–21, 1912, one of eighteen regional meetings sponsored by the Continuation Committee of the 1910 World Missionary Conference in Edinburgh.[21] The Calcutta meeting of fifty missionary leaders deliberated over how to foster evangelism, the Christian church, indigenous leadership, missionary training, Christian education, medical missions, and outreach to women.

Christlieb and two other women joined twenty-eight men on an interim committee charged with creating a National Missionary Council

---

20. James Edwin Orr, *The Fervent Prayer: The Worldwide Impact of the Great Awakening of 1858* (Chicago: Moody Press, 1974), 120.

21. For more information on the 1910 World Missionary Conference held in Edinburgh, Scotland, see chapter 13.

for India under the auspices of the International Missionary Council. Under John R. Mott's leadership, the International Missionary Council laid the groundwork for the worldwide ecumenical movement.

Christlieb was listed as living in England in 1945. She died in 1946 in Oxford at age seventy-eight and left behind £2,517, which would have been worth £98,163 in 2016.

Christlieb wrote many articles and books.[22] She tended to use the sociological approach to understand cultures and religions. For example, in her 1930 book, *If I Lived in India,* she details the religious beliefs and practices of the Telugus of Rayalaseema in South India.

An even clearer example of Christlieb's use of the sociological method, was the book coauthored with Edyth Hinkley, *A Struggle for a Soul, and Other Stories of Life and Work in South India.* In his introduction to the book, the Reverend R. Wardlaw Thompson described first how the authors were "careful observers" and "broad-minded enough" to understand "their ways of thinking" (i.e., the residents of South India). He said that the authors have provided "incidents and experiences as might best illustrate the lives of the people" and "vivid pictures from real life."[23]

The authors did exactly what Thomas wrote. In a detailed and objective manner, they described the daily life of people in various towns. They used local terms for this, such as the "komaties," or merchants, who were managing their shops in the bazaar. They described religious customs of individuals in South India, and they included several photographs.

For Christian sociologists of religion such as Christlieb, the ultimate aim of the use of the field was to evangelize more effectively. Having an objective understanding of a particular community was important. But without the goal of reaching these people with the Gospel, sociological analysis was incomplete. At the end of their book, Hinkley and Christlieb were true to their missionary calling by preaching the Christian faith, "the evangel of authentic hope."[24]

---

22. Some of Christlieb's books are *A Struggle for a Soul and Other Stories of Life and Work in South India* (with Edyth Hinkley) (Philadelphia: Union Press, 1907); *The Way of Christ in the Mission Field* (Madras: CLS, 1924); *An Uphill Road in India* (London: George Allen and Unwin, 1927); *Lalappa: An Indian Story* (London: London Missionary Society, 1928); *If I Lived in India* (London: Edinburgh House Press, 1930); and *Indian Neighbours* (London: Student, 1930).

23. Christlieb and Hinkley, *Struggle for a Soul,* vi.

24. Ibid., 190.

BIBLICAL CRITICISM

From the beginning, Bible study had a central and fundamental place in the SCM. Originally, the movement took a devotional approach. Bible study meant prayerful individual reading of selected passages for an inspirational thought (e.g., "The Morning Watch") or listening to readings of Bible passages or devotional Bible talks. Increasingly, investigations and the application of the new biblical criticism appeared in SCM circles, and by 1910, came to dominate the movement's approach to the Bible.

This new biblical criticism, arose from nineteenth-century European rationalism. Rationalism used human reason not revelation to understand things. Rationalists handled the Bible differently than their pietistic colleagues. The pietistic approach asked how a particular Bible passage provided a spiritual and personal message. The new approach, historical-critical criticism, asked several other questions, such as when, where, and why it was produced, who was the text's audience, and what oral or written sources might have been used in its composition. In essence, it treated the Bible as any other ordinary piece of literature instead of a divinely inspired text. And this bothered those who first viewed the text as the revealed truth of God in inspired text. As part of this new approach to the Bible, the SCM had to "shake itself free of the theory of the verbal inspiration of the Bible."[25]

The new approach was developed in Germany in the late eighteenth century and most of the nineteenth century. Friedrich Schleiermacher, Ludwig Feuerbach, and David Friedrich Strauss were pivotal figures. The work of these men and others spread across continental Europe, the United Kingdom, and North America.

SUPPORTERS OF THE NEW BIBLE CRITICISM

Four SCM women supported the new approach to the Bible, Clara Ruth Rouse, Anne Wakefield Richardson, Suzanne de Dietrich, and Margaret Wrong.

CLARA RUTH ROUSE

Ruth Rouse prepared Bible study materials using historical-critical methods, and these were adopted by many national movements. She observed how the Russian SCM had decided to use her studies: "After

---

25. Tatlow, *Story*, 213.

an interminable discussion, the Committee, to my vast amusement, announced: 'We shall study the Epistle to the Philippians, using the British SCM text-book of Ruth Giorgievna (my Russian name) and the commentary of St. Chrysostom.' This is the only occasion when I was rated with a Father of the Church."[26]

ANNE WAKEFIELD RICHARDSON (1859–1942)

Anne Wakefield Richardson was born in Northern Ireland to John Grubb (1813–1890) and Jane Marion Wakefield (1831–1909) Richardson. Anne Richardson had fourteen siblings. John Grubb Richardson inherited a great deal of wealth and was himself a linen manufacturer and philanthropist. At one time, his linen was considered among the finest in the world.

The Richardson family was a wealthy and prominent Quaker family. Quakerism influenced everything the Richardsons did. Her father refused an offer of a baronetcy because he said all humans were born equal. Anne Wakefield Richardson also believed and argued that men and women were created totally equal. She also supported temperance because of her Quaker value of respect for human life.

The Richardson family was known for its role in creating the model village of Bessbrook, County Amagh, Ireland, in 1845. This village had spacious streets and squares along with a large linen mill. Among the principles of the village were the "Three Ps": no public houses, no pawn shops, and no police. Bessbrook had religious houses for Anglicans, Methodists, Presbyterians, Roman Catholics, and Quakers.

Anne Wakefield Richardson attended Newnham College, Cambridge, from 1881 to 1883. The 1881 British Census has her as a boarder among many boarders of Dr. Henry Sidgwick. He was a well-known advocate for women's higher education and a praelector in moral and political philosophy at Trinity College.[27] He is also listed as the founder of Newnham College at Oxford University.

In 1883, Constance Maynard invited Richardson to join the student body of Westfield College.[28] The college was founded in 1882 to educate women. Westfield was modeled after Mount Holyoke and Girton

---

26. Rouse, *World's Student Christian Federation*, 85.

27. A praelector at Oxford University was either a fellow of the college or a college tutor responsible for directing the Honors School in the absence of a fellow, and possibly a holder of a college fellowship.

28. For more information on Westfield College, see Janet Sondheimer, *Castle Adament in Hampstead: A History of Westfield College, 1882–1982* (London: Westfield College, 1983).

College, Cambridge. Mount Holyoke provided the model for rigorous education combined with spiritual development and Girton for rigorous education. It was among a select group of higher education institutions established for women in the late nineteenth century and offered new opportunities for women to reside and study in London. Westfield admitted male students starting in 1965 and later became part of the University of London.

As one of first students to attend Westfield College, Richardson earned a BA First Class in Classics in 1886. Two of her sisters attended Westfield College, Ethel (1889) and May (1894), but neither took a degree.

Richardson was one of Westfield College's first five college staff members and she remained associated with the institution for her entire life. She was lecturer in classics from 1887 to 1925 and then a senior residential lecturer from 1903 onward. In 1918, she became vice principal and also acting principal from 1917 to 1919 after the sudden death of Agnes de Selincourt. From 1920 to 1928, Wakefield was president of the Westfield College Association.

When her widowed mother died in 1909, Anne and her siblings divided up a substantial estate. She never married and died at eighty-three in 1942. Richardson was buried among other Richardson family members in the cemetery next to the Bessbrook Friends' Meeting House in Northern Ireland.[29]

Richardson was a noted author, educator, and speaker.[30] Because she felt that the British movement needed to deal with the new biblical criticism, Anne Wakefield Richardson gave a speech at the 1902 summer conference for men and women titled "Students' Attitudes to Biblical Criticism." Her address was the only one given by a woman at the conference. It was so popular that the British Executive printed it with the title "Criticism and Inspiration."

In a *Student Movement* editorial, the executive praised the pamphlet by saying:

---

29. For a video of her grave, see http://derrymoreestate.blogspot.com.

30. Some of Anne Wakefield Richardson's books are *The Practical Side of Scientific Temperance: A Paper Read at the Autumnal Conference of the British Women's Temperance Association Held at York, October, 1892* (British Women's Temperance Association, 1892); *Lectures on Moderate Drinking, etc.* (n.p., 1893); *The Quaker View of War* (London: Headley Brothers, 1900); Review of "*Jesus Christ and the Social Question: An Examination of the Teaching of Jesus in Its Relation to Some of the Problems of Modern Social Life,*" by Francis Greenwood Peabody, *Student Movement* 5, no. 5 (February 1903): 113–16; *The Nation and Alcohol* (London: SCM Press, 1920); and *The Spiritual Application of Quakerism* (London: privately printed, 1929).

Students will read with attention what so thoughtful a writer as Miss Richardson has to say on a subject which has given rise to so much controversy. . . . We believe this clear statement is calculated to be of very great help at this time when "the numbing effect on the Christian life and activity of theories apparently destructive, however vaguely understood," is strongly felt by many.[31]

SUZANNE DE DIETRICH (1891–1981)

Suzanne de Dietrich was a strong advocate of applying the new criticism to Bible study. She argued for the use of the "historical-critical approach which frees the texts from our presuppositions."[32] By 1922, her influence on Bible study was so strong that she confided, "Intellectually, I have become a machine producing Bible study plans."[33] Although her approach is common today, it was revolutionary in its day.

Suzanne Anne de Dietrich was born into a wealthy family of metal founders dating back to 1684 in Niederbrown, Alsace, France. Her mother was a baroness. She was the youngest of seven girls. Because de Dietrich suffered from genetic deformities of short arms and legs, she walked with two canes and experienced chronic pain. A member of the Eglise Reforme de France, de Dietrich became a Christian in 1907. She spoke French, English, and German fluently. At the University of Lausanne, de Dietrich studied engineering (one of three women in a class of eighty) and philosophy. She was one of the first French women to graduate in engineering (BS, 1909, and Diploma in Engineering, 1913).

Instead of pursuing an engineering career, de Dietrich decided to work for the SCM. During World War I, she was a traveling secretary for the French movement and worked also with soldiers and students in Paris. Despite what seemed to be her lack of ability in practical matters, she had a tremendous gift with individual work. At the time it was noted, "She does good to all those who come to her. . . . She can speak to souls; she does them good, she instructs them; she encourages them, she comforts them; . . . She is a force in the spiritual work of the Federation."[34] She also joined the Russian SCM and served as a nurse.

In 1929, de Dietrich was appointed vice president of the Universal Federation of Christian Students. She attended World Student Christian

---

31. Editorial, *Student Movement 5*, no. 3 (December 1902): 58.

32. Hans-Ruedi Weber, *The Courage to Live: A Biography of Suzanne de Dietrich* (Geneva: WCC Publications, 1995), 59.

33. Ibid., 60.

34. Johanna M. Selles, *The World Student Christian Federation 1895–1925; Motives, Methods and Influential Women* (Eugene, OR: Pickwick Publications, 2011), 181.

Federation (WSCF) conferences at St. Beatenburg (1920), Oxford (1937), and six others (1920–1946). De Dietrich was a WSCF executive committee member (1920–1935), vice-chair (1928–1932), and staff member (1935–1946). She developed the first meeting of Roman Catholic, Protestant, and Orthodox theologians in 1932.

In September 1939 de Dietrich helped found CIMADE (Inter-Movement Committee Along With Evacuees), and in 1941 she and sixteen pastors and laypeople, including three women, proclaimed the Thèses de Pomeyrol, which called on the French Reformed Church to resist Nazism. During World War II, de Dietrich lived in Geneva. There she helped with SCM groups and wrote her most famous book, *Le Dessien de Dieu* (God's Will). It was published in 1945 and translated into thirteen languages.[35]

At the end of World War II, de Dietrich became a staff member at the Ecumenical Institute at Bossey (1946–1954). From its start in 1946, this institute brought together people from different denominations, cultures, and backgrounds for ecumenical leadership, academic study, and personal exchange.

In 1954, de Dietrich moved to Paris. She traveled to the United States and Canada and taught courses at several universities and seminaries. De Dietrich was nominated Doctor Honoris Causa in Theology by several universities in North America and Europe.

In 1979 she moved into the Deaconess House in Strasbourg, where she lived until her death on January 24, 1981. The words on her tombstone fit her life, "Praise the Lord Oh My Soul."

Despite her many interests, de Dietrich's main focus was on developing Bible study materials for small groups in the WSCF. A small group format was used with twelve to fifteen members. De Dietrich had several goals for Bible study. First, Bible study promoted good fellowship. In these small groups, members not only talk about particular Bible verses but also about their lives, interests, and needs. Next, Bible study was the

---

35. Suzanne de Dietrich, *Dessien de Dieu: God's Unfolding Purpose: A Guide to the Study of the Bible*, trans. Robert McAfee Brown (Philadelphia: Westminster Press, 1960). She also wrote many other works: Suzanne de Dietrich, *Rediscovering the Bible* (Geneva: WSCF, 1942); *The Witnessing Community: The Biblical Record of God's Purpose* (Philadelphia: Westminster Press, 1958); *The Word and His People: A Bible Study Guide* (Greenwich, CT: Seabury Press, 1958); *Free Men* (Philadelphia: Westminster Press, 1961); *This We Know: A Study of the Letters of John* (Richmond, VA: John Knox Press, 1963); *The Word with Power* (New York: Friendship Press, 1965); *Toward Fullness of Life: Studies in the Letter of Paul to the Philippians* (Philadelphia: Westminster Press, 1966); *God's Word in Today's World* (Valley Forge, PA: Judson Press, 1967); and *Heure l'élévation: And He Is Lifted Up: Meditations on the Gospel of John*, trans. Dennis Pardee (Philadelphia: Westminster Press, 1969).

perfect place to bring new students and non-Christians because in these small groups, individuals could question texts and have issues with the Christian faith addressed. Third, Bible study fostered spiritual growth and made believers stronger. De Dietrich's method let biblical passages speak for themselves. Assigned members of the group would research a particular passage's background. A study outline was also provided with leading questions for group discussion.

A large number of requests for de Dietrich's Bible studies programs were made. Beginning in 1914, de Dietrich taught students in the French SCM and YWCA to discover the original meanings of biblical texts, using extra study materials, such as commentaries.[36] Her Bible studies programs were even used in groups of mixed Protestants, Roman Catholics, and Orthodox members.

In 1922, de Dietrich attended a WSCF-sponsored consultation in Hardenbroek, Netherlands. The purpose of the meeting was to develop an intellectually honest and open kind of Bible study.

By that time, de Dietrich had written studies on the Prophets for high school students, on the parables of Jesus for the French YWCA, and on Paul for a Paris student group. Each study had a two- or three-page outline including the literary and historical contexts of passages to be studied and a series of questions.

In 1937, she took part in the first world youth conference that emphasized Bible study. Later she joined the consulting committee for the creation of a "method for Bible studies," later known as Biblical Renewal.

De Dietrich's influence over the SCM was tremendous thanks to these Bible studies. Her studies were popular with students, and they became the basic materials for SCM small group and Bible work. Her studies unified the movement because many students were using these materials.

MARGARET CHRISTIAN WRONG (1887–1948)

Like de Dietrich, Canadian Margaret Wrong argued that a more critical approach should be used in Bible study.[37] She was a single career

---

36. For more information on de Dietrich, see Weber, *Courage to Live*, and Archives of the WSCF, Record Group No. 46 (Box 149, Folder 1095, and Box 150, Folder 1104), Special Collections, Yale Divinity School.

37. For more information on Wrong, see Ruth Compton Brouwer's following three works: "Margaret Wrong and the Gendering of African Writing, 1929–1963," *International Journal of African Historical Studies* 31, no. 1 (1998): 53–71; "Margaret Wrong's Literacy Work and the 'Remaking of Woman' in Africa, 1929–1948," *Journal of Imperial*

Margaret Christian Wrong with Reverend S. Moore and three teacher
trainers at the border of Uganda, a few miles from Nimule, on April
10, 1948, hours before her sudden death the following morning.
(University of Toronto Archives)

woman and an intellectual, missionary, and educator with a profound
interest in Africa, its culture, and in particular its women. Wrong was
a hard worker. As she aged, it was suggested that she slow down. Her
answer was always, "There is too much waiting to be done."[38]

Margaret Wrong (known as Marga by her family and close friends)
was the eldest daughter of a distinguished, well-connected Canadian
family that was featured in chapter 2. She completed her secondary
education at Havergal College, a Church of England Ladies' College,
founded in 1894. The school was named after the famed Evangelical
hymn writer, author, and humanitarian Frances Ridley Havergal. This
suggests something about the religious atmosphere of the institution.
When she was there, the motto was "What are you going to do?" (i.e.,
How are going to make a difference in the world?). The school had
120 boarders and 200 day students, a staff of twenty resident teachers,
chiefly from English universities, and a number of nonresident visiting
teachers.

---

and Commonwealth History 23, no. 3 (1995): 427–52; and *Modern Women Modernizing Men: The Changing Missions of Three Professional Women in Asia and Africa,
1902–1969* (Vancouver, BC: UBC Press, 2002).

  38. Agnes Wrong Armstrong, "There's Too Much Waiting to Be Done," *Food for
Thought* 16 (March 1956): 258–63.

After attending the University of Toronto on and off (1906–1907 and 1910–1911), Wrong attended Somerville College, Oxford (1911–1914), where she earned a BA in modern history (Honors, Modern History, Class II, 1914). She won the school's Margaret Evans History Prize (1912) and the Coombs Prize (1913). Wrong earned an MA at the University of Toronto in 1919. After 1926, she maintained a home in London. There she entertained visitors from all over the world until the World War II Blitz brought a bomb to her backyard. This bomb was later detonated by experts with no loss of life.

Wrong took on many roles in SCM circles. She was intercollegiate secretary of the Student YWCA at the University of Toronto (1914–1916), traveling secretary for the WSCF (1921–1925), and a secretary for the British SCM (1926–1929).

Outside of SCM circles, Wrong was head of the University College Women's Union and a lecturer in the Departments of History and English at the University of Toronto (1916–1921). She was also secretary of the International Commission on Christian Literature for Africa (1929–1948). Wrong was an editor and writer.[39] She was also a contributor to *International Review of Missions*, *Canadian Forum* and other missionary magazines.

Wrong was a fellow and member of the Library Committee, a member of the Royal Empire Society, and a member of the executive of the Church Missionary Society.

Listed as a spinster, Wrong died in 1948 in Gulu, Uganda, which is in the less developed northern part of the country. She left £3,035 pounds, which would have been worth £107,135.50 in 2016.

After her death, the Margaret Wrong Memorial Fund and Prize for African Literature was established. Awarded from 1949 to at least 1962, it honored the best African writing in all genres. It was awarded annually for works in African vernacular or European languages. A prize and medal were occasionally awarded separately.

In the *Canadian Student*, Wrong argued that intellectual study of the Scriptures was a necessity and a duty for Christians. This was different from the popular devotional approach or "casual reading of

---

39. Books by Margaret Wrong include *Ideals and Realities in Europe* (London: SCM Press, 1925); *Africa and the Making of Books* (London: Intentional Committee on Christian Literature, 1934); *The Land and Life of Africa* (London: Edinburgh Press, 1935); *Five Points of Africa* (London: Edinburgh House Press, 1942); (with Jackson Davis and Thomas M. Campbell), *African Advancing: A Study of Rural Education in West Africa and the Belgian Congo* (London: Friendship Press, 1945); *For a Literature of West Africa* (New York: Friendship Press, 1946); and *West African Journey, in the Interests of Literacy and Christian Literature, 1944–1945* (London: Livingstone Press, 1946).

a few familiar passages and then drawing a few moral lessons" from them. Instead, Wrong maintained that Christians should use their minds to the "highest level of development." She said that Christians should "transport ourselves into the time we are studying and look through the eyes of the people of that time. Under what circumstances were different books of the Bible written? What was the individual outlook of the writer on his time?" This intellectual approach was the foundation for the devotional approach to Bible study. She said that without this approach, much of the Bible would remain unintelligible. The promotion of this type of Bible study was the most important work of the SCM in and college and university.[40]

OPPONENTS OF THE NEW APPROACH TO BIBLE STUDY

As noted in chapter 4, the SCM had its own fundamentalist-modernist controversy, which split the movement into two groups that exist today. A sample of this division was seen in the dustup between an English woman Dorothea Warner and Tatlow.

DOROTHEA LOUISA WARNER (1884–1948)

Dorothea Louisa Warner was born in London, England, to Francis (1848–?) and Louisa Loder (1853–1926) Warner. Her father was a physician-surgeon, as was her brother. Her mother's father was a banker. Warner had one brother and one sister. She was educated at Kensington High School, Livinghold (a private boarding school), Bedford College, the Froebel Institute (1901–1905 on and off), and Manchester University. She taught at the demonstration school associated with this institution in 1906. Warner majored in science and education (kindergarten teaching). The 1911 British Census has her working as a private family teacher in London. When she died in 1948, she was identified as a spinster with an estate worth £11,925, which would have been worth £420,952 in 2016.

Warner's involvement with the SCM began as president of the Froebel Institute's Christian Union (1904). She was then a member of the General College Department's Executive (1907–1908), a traveling secretary in the training colleges (1908–1909), and a nonexecutive committee member of the Bible Study Standing Committee. Warner was also secretary of the London Interchurch Women's Committee (1904–1906).

---

40. See Margaret Wrong, "The Value of Bible Study II," *Canadian Student 1*, no. 2 (October 1918): 16–17.

Warner's trouble with the new approach to the Bible spilled over into a controversy with Tatlow. Opposed to intellectual questioning, Dorothea Warner believed that gaining an inspirational thought from a passage would warm a person's heart and best prepare them for their daily tasks. She argued that any other approach to the Scriptures would take Christians away from their primary tasks of personal spiritual growth and evangelism.

Tatlow criticized Warner for what he felt was her desire to eliminate the intellectual grind of Bible study and substitute it with the finding of these "best thoughts" from a Scripture passage.[41] To him, a person who studied Scripture intellectually had a stronger foundation than the person who looked for merely "best thoughts."

---

41. Tatlow, *Story*, 262.

13

Social Gospel Pioneers

On a tour of the Georgia State Capitol Building, one might note the striking painting of an African American woman located on the third floor. She is a gray-haired older woman holding a magazine, and she is looking nobly out to the horizon. Next to her are two African American children. On August 11, 1974, this portrait of Lucy Craft Laney along with one of Bishop Henry McNeal Turner was hung in the Georgia State Capitol Building six months after the portrait of the Reverend Martin Luther King Jr. had been placed. These three were the first African American people to be so honored.

Lucy Craft Laney was one of the many Student Christian Movement (SCM) women leaders who helped shape the movement's response to contemporary social issues. While these women worked in the realm of ideas similar to the intellectual pioneers of the previous chapter, they also were social activists pushing the SCM to take action on these issues. And like their sister leaders, they worked with men as much as with women.

THE SOCIAL GOSPEL

The social gospel fueled this interest in social activism. This late nineteenth- and early twentieth-century movement applied Christian ethics to a number of social issues, including poverty, alcoholism, family and home life, racial tensions, slums, child labor, war, labor unions, and education. Important leaders include Richard T. Ely, Josiah Strong, Washington Gladden, and Walter Rauschenbusch. The last man was one of the most important theologians of the social gospel.[1] By World War I,

---

1. Arguably the main proponent of the social gospel, Walter Rauschenbusch (1861–1918) was a Baptist pastor and theologian. He taught at Rochester Theological Seminary. Born in Rochester, New York, he had a personal conversion experience at age seventeen. While attending Rochester Theological Seminary, he dropped his childhood beliefs in the inerrancy of the Bible and the substitutionary atonement of Jesus Christ. In 1885, he became pastor of Second German Baptist Church located on the edge of Hell's

188

Rauschenbusch was a very popular speaker in SCM circles, and his writings were enthusiastically read and studied by student groups.[2]

This was a huge change from the earliest days of the SCM. Influenced by D. L. Moody and the like, the earliest SCM's primary interest was individual conversion followed by social activism, such as temperance. The social gospel movement transformed the SCM's primary interest to social evangelism or social improvement.

ANNE WAKEFIELD RICHARDSON

An example of this changing emphasis was seen in Anne Wakefield Richardson's ministry. In the previous chapter, her ministry as an intellectual pioneer was featured. In this chapter her work as a social gospel advocate is emphasized.

She gave convincing speeches, led discussions, and wrote reviews to spur interest in social questions. Women students asked her to speak on the issue at the 1900 British summer conference. According to the *Student Movement*:

> The subject of work for the poor at home has perhaps been rather neglected hitherto by the [British College Christian] Union, but at Matlock this was rectified. The keen interest in social work felt by many of the delegates was shown as much by the constant discussion of its problems with Mr. Leonard and Miss Richardson in conversation, as by close attention to their addresses on the subject.[3]

To argue for a new approach to Christianity's social responsibilities, Richardson wrote a review of Francis Greenwood Peabody's *Jesus Christ and the Social Question: An Examination of the Teaching of Jesus in Its*

Kitchen, a very depressed area of New York City. From 1891 to 1892, Rauschenbusch studied economics and theology at the University of Berlin. Because of his education and experience as a pastor, he started to argue for the social implications of the Gospel. In 1892, he and others formed the Brotherhood of the Kingdom, a group which sought to refocus Christian faith from personal piety to social change. Rauschenbusch died on July 25, 1918, at fifty-six years of age.

2.   Particularly popular were Rauschenbusch's books *Christianity and the Social Crises* (New York: Macmillan, 1907); *For God and His People: Prayers of the Social Awakening* (Boston: Pilgrim Press, 1910); *Christianizing the Social Order* (New York: Macmillan, 1912); *A Theology for the Social Gospel* (Nashville, TN: Abingdon, 1917); and *The Social Principles of Jesus* (New York: Association, 1918).

3.   Tissington Tatlow, *The Story of the Student Christian Movement of Great Britain and Ireland* (London: SCM Press, 1933), 339.

Relation to Some of the Problems of Modern Social Life.[4] In it, she wove a thorough knowledge of Scripture, contemporary theologians (Harnack and Maurice), political movements (Christian socialism and the social gospel), and contemporary issues (the impact of industrialization, the family, the poor, and wealth).

THE CONFERENCE ON SOCIAL PROBLEMS

The Council of North American Student Movements sponsored the Conference on Social Problems held at Garden City on Long Island between April 17 and 20, 1914. It was another demonstration of this new focus on social evangelism. Similar meetings were also held throughout the SCM world.

At the Garden City meeting, more than twenty-five of the leading social workers in North America met with the leaders of the SCM to discuss how to foster student involvement in solving existing social problems. Those invited among social gospel notables included Walter Rauschenbusch and socialist Vida Scudder. Topics included "Our Unchristian Civilization and How to Change It," "Unsocial Practices among Students," "Some Issues on Which an Enlightened Social Conscience Is Needed," and "The Church and Industrial Life."[5]

JULIA VIDA DUTTON SCUDDER (1861–1954)

Julia Vida Dutton Scudder was an educator, writer, and social activist. She was born to American Congregationalist missionaries in Madurai, India. She was raised in Boston, Massachusetts. In 1884, Scudder graduated with a BA from Smith College. In 1885, she was one of the first two American women to be admitted to the graduate program at Oxford University. She received DHL from Smith College (1932) and an LLD from Nashota House, an Episcopal seminary (1942). She died in Wellesley, Massachusetts, in 1954 at the age of ninety-three.

Scudder taught English literature at Wellesley College from 1887 to 1927. In 1888, she joined the Society of the Companions of the Holy Cross, a group of Episcopal women committed to intercessory prayer and social activism. Also in 1888, she became a member of the Society

---

4. Anne Wakefield Richardson, review of Francis Greenwood Peabody's *Jesus Christ and the Social Question: An Examination of the Teaching of Jesus in its Relation to Some of the Problems, of Modern Social Life* (New York: Macmillan, 1900). The review appeared in the *Student Movement* 5, no. 5 (February 1903): 113–16.

5. "Social Problems," *North American Student* 2, no. 9 (June 1914): 411–12.

of Christian Socialists. In 1890, Scudder was one of the founders of Denison House, a settlement house in Boston. She was its director from 1893 to 1913. In 1911, Scudder joined the Episcopal Church Socialist League and the Socialist Party.

Her views on war changed through the years. Scudder supported Wilson's decision to intervene in World War I, but then in the 1920s she became a pacifist. In 1923, she joined the Fellowship of Reconciliation linked with Lilian Stevenson, written about in chapter 8.

Scudder was involved in the American labor movement. In 1903, she helped organize the Federal Labor Union and the Women's Trade Union League. Scudder supported striking textile workers in 1912. Scudder never married. Instead, she lived with several women in her lifetime. She was the author of many books and articles, including her autobiography *On Journey* and several books linking Christianity and socialism, such as *Socialism and Spiritual Progress: A Speculation*; *Socialism and Character*; and *The Christian Attitude toward Private Property*.[6]

INTERRACIAL RELATIONS

By the second decade of the twentieth century, the SCM's pioneers argued persuasively for the integration of races, challenging accepted theories of racial separation.

By this time, the SCM movement had become a mixed-race organization, having moved beyond the narrow confines of the white, Anglo-American student world to include other groups. The SCM had come a long way after the debacle at the 1906 Student Volunteer Movement for Foreign Missions (SVMFM) Conference held in Nashville. At that gathering, the movement's leadership had caved in to pressure from city leaders and required that blacks sit in the gallery and whites sit on the main floor of Ryman Auditorium where the meetings were held.[7]

Indications of SCM interest in interracial issues were seen in Bertha Condé's writing and in the movement's conference ministries. In these cases, the question of fostering better interracial relations included not only blacks and whites but also Native Americans. And as with all the women found in this book, the SCM women social gospel pioneers worked with both men and women.

---

6. Julia Scudder, *On Journey* (London: J. M. Dent and Sons, 1937); *Socialism and Spiritual Progress: A Speculation* (Boston: Church Social Union, 1896); *Socialism and Character* (Boston: Houghton Mifflin, 1912); and *The Christian Attitude toward Private Property* (Milwaukee: Morehouse, 1934).

7. Addie Waites Hunton, *William Alphaeus Hunton: A Pioneer Prophet of Young Men* (New York: Association Press, 1938), 93–94.

BERTHA CONDÉ

Bertha Condé wrote an article for the monthly *Fisk University News* of the historically black Fisk University in Nashville, Tennessee. To do this was itself a bold act. Here a white New Yorker wrote for an all-black audience. Although this was applauded by many blacks and whites, there were probably those in both groups who objected. In this 1919 piece, Condé wrote, "There is no question more worthy of our earnest study and sympathy than the negro question; and in these days of reconstruction and shaping our principles of democracy, we need, as a country, and as a student movement, to do our share of thinking."[8] Her influence was felt at the upcoming YWCA National Convention in 1920. This conference declared that the time had come for educated women to use their networks to encourage society to rethink its racial attitudes. They should take action to combat racism since women had come into a new era in which they could stand together and achieve impossible goals.[9]

HANDLING OF RACIAL ISSUES AT SCM CONFERENCES

Some SCM social gospel pioneers used conferences to advocate for new interracial relations. Two conferences of particular interest were the 1913 World Student Christian Federation (WSCF) Lake Mohonk meeting and the 1914 Negro Student Christian Conference. At both of these meetings, SCM women pioneers played significant roles.

THE WSCF MEETING AT LAKE MOHONK, JUNE 2–8, 1913

Developing healthy relationships between Caucasians, blacks, and Native Americans was a theme of the WSCF conference held at Lake Mohonk, New York, between June 2 and 8, 1913. Prior to the gathering, the WSCF General Committee informed American SCM leaders that if they wanted to host this meeting, whites and nonwhites needed to be together on an equal footing. Whether this threat had any influence on the meeting, one will never know. But, in location and policy, the meeting emphasized integrated activities. The meeting was held at the Lake Mohonk Mountain House on the shores of Lake Mohonk. Founded by the Smiley brothers, the lodge hosted conferences on international arbi-

---

8. Bertha Condé, "Hopeful Signs," *Fisk University News* 6 (February 1919): 30.

9. See "Report of the National Board of the YWCA of the USA to the Sixth National Convention at Cleveland, Ohio," April 13–20, 1920, 55, 59.

tration and on the American Indian. It had earned the reputation as a moral citadel and a place of welcome for African Americans and Native Americans, and for the cause of international peace.

Out of 275 in attendance, there were 13 African Americans, 20 Chinese, 3 "British Indians," 5 Native Americans, 2 citizens of the Philippines, 9 Japanese, and 1 Korean. The Chinese delegation hosted a tea for all present. Chinese tea, cakes, and candies were served. Each delegate was given a Chinese coin with five ribbons to mark the five races that made up the Chinese Republic.

Three WSCF women were involved in furthering interracial relationships at the Lake Mohonk meeting: Grace Hoadley Dodge, Addie D. Waites Hunton, and Ella Cara Deloria. Just like other SCM women pioneers, these women had a substantial influence on the movement and the handling of interracial activities at this meeting. And like other SCM women, they worked with and even led men.

GRACE HOADLEY DODGE (1856–1914)

Grace Hoadley Dodge was a social welfare worker, educator, philanthropist, and Presbyterian with extensive connections with the SCM. Born into an upper-class family, her parents were William Earle Jr. (1832–1903) and Sara Hoadley (1832–1909) Dodge. Both parents came from wealthy, distinguished families. Her father was a controlling partner in one of the largest copper mining companies in the United States in the nineteenth century (Phelps, Dodge and Company), and her mother's father was president of the Panama Railway Company. Dodge was the eldest child of six; she had three brothers and two sisters. Her family included well-known philanthropists and social activists. Dodge was educated at home by private tutors and then at Miss Sarah Porter's School from 1872 to 1874. She never married.

Dodge was a committed Christian and although a supporter of a variety of Christian groups, was an active supporter of two Presbyterian churches, Brick Presbyterian Church and Riverdale Presbyterian Church, both in New York City.

After an 1876 visit of D. L. Moody to her family home, Dodge chose a life of service rather than a life in society as her family had expected. From the first, she regarded social service as a full-time occupation, obliging her to give up many social obligations and limiting herself to a two-week vacation each year.

Dodge donated approximately $1.5 million, which was worth approximately $35,817,300 in 2016. Dodge died in 1914 of apoplexy, a term used in the late nineteenth century for any sudden death that almost immediately followed a loss of consciousness. She was buried in Woodlawn Cemetery in the Bronx with other family members. Dodge left an estate worth $6,977,747. In 2016 this amount was worth approximately $166,616,038.

Inside SCM circles, Dodge was very active. She was Ruth Rouse's major financial backer, and as such was one of the first women to have the vision to finance a woman who was appointed to minister to women. Yet as this book has demonstrated, Rouse, although appointed to work with women, worked with men extensively as well.

Outside of SCM circles, Dodge was a Sunday school teacher (beginning in 1874) and a Civil War relief worker. She helped establish and direct the Kitchen Garden Association (1880), the Industrial Education Association (1884, which became the New York College for the Training of Teachers and was eventually absorbed into Columbia University), and a national working women's society (1885). She was a member of the City of New York Board of Education (1886–1889), the Girls' Public School Athletic League (1905), the New York Travelers' Aid Society (1907), and the American Hygiene Association (1912).

In probably her most memorable work in 1905, Dodge was chosen to act as a mediator between two rival YWCA groups—the International Board (dominated by Eastern upper-class women of liberal persuasion) and the American Committee (based in Chicago, much more evangelical and desirous of more centralized control).

As a result, in 1906, Dodge was named president of the National Board of the YWCA of the United States. She pushed the YWCA to move into new areas of social service, kept in constant touch with working girls, regularly made up financial deficits of the organization, and with her brother gave $625,000 to the YWCA's 1913 building fund drive.

Dodge authored *A Bundle of Letters to Busy Girls on Practical Matters* and, with Thomas Hunter et al., *What Women Can Earn: Occupations of Women and Their Compensation*.[10]

Her pioneering efforts at Lake Mohonk came before the meeting. Dodge hosted a garden party at her summertime Hudson River estate, Greystone, for all delegates, and the then mostly white West Point Military Academy held a dress review for everyone.[11] Both of these were

---

10. Grace Hoadley Dodge, *A Bundle of Letters to Busy Girls on Practical Matters* (New York: Funk and Wagnalls, 1887); and with Thomas Hunter et al., *What Women Can Earn: Occupations of Women and Their Compensation* (New York: F. A. Stokes, 1889).

11. For more information about Dodge, see Margaret E. Burton, *Comrades in Service* (Nashville, TN: Smith and Lamar, 1915); Mrs. Robert E. Speer, "She Remembers His Commandments to Do Them," *North American Student* 3, no. 5 (February 1915):

bold interracial statements. In Dodge's restricted exclusive neighbor-hood, some may have objected. Hosting an interracial collection of delegates at the mostly white West Point was also a daring statement.

ADDIE D. WAITES HUNTON (1875–1943)

A second woman, Addie D. Waites Hunton, joined Dodge in fostering better racial relationships in the SCM at Lake Mohonk. Like Dodge, Hunton was a leader of men as well as women. Educated and cultured, Hunton was born in Norfolk, Virginia, the daughter of Jessie and Adeline Waites. Their birth and death dates are unknown. Her father was the owner of a wholesale oyster and shipping business, co-owner of a black amusement park, and co-founder of the Negro Elks Benevolent Protection Order of the Elks of the World (IBPOEW). She had one sister and one brother. Hunton was fluent in English, French, and German. She lived in Norfolk, Virginia; Atlanta, Georgia; and New York City. She traveled in the United States and Europe.

In childhood, Hunton was a member of the African Methodist Epis-copal Church. Later she became an Episcopalian. When her mother died during her childhood, Hunton was sent to Boston to be reared by a maternal aunt. She attended Boston's Latin School and Spencerian Business College of Philadelphia, where she was the first black student in 1889. Around 1909, Hunton studied for three semesters at Kaiser Wilhelm University and in 1910 took courses at the College of the City of New York.

After graduation, Hunton taught in the public schools of Ports-mouth, Virginia; she taught and became principal at a vocational school between 1890 and 1893. This institution became the Alabama Agricul-tural and Mechanical College in Normal, Alabama.

In 1893, Addie Waites married William A. Hunton, the first "colored man's" secretary for the YMCA.[12] She eventually had four children, two

---

189–93; "In Memory of Grace Dodge," *Association Monthly* (May 1918): 63–115; Abbie Graham, *Grace Dodge: Merchant of Dreams; A Biography* (New York: Woman's Press, 1926); and Marion O. Robinson, *Eight Women of the YWCA* (New York: National Board of the YWCA, 1966).

12. William Alphaeus Hunton (1863–1916) was born in Chatham, Ontario, Canada. His father had purchased his freedom around 1840 and come via the Under-ground Railroad to Chatham. In 1858, John Brown consulted with Hunton's father about his upcoming raid on Harper's Ferry. After attending the Wilberforce Institute in Ontario, he worked as a teacher in Canada and joined the YMCA. In 1888, Hunton was hired as the first secretary for the Norfolk, Virginia, YMCA. He was the first black YMCA secretary, and he gave up his relative freedom in Canada for the world of diffi-cult race relations in the United States after the American Civil War. Hunton felt he had

of whom died in infancy. Hunton combined motherhood, YWCA and YMCA work, and women's club work.

After serving as registrar and accountant for Clark College, Atlanta (1905–1906), Hunton and her family moved to Brooklyn, New York. She did this because of her husband's ill health and also because of the aftershocks of the 1906 Atlanta race riots, which occurred between September 22 and 24. White mobs killed twenty-five to forty blacks and wounded others and caused considerable property damage. Families, like the Huntons, who could leave the city moved to safer locations.

Once in New York, she was appointed as the advisory secretary for the National YWCA's ministry with African American women. Between 1906 and 1910, Hunton was the organizing secretary for the National Association of Colored Women. And, from 1907 to 1908, she traveled throughout the South for the YWCA. Hunton would do traveling work for the YWCA on several occasions.

Hunton often traveled with her husband, acting as his secretary, handling trip details and correspondence and editing his magazine, *The Messenger*, although the public saw D. Webster Davis as editor. During World War I in 1916, Hunton was widowed when her husband died of tuberculosis in New York.

In 1917, Hunton gave an address at the Pan-African Congress in Paris, and she served with the YMCA with troops from the United States in Europe during World War I in 1918. She was one of only three women workers with over 200,000 African American soldiers stationed there. Hunton took charge of the canteen at Saint-Nazaire, in Brittany in western France. There she added a Sunday night discussion group and a literacy course. In 1919, Hunton was transferred to the YWCA work in Challes-les-Eaux, in southeastern France, where she arranged activities for over one thousand black troops.

After returning home in 1919, she served on several national boards, sometimes as an officer: the Council on Colored Work of the YWCA National Board, International Council of the Women of Darker Races (president), Empire State Federation of Women's Clubs, the NAACP (vice president and field secretary), and National Association of Colored Women (parliamentarian). Hunton spoke out frequently against segre-

---

to go because for him, it was "God's leading." In 1891, the International and American YMCA hired him as the first "colored secretary," and he was for years the only person working in this area. In 1905, he reported that there were 116 "colored associations" with 8,000 members, and 50 percent of men at historically black colleges were YMCA members. Hunton was a speaker at the 1907 WSCF Conference in Tokyo, Japan. He contracted tuberculosis in 1914 and died in 1916. For more information on Hunton's YMCA ministry, see Addie Waites Hunton, *William Alphaeus Hunton*.

gation. Her other interests included women's suffrage and the peace movement. Hunton wrote several books and articles.[13]

During the Lake Mohonk conference, men and women of different nationalities and races were assigned seating at meals together. Each table had eight to ten people and was numbered. Between meals, these numbers were mixed, and each person drew one as he or she entered the room. Delegates then went to their numbered table where a permanent host and hostess sat. According to one anecdote, a southern woman drew a number which sat her next to a black. Though initially uncomfortable, she sat through the meal graciously, and thereby began to learn to mix with blacks.[14] Addie Hunton joined her husband, William Alphaeus Hunton, then head of the YMCA's "colored division," as permanent hosts of one table.[15]

Addie Hunton died after surgery at age sixty-eight and was buried at Cypress Hill Cemetery in Brooklyn, New York.

ELLA CARA DELORIA (1889–1971)

A third SCM pioneer joined Grace Dodge and Addie Hunton in fostering better interracial relations at Lake Mohonk. Ella Cara Deloria, also called Aŋpétu Wašté Wiŋ (Beautiful Day Woman), changed the meeting and the SCM by her presence and ministry as a Native American. Like Dodge and Hunton, Deloria led men as well as women.

Deloria, a Yankton Sioux, had the unique combination of Christian faith, a Sioux upbringing, and a career as a linguistic anthropologist and ethnologist. Throughout her life, she collected folklore, linguistic materials, and translations. In 1943, Deloria received the Indian Achievement Award.

In *Ella Deloria: A Biographical Sketch*, the following comments are made about her:

---

13. Addie D. Waites Hunton, "Negro Womanhood Defended," *Voice of the Negro* (July 1914): 280–82; *William Alphaeus Hunton*; and with Kathryn M. Johnson, *Two Colored Women with the American Expeditionary Forces* (Brooklyn: Eagle Press, 1920).

14. C. Howard Hopkins, *John R. Mott, 1865–1955: A Biography* (Grand Rapids, MI: William B. Eerdmans, 1979), 412.

15. For more details on Hunton, see Jean Blackwell Hutson, "Addie D. W. Hunton," in *Notable American Women, 1607–1950: A Biographical Dictionary*, ed. Edward T. James (Cambridge, MA: Belknap Press of Harvard University Press, 1971), 240–41; Rayford W. Logan, "Addie D. W. Hunton." In *Dictionary of American Negro Biography*, ed. Rayford W. Logan and Michael R. Watson (New York: Norton, 1982), 337–38; and Paula Giddings, *When and Where I Enter: The Impact of Black Women on Race and Sex in America* (New York: W. Morrow, 1984).

Ella Deloria was a scholar through and through, yet she never let her dedication to scholarship overwhelm her sense of responsibility as a Dakota woman, with family concerns taking precedence over her work. Nor did she ever lose her deep faith in Christianity. She was a warm and gracious individual, whose kindness and personality were inspirational. Her constant goal was to be an interpreter of an American Indian reality to other peoples. Her studies of the Sioux are a monument to her talent and industry.[16]

Deloria was born at White Swan, South Dakota, at the Yankton Sioux Reservation. Her parents were Philip Joseph (Indian name Tipi Sapa, or "Black Lodge," 1853–1931) and Louisa Mary Sully Bordeaux (Indian name Akicita Win, or "Soldier Woman," 1858–1916) Deloria. From French and Yankton lineage, Ella Deloria's given name was Aŋpétu Wašté Wiŋ (Beautiful Day Woman) because of the blizzard that occurred on the day of her birth. She had one sister and one brother.

Deloria's presence at the 1913 meeting highlighted an interesting change in the SCM narrative. Frances Cousens Gage, the SCM traveling secretary featured in chapter 5, lived in Mankato, Minnesota, less than twenty years after the tragic Dakota War of 1862. This war was fought between whites and the Eastern Sioux. Deloria was a Western Sioux and was a welcome member of the 1913 WSCF conference.

In 1890, Deloria's family moved to Standing Rock Reservation when her father was assigned to St. Elizabeth Church and Boarding School at Wakpala, South Dakota, as a deacon of the Protestant Episcopal Church. He became the first Sioux Episcopal priest in 1892. This reservation, in both North and South Dakota, was home to the Lakota, Yankonai, and Dakota Indians. The famed Indian chief Sitting Bull was shot here on December 15, 1890. Prior to his death, Deloria's father attempted to convert him to Christianity. Records indicate that "Sitting Bull, aloof and distant, ignored the efforts of Philip Deloria to convert him to Christianity."[17] Although there is no record of Ella Deloria's presence, she was in the immediate area and may in fact have seen or met Sitting Bull.

Deloria was educated at St. Elizabeth Mission, Wakpala, South Dakota, until 1902, and All Saints' School, Sioux Falls. At the latter, she

---

16. *Ella Deloria: A Biographical Sketch* (Chamberlain, SD: Dakota Indian Foundation, n.d.). See http://zia.aisri.indiana.edu.

17. Joseph E. Bennett, "The Prince of Dakota Sioux," *Northern Light: A Window for Free Masonry* 30, no. 2 (May 1999): 6.

took college preparatory courses between 1906 and 1910. Although she began her higher education at Oberlin College between 1910 and 1913, she graduated from the Teachers College, Columbia University with a BS (1915).

Deloria taught at All Saints' School (1915–1919), and then accepted a position with the YWCA in an experimental program to show Indian bureaus the value of physical education for Native American girls. She worked there from 1919 to 1923. Deloria taught dance and physical education at Haskell Indian School in Lawrence, Kansas (1923–1927).

In 1927, Deloria became a research assistant for Frank Boas, a professor at Columbia University and leader in the field of American anthropology. Specializing in American Indian ethnology and linguistics, she worked with Frank Boas until his death in 1942.

From 1928 to 1938 with the support of Columbia University, Deloria studied the language of and recorded stories and ethnographic material from Lakota and Dakota elders throughout South Dakota and Minnesota. She also translated historic texts written by tribal members. In 1941 Deloria and Boas jointly published a grammar of the Dakota language, which became an important text in American Indian language studies.

From 1955 to 1958, Deloria was director of the St. Elizabeth Mission. She was also employed by the Sioux Indian Museum in Rapid City, South Dakota, and was the assistant director of the William Henry Over Museum at the University of South Dakota. She received a grant from the National Science Foundation from 1962 to 1966 for work on a Lakota dictionary.

Deloria died at age eighty-two from a pulmonary embolism after suffering a stroke one year earlier. She was buried in St. Philips Episcopal Cemetery in Lake Andes, South Dakota.[18]

Of all her books, probably the most popular was *Waterlily*, an ethnographic novel of three generations of pre-reservation Lakota women.[19] It has been the only written source that explores the religious life of Lakota women. It was published posthumously.[20]

---

18. For more information on Deloria, see Bea Medicine, *Reminiscences of Ella Deloria: Standing Rock Sioux Tribe of South Dakota* (Sanford: Microfilming Corp. of America, 1979); and the Ella Deloria Archives, Dakota Indian Foundation, Chamberlain, SD.

19. Other books of Deloria's are *Dakota Texts* (New York: G. E. Stechert, 1932); *Speaking of Indians* (New York: Friendship Press, 1941); with Frank Boas, *Dakota Grammar* (Washington, DC: United States Government Printing Office, 1941); Julian Rice, *Deer Women and Elk Men* (Albuquerque: University of New Mexico Press, 1992); *Ella Deloria's the Buffalo People* (Albuquerque: University of New Mexico Press, 1993); and *Ella Deloria's Iron Hawk* (Albuquerque: University of New Mexico Press, 1993).

20. Ella C. Deloria, *Waterlily* (Lincoln: University of Nebraska Press, 1988).

At the Lake Mohonk meeting, Ella Cara Deloria along with four fellow Native Americans in attendance, sent a WSCF-sponsored message to their community in North America. After declaring that only Christianity could save "red men," the Native American contingent challenged all Christian agencies working with Native American students to work harder to bring them to Jesus Christ and to foster settlement of Indian problems along Christian lines.

THE NEGRO CHRISTIAN STUDENT CONFERENCE

The Negro Christian Student Conference was held in Atlanta, May 14–18, 1914.[21] Between five hundred and six hundred people attended, and over forty colleges and universities were represented. Though mostly attended by blacks, 10 percent of those present were white. All student delegates (men and women) were blacks, while there were black and white YMCA and YWCA secretaries, social workers, bishops, missionaries, pastors, editors, church board secretaries, college presidents, and teachers present.

Meeting purposes, prayers, and topics emphasized the equal mixing of blacks and white.[22] One of the four purposes for the conference was "to consider what light Christian thought may throw on present and future cooperation between the races." The other three were to give the spiritual and moral direction to blacks, to study the black student's responsibility for Christian leadership and life callings at home and abroad, and to face the responsibility of black churches of America with the claims and needs of Africa.[23]

Conference prayers contained statements calling for equality of the races: "Pray that this may be a nation in which each man may wish for all men such a fair chance at all good things as every man would like his brother to have. Pray that all problems growing out of race antipathy may be settled in the light of the Gospel and in the Spirit of Christ."[24]

Conference topics included "The Basis of Race Progress in the South," "Christianity as the Basis of Common Citizenship," "Signs of

---

21. For more information, see A. W. Trawick, ed., *The New Voice in Race Adjustments: Addresses and Reports Presented at the Negro Christian Student Conference, Atlanta, Georgia, May 14–18, 1914* (New York: SVMFM, 1914); Harlan P. Beach, "The Atlanta Negro Christian Student Conference," *Student World* 7, no. 2 (April 1914): 109–14; and Council of North American Student Movements, *The Social Needs of Today and the Colleges of North America* (New York: YMCA, 1914).

22. Trawick, *New Voice*, v, vi.

23. Ibid., 1.

24. Ibid., 6.

Growing Cooperation," "Cooperation of Southern White People," "Signs of Growing Interest on the Part of the Southern White Man," "Ministers in Cooperation," "Cooperation between Pastors of White and Colored Churches," and "Cooperation of White and Negro Ministers for Social Service."

At this conference, Lucy Laney, Belle Harris Bennett, Mrs. John Hope, and Addie Waites Hunton provided leadership. Laney and Bennett served on the conference planning committee, and Mrs. John Hope gave a speech.

Laney and Bennett were the only women who served on the ten-member planning committee. This group had had an even split between southern blacks and whites. No one who served was from outside the South except John R. Mott, who represented the WSCF. The group set the agenda, invited the speakers, arranged for the facilities, and publicized the meeting.

LUCY CRAFT LANEY (1854–1933)

Lucy Craft Laney is the state of Georgia's most famous African American woman educator. She believed that to be successful both men and women, particularly African Americans, had to be educated. Laney never married, but because of her interest in children, she was seen as a mother figure. She also was a deeply committed Christian whose faith motivated her to be an activist.

"Miss Lucy" was born in 1854 to David (1809/1810?) and Louisa (1832?–?) Laney, who had a total of ten children. Her father was a Presbyterian minister and carpenter. Laney's parents were free blacks who had purchased their freedom. Laney was educated to read and write by age four and could translate difficult passages in Latin at the age of twelve. She attended Lewis (later Ballard) High School in Macon, Georgia, which was supported by the American Missionary Association. This northern Protestant Abolitionist Society was active in African American education in the South during the Reconstruction era. In 1869, Laney became a member of the first class at Atlantic University (later Clark Atlanta University). This university was one of the historically black educational institutions. It had begun granting bachelor's degrees in the 1870s, and it supplied teachers and librarians for African American schools in the South at that time. She graduated in 1873 in the first class from the Normal Department (teacher training). Women were not allowed to take classics courses at the university at that time, which really upset Laney.

After teaching in Macon, Savannah, Milledgeville, and Augusta for ten years, Laney launched a school in the basement of Christ Presbyterian Church in Augusta in 1883. In 1886, it was chartered by the state of Georgia as the Haines Normal and Industrial Institute. The school grew to include a kindergarten to junior college curriculum, the Lamar School of Nursing, and a teaching training program. This institution had the first kindergarten and training program for African Americans in Augusta. Originally intended as an all-girls institution, Laney began to admit boys where they appeared at her school and she could not send them away. Some of its most famous students and teachers were John Hope and Mary McLeod Bethune, who went on to found Bethune-Cookman College for Blacks in Daytona Beach, Florida.

Laney started a lifetime of appeals for funding by seeking funds at an 1886 meeting of the Northern Presbyterian Church. She gave a speech but received no money, except train fare home. One person at the assembly, Francine E. H. Haines, did decide to support her, and the school was named for her. Haines donated $10,000 at this time and became a lifetime supporter of the school.

By 1912, the institute had thirty-four teachers and nine-hundred students. Laney taught Latin for its fifth-year college preparatory high school. Graduates soon went on to many prestigious schools, such as Yale University. Her institution became the center of the local African American community with orchestra concerts, lectures, and other social events. The school closed in 1949, and the Lucy C. Laney High School was built on its site.

In 1918, Laney helped found a local chapter of the National Association for the Advancement of Colored People. She was active in the Interracial Commission, the National Association of Colored Women, the Niagara Movement, and the YMCA and YWCA, which she worked to integrate.

She was inducted into the Georgia Women of Achievement in 1992.

Laney died in 1933 and is buried at the Lucy Craft Laney Burial Site in Augusta, Georgia. The city has established the Lucy Craft Laney Museum of Black History.[25]

BELLE HARRIS BENNETT (1852–1922)

Along with Lucy Craft Laney, Belle Harris Bennett was involved with the 1914 Negro Student Christian Conference. Bennett had extensive connections with the SCM due to her interest in missions. The daughter of

---

25. The Lucy Craft Laney Museum of Black History, 1116 Phillips Street, Augusta, GA 30901.

a successful planter, Samuel (1805–1888) and his wife Elizabeth Chenault (1815–1897) Bennett, she hailed from a distinguished and wealthy family. Bennett grew up at the Homelands estate near Richmond, Kentucky. Bennett had six brothers and one sister. She never married.

She had an early education at the local grammar school, and then went to private schools in Richmond and Bardstown, Kentucky, and College Hill, Ohio. Though she never attended college, she received an honorary doctorate from Kentucky Wesleyan College in 1916.

Bennett was actively involved in the Methodist Episcopal Church, South. Her grandfather had been a Methodist Church circuit rider. She attended Providence Church on land donated by the family where she taught Sunday school and sang in the choir.

In 1875, Bennett become a follower of Jesus, and later in 1884, Bennett claimed to experience a Baptism of the Holy Ghost.

In 1887, Bennett went to a Methodist meeting where she first felt a call to prepare women for missionary work, and in 1888, she felt called to establish a school for that purpose. Overcoming her timidity, Bennett presented her idea to the Southern Methodist Board of Missions in 1889. This group commissioned her to travel throughout the South, speaking at church meetings describing her vision. Armed with dignity, deep conviction, a keen sense of humor, and an effective use of anecdotes, Bennett raised over $25,000 for her proposed institution.

In 1892, the central committee of the Woman's Parsonage and Home Mission Society (later the Women's Home Missions Society) decided to establish her school. The Scarritt Bible and Training School opened officially on September 11, 1892, in Kansas City, Missouri. Bennett dominated school life for over thirty years. She selected her own principals and made up budget deficits with her own money until 1901. In 1924, this school was moved to Nashville, Tennessee next door to Vanderbilt University where its name was changed to Scarritt College for Christian Workers. Its name changed several times, and then the school closed down in 1988. Since that time, it has been called the Scarritt-Bennett Center.[26] Its beautiful facility is often used for conferences, weddings, and other special events.

In 1897, Bennett also established a small Methodist college to serve low-income students, Sue Bennett Memorial College (1897–1997), in the name of a recently deceased sister.

That year she traveled to London to study urban missions and became an avid supporter of settlement houses, eventually establishing about forty (Wesley Community Houses or Bethlehem Houses). In

---

26. Scarritt-Bennett Center, 1008 19th Ave. S, Nashville, TN 37212.

1902 she convinced the Methodist General Conference to establish a deaconess program.

Bennett fought to eradicate racism by expanding Paine College, a historically black institution in Augusta. She preached sermons on ending racism, held a weekly Bible study for black church leaders (Richmond, Kentucky, 1900–1904), and organizing a "Colored Chautauqua." Between 1910 and 1922, she was president of the Women's Missionary Council. Bennett helped spur the development of new mission fields in the Belgian Congo, Japan, Rio de Janeiro, and China, where she helped create a women's medical college.

In 1906, Bennett began a drive for full lay rights for women in the Methodist Episcopal Church, South, because women had no voice in the church's councils. In 1922, Bennett was named the first woman delegate from the Kentucky Conference to the General Conference of the Methodist Church, but she was too ill to attend. She was a member of the National Child Labor Committee, an early advocate of suffrage and a strict sabbatarian.

Bennett attended the 1910 World Missionary Conference at Edinburgh presided over by Mott.[27] After the 1910 Edinburgh Conference, Bennett had the unusual experience of attending a reception hosted by Pope Pius X at the Vatican.

Along with Rouse, Bennett attended the 1916 Congress on Christian Work in Latin America. Her interest in missionary preparation brought about her selection as a member of the International Missionary Council chaired by Mott, and she attended the group's 1921 meeting with him. Bennett served as chair of the council's Committee on Women's Work. She was a member of the YWCA and the Federation of Foreign Mission Boards. Bennett served on the Committee of Reference and Council of the Foreign Mission Conference of North America along with Fennell P. Turner and Mott.

Although she traveled globally, Bennett spent her entire life in and around Richmond, Kentucky. She died there after a lengthy fight against cancer in 1922 and was buried in the Richmond Cemetery near her sister's grave.[28]

---

27. Meeting in Edinburgh, Scotland, June 14–23, 1910, the 1910 World Missionary Conference or the Edinburgh Missionary Conference had 1,200 representatives attending from major North America and Northern European missionary societies and missionary organizations to hear presentations on a variety of topics dealing with missions. For more information, see Brian Stanley, *The World Missionary Conference: Edinburgh 1910*, Studies in the History of Christian Missions (Grand Rapids, MI: William B. Eerdmans, 2009).

28. For more information on Belle Harris Bennett, see Mrs. R. W. MacDonell, *Belle Harris Bennett: Her Life Work* (Nashville, TN: Board of Missions, United Meth-

LUGENIA BURNS HOPE (1871–1947)

Lugenia Burns Hope was a social activist and community organizer, who worked to improve local black communities, mostly in Atlanta. Hope was a competent administrator and could be quite confrontational, headstrong, and demanding. She was a supporter of women's suffrage. In 1996, Hope was inducted into Georgia Women of Achievement. Although she was involved in many organizations, she is most remembered for her work with the Neighborhood Union of Atlanta.[29]

Hope was born in St. Louis, Missouri, to Ferdinand and Louisa Burns in 1871. Their birth and death dates are unknown. Her father was a successful carpenter. Hope was the youngest of seven children. In the 1880s, after the death of her father, Hope's family moved to Chicago. From 1890 to 1893, she studied at the Art Institute of Chicago, the Chicago School of Design, and the Chicago Business College. Hope was active with the King's Daughters and Hull House.

In 1897, Lugenia Burns married John Hope and moved to Nashville, Tennessee, where her husband taught at Roger Williams University. In 1898, the Hopes moved to Atlanta with their two sons. Her husband began teaching at Atlanta Baptist College (later Morehouse College). In 1906, he became the school's president.

During World War I, Hope was the Special War Work Secretary for the YWCA's War Work Council. She organized services for returning black and Jewish soldiers and oversaw the training of hostesses for Camp Upton in New York. After the war, Hope fought against the YWCA's racial policies. After the Great Flood of 1927, she was appointed to serve on President Herbert Hoover's Colored Advisory Commission. In 1932, Hope became the first vice president of the National Association for the Advancement of Colored People's Atlanta chapter.

After her husband's death in 1936, Hope moved to New York City. She died in 1947 at the age of seventy-six. Her cremated remains were spread near the grave of her husband on the Morehouse College campus.[30]

---

odist Episcopal Church, South, 1928); and Douglas R. Chandler, "Bennett, Belle Harris," in *Notable American Women, 1607–1950* 1, ed. Edward T. James (Cambridge, MA: Belknap Press of Harvard University Press, 1971), 132–34.

29. Hope was involved with the Commission on Interracial Cooperation, the National Association of Colored Women's Clubs, the Association of Southern Women for the Prevention of Lynching, the International Council of Women of the Darker Races, and the National Association of Colored Graduate Nurses.

30. For more information on Hope, see Jacqueline Anne Rouse, *Lugenia Burns Hope: Black Southern Reformer* (Athens: University of Georgia Press, 1992).

At the Negro Student Christian Conference, Hope gave a speech titled "The Work of a Neighborhood Union."[31] In conference literature, she was identified by her married name, Mrs. John Hope and was listed as from Morehouse College. In her presentation, Hope began by talking about how rare an opportunity it was to speak to hundreds of students. Although she did not mention it, her audience was made up of men and women. Hope then talked about the needs of the city of Atlanta and what was being done to meet those needs. A huge portion of her speech contained descriptions of the black slums of Atlanta. Interspersed between these descriptions were personal stories about everyday citizens living there. Hope stated that the Neighborhood Union planned to establish neighborhood centers in each area of the slums. Day care facilities, kindergarten classes, recreation centers, and educational programs would be established at the centers. The goal would be to create good citizens.

---

31. See A. W. Trawick, ed., *The New Voice in Race Adjustments: Addresses and Reports Presented at the Negro Christian Student Conference, Atlanta, Georgia, May 14–18, 1914* (New York: SVMFM: 1914).

14

Pioneers of the Women's Movement

For the Courage to Rise to the Call of God

Let us pray: For all societies and movements for the uplifting of womanhood, for the woman's movement in all lands, that it may stand for whatsoever things are true, reverent, just, pure, lovely, and gracious; for the singleness of purposes for the righting of wrong, the defense of the weak.[1]

Whether the women pioneers of the Student Christian Movement (SCM) made sure that this prayer was included in the British SCM's 1915 *A Book of Prayer for Students* may never be known. This prayer book was created for all SCM groups, whether all-male, all-female, or mixed. Its presence points to the visibility and importance of the women's movement within SCM circles. This petition listed the objectives that SCM women pioneers promoted. Not only did this prayer ask for the "uplifting of womanhood," but it also prayed for the international "woman's movement . . . that it may stand for whatsoever things are true, reverent, just, pure, lovely, and gracious."[2]

THE WOMEN'S MOVEMENT

The first of three eras of feminism, lasting from 1840 to 1925, was called by SCM women "the woman's movement."[3] Some SCM leaders

---

1. *A Book of Prayer for Students* (London: SCM Press, 1915), 61–62. SCM women used the terms *women's movement* and *woman's movement* interchangeably. I will use the term *women's movement*.

2. Ibid.

3. Second-wave feminism occurred in the 1960s and 1970s and third-wave feminism in the 1990s and beyond. For an examination of Christianity and first-wave feminism, see Betty A. DeBerg, *Ungodly Women: Gender and the First Wave of American Fundamentalism (Three Indispensable Studies of American Evangelicalism)* (Macon, GA: Mercer University Press, 2000); and Diane Capitani, "Imaging God in Our Ways:

207

used the word *feminism,* which first appeared in the 1895 edition of the *Oxford English Dictionary.* By the turn of the century, it had become an acceptable term, though its use was rare.

According to the National Women's History Project, a tea party launched a movement.[4] This tea party is just one of many, including the Boston Tea Party and the contemporary Tea Party movement. All of these have been attempts to enact social change. On July 13, 1848, a young housewife and mother, Elizabeth Cady Stanton, was invited to tea with four friends. At tea, the group talked about the status of women in society. One week later, between July 19 and 20, 1848, the Seneca Falls Convention was held to discuss "the social, civil and religious condition and rights of women."

It is no coincidence that this meeting took place in the Wesleyan Chapel in Seneca Falls, New York. This is because first-wave feminism had close connections with Christianity, especially evangelical Protestantism.[5] Later on, SCM women made the same point. Suzanne de Dietrich wrote that to have the benefits of this emancipation, it "must be realized in the Spirit of Christ if it is to be truly liberating."[6] Zoe Fairfield and Annie Caroline Macdonald both included the spiritual life as an important component of women influenced by the women's movement.[7] Ruth Rouse contended that "Christ's teaching on the law of love is working out in the movement, unconsciously or consciously."[8]

On day one of the Seneca Falls Convention, Stanton's "Declaration of Sentiments and Grievances" was read. This statement listed the injustices women have suffered using the Declaration of Independence as a model. On day two, twelve resolutions were passed, eleven unanimously, that called for equal rights for women.[9]

The Journals of Frances E. Willard," *Feminist Theology: The Journal of the Britain and Ireland School of Feminist Theology* 12, no. 1 (2003): 57–88.

4.   Bonnie Eisenberg and Mary Ruthsdotter, "Living the Legacy: The Women's Rights Movement 1848–1998," History of the Women's Rights Movement (Santa Rosa, CA: National Women's History Project, 1998), n.p. See http://www.nwhp.org.

5.   See Donald W. Dayton, "Evangelical Roots of Feminism," *Covenant Quarterly* (November 1976): 41–56.

6.   Hans-Ruedi Weber, *The Courage to Live: A Biography of Suzanne de Dietrich* (Geneva: WCC Publications, 1995), 31.

7.   Zoe Fairfield, "Some Aspects of the Woman's Movement," *North American Student* 3, no. 1 (October 1914): 60. Fairfield wrote both an article (1914) and a book with the same title.

8.   Ruth Rouse, "The Ideal of Womanhood as a Factor in Missionary Work," *International Review of Missions* 2 (1913): 153.

9.   For more information on the Seneca Falls Convention, see Judith Wellman, *The Road to Seneca Falls: Elizabeth Cady Stanton and the First Woman's Rights Convention* (Urbana: University of Illinois Press, 2004); and Sally McMillen, *Seneca Falls and the*

The Seneca Falls meeting spawned the wide-ranging, international women's movement, involving all nationalities, classes, races, religions, and both men and women. By the early twentieth century, feminists in Germany, Great Britain, the United States, and other countries read each other's works, watched each other's progress, and worked for each other's causes. The women's movement pursued its agenda through national and international organizations, conferences, and writings.[10]

The women's movement had a broad agenda that encompassed all aspects of women's lives. Partially through it, women had achieved access to higher education in women's and colleges and universities. New developments in the century-long battle for social reform came to fruition, such as the repeal of the Contagious Diseases Acts, changes in marital, property, and divorce laws, and the enhancement of the prestige of motherhood. Opportunities were expanded in the professions, such as education, medicine, journalism, and government. By 1920, the women's movement focused its energies on suffrage and temperance.

Like most observant people, SCM women pioneers noted that the women's movement was occurring around them. Japanese SCM leader Ume Tsuda observed the "unleashed woman." Accordingly, she said, to many Japanese women "no less than to men has come the new life, calling them out into a new and stirring world with changed responsibilities and duties, new thoughts and ambitions. . . . Ambitions hitherto unheard of are being developed and women are seeking self-expression and excitement."[11] In a 1916 YWCA report about Indian women, one author, most likely Rena Carswell Datta, wrote, "They are rising up today and throwing off those shackles and demanding freedom. This desire and demand find expression in varying ways."[12] If married, they were their husband's helpmate, not a plaything.

Origin of the Women's Rights Movement (Oxford: Oxford University Press, 2009).

10.   SCM women pioneers identified the eight most important international women's organizations, all of which were involved with the women's movement. These included the International Council of Women with seven million members in twenty-two nations, the International Women's Suffrage Alliance, the Traveler's Aid Society, Les amies de la jeune fille (working in thirty-nine nations), Le secretariat internationale de l'action sociale de la femme, l'association catholique internationale des oeuvres de protection de la jeune fille, the World's YWCA (with 670,000 members in twenty-two nations), and the World's Women's Christian Temperance Union (with auxiliaries in fifty nations). See Zoe Barbara Fairfield, ed., *Some Aspects of the Woman's Movement* (London: SCM, 1915), 132–33.

11.   Ume Tsuda, "Japanese Women and the Problems of the Present Day," in "The Ideal of Womanhood," *International Review of Missions* 2 (1913): 293, 297.

12.   *The YWCA and Non-Christian Indian Women,* June 2, 1916, 1, Archives of the WSCF, Record Group 46 (Box 49, Folder 392), Special Collections, Yale Divinity School. In a handwritten notation on the article, Rouse writes, "By whom R.C. [I don't think so. RR.]" Was R. C. Rena Carswell Datta? The reader assumed so.

UME TSUDA (1864–1929)

Ume Tsuda, a woman with a sense of noblesse oblige and great wealth, was an English scholar and Japanese educator of the Meiji and Taisho eras.[13] As noted in chapter 2, she was the second daughter of Sen (1837–1908) and Hatsuko (1843–1909) Tsuda. Sen Tsuda had a profound respect for Western education and traveled to the United States in 1860. He was a low-ranking samurai or a member of the military nobility. He is identified as an agriculturalist, early environmentalist, and entrepreneur. Most important, Tsuda played a prominent role in establishing Christian schools in Japan, such as Ayomana Gakuin, Doshisha University, the Friends' Girls' School, and Tokyo School for the Blind and Deaf.

Ume Tsuda was originally named Tsuda Mume (mume or ume refers to the Japanese plum) and she went by the name Ume Tsuda in the United States. In 1902, she changed her name to Ume Umeko.

As noted in chapter 2, the Japanese government sent her at age six to the United States to study as part of a modernizing program that was hoped to help Japan catch up with Americans through education (1871). Tsuda went with four other girls from age fourteen to eighteen. She attended Georgetown Collegiate Institute in 1878 and the Archer Institute, both in Washington, DC.

During her first stay in the United States, Tsuda converted to Christianity. After the Japanese government legalized Christian rites in 1873, she was baptized at the Old Swede's Church, Bridgeport, Pennsylvania. The rites used were those of the Episcopal Church.

During a second stint in the United States, Tsuda attended Bryn Mawr College, where she studied biology and education. She turned down M. Carey Thomas's offer to teach at that institution, saying, "Japan needed me."

After returning home, Tsuda taught at Peeresses' School, Kazoku Girls' English School, and the Women's Higher Normal School. In 1900, she founded the Tsuda Girls' English School, which was the first professional school for women in Japan. By 1905, the graduates of her school

---

13. During the Meiji (1868–1912) and the Taisho (1912–1926) eras, Japan moved from being an isolated feudal society to its modern form with a less rigid social structure, open relations with outsiders, and limited liberal democracy ("Taisho Democracy"). It was followed by the militarism, totalitarianism, ultranationalism, and fascism of the first part of the Showa Period (1926–1945). For more information on Tsuda, see Yoshiko Furuki, *The White Plum: A Biography of Ume Tsuda: Pioneer in the Higher Education of Japanese Women* (New York: Weatherhill, 1991); and Janice P. Nimura, *Daughters of the Samurai: A Journey from East to West and Back* (New York: W. W. Norton, 2015).

were permitted to teach English without exams due to the institution's reputation.

In Japan, Tsuda attended a Union Church and Episcopal churches. On Sunday afternoons, she held Bible readings.

Tsuda rejected several arranged marriages and never married. She felt that a man and woman should be equal partners in a marriage and that a woman could have a career and be married. Instead, in 1902, Tsuda set up her own household, which made her the legal head of a home in Japan. This was a radical step in her day.

After suffering a stroke in 1919, Ume Tsuda retired. She died in 1929 after a long illness at age sixty-five and is buried on the grounds of Tsuda College in Tokyo.

Tsuda had extensive connections with the SCM in Japan and world-wide. SCM workers such as Annie Caroline Macdonald taught a YWCA Bible class in her school. Tsuda attended the 1907 and 1914 World Student Christian Federation (WSCF) Conferences. At the 1914 meeting, she spoke on "The Presentation of the Gospel in Japan." Tsuda was the first chair of the Japanese YWCA.

ACTIVE PARTICIPATION OF SCM WOMEN PIONEERS

SCM women were active participants in women's movement activities. As already noted in chapter 10, the Reverend Barbara Ellen Groenendyke was very active in the Woman's Christian Temperance Union activities on the local level in Decatur, Alabama, and on the national level. Although temperance will not discussed here, it was supported by SCM women with great vigor.

SCM women pioneers were also involved in the suffrage movement. Swedish SCM leader Lydia Wahlstrom reported that "several ladies of the YWCA were suffragists."[14] Zoe Fairfield wrote, "I am myself a convinced suffragist."[15] In 1909, popular SCM speaker Agnes Maude Royden became the first chair of the Church League for Women's Suffrage.

SCM women also arranged for speakers to lecture on suffrage. For example, while principal of Westfield College between 1913 and 1917, Agnes de Selincourt organized public lectures. The most important of these occurred on Annual Commemoration Day. One of the first speakers was Millicent Fawcett, a leading nonmilitant suffragist.[16]

---

14. Lydia Wahlstrom, *Questions with Regard to the Women's Movement:* 1, Archives of the WSCF, Record Group No. 46 (Box 56, Folder 445) Special Collections, Yale Divinity School Library.

15. Fairfield, "Some Aspects of the Woman's Movement," 60.

16. Although Millicent Fawcett (1847–1929) was an English feminist, intellectual,

However, some SCM women leaders, such as Mary Pauline Root and Ume Tsuda, did not support the movement to gain voting rights for women.

WRITTEN MATERIALS
ON THE WOMEN'S MOVEMENT

SCM women pioneers and the SCM itself created an astounding number of written materials on the subject of the women's movement.[17] The most important of these writings was Fairfield's 1915 book *Some Aspects of the Woman's Movement*. According to Fairfield, the book was "an attempt to estimate the actual position of women in the past and in the present, and to suggest some of the guiding principles upon which the future may most hopefully be built."[18]

To carry out the book's objectives, Fairfield included examinations of women and history, women and higher education, women and economic freedom, women's contributions to morality, the internationalism of the women's movement, women's unique contribution to government, women and individualism, and women and the family. Appendixes had discussions on the position of women in a variety of English churches, ranging from Anglican churches to the Salvation Army, an extensive bibliography on women's issues, and a list of political groups for women.

Contributors were mostly professional women, joined by two male writers.[19] The women were Cecilia M. Ady, vice-principal of St.

---

political and social activist, unionist, and writer, she was best known as a suffragist. In 1871, she co-founded Newnham College, Cambridge, and between 1897 and 1919, she was president of the National Union of Women's Suffrage Societies (the NUWSS). This organization (called "the law-abiding suffragists") took a nonconfrontational approach using popular public speeches and written articles. It was more widely supported than the Women's Social and Political Union (WSPU) headed by Emmeline Pankhurst (1858–1928) and her daughter Christabel (1880–1958). The Pankhurst organization was known for its physical confrontations, such as smashing windows and assaulting police officers. Fawcett supported many issues, such as curbing child abuse and raising the age of consent. By 1915, the NUWSS had 305 societies with 50,000 members as opposed to 2,000 members in the WSPU.

17.   Examples of SCM writings on the women's movement include Eleanor McDougall, "The Influence of Christianity on the Position of Women," *International Review of Missions* 1 (1912): 435–51; Rouse, "Ideal of Womanhood"; Zoe Barbara Fairfield, "The Woman's Movement," *Student Movement* 15, nos. 4, 5, 7 (January, February, and April 1913): 78–80, 92–95, 128, 130–31; reprint edition (London: SCM Press, 1913); Fairfield, "Some Aspects" (1914): 59–64; Zoe Fairfield, *Some Aspects of the Women's Movement* (London: SCM Press, 1915); and A. Estelle Paddock, *Overtaking the Centuries: Modern Women of Five Nations* (New York: National Board of the YWCA, 1915).

18.   Fairfield, *Some Aspects* (1915), 8–9.

19.   Male writers include Ernest Barker, Fellow of New College, Oxford, and

Hugh's College, Oxford; Clara E. Collet, Fellow of University College, London; Helen Wilson, honorary secretary of the British Branch of the International Abolitionist Federation; Una Mary Josephine Saunders, general secretary of the YWCA of Canada; and, of course, Zoe Barbara Fairfield.

TOPICS OF INTEREST FOR SCM WOMEN PIONEERS

In their writings, the SCM pioneers explored a variety of topics related to the women's movement. Of these, two were particularly important: what were its causes and what were its benefits? Its causes will be dealt with in the rest of this chapter. The benefits of the woman's movement will be described in chapter 15.

THE SECULAR AND SPIRITUAL CAUSES
OF THE WOMEN'S MOVEMENT

SCM women spilled a lot of ink discussing the causes of the woman's movement. From two different sources a list can be compiled of Zoe Barbara Fairfield's causes. She identified economic changes, altered international relationships (the shrinkage of the world and the contact of East with West), materialism, the spread of education, the discoveries of modern science, the rise of new schools of thought, and a general unrest and stirring of life.[20]

In a Swedish SCM survey, one student wrote that the movement arose as a result of the Aufklärung or the Enlightenment of the eighteenth century and feelings of social responsibility.[21]

Similarly, Rouse wrote that the women's movement was a "true product of the Zeitgeist."[22] Zeitgeist refers to "the spirit of the age," the beliefs and ideas that dominate a particular era of time. Along similar lines, Una Saunders wrote that the women's movement caused other women's movements. It spread when those who fought for suffrage in one nation discovered that the suffrage fight needed help in other nations.[23]

William Temple, formerly headmaster of Repton School and rector of St. James, Piccadilly, and later, Archbishop of Canterbury (1942–1944).

20. See Fairfield, "Some Aspects" (1914), 60.
21. See Wahlstrom, *Questions with Regard to the Women's Movement*, 1.
22. See Rouse, "Ideal of Womanhood," 148.
23. See Fairfield, *Some Aspects* (1915), passim.

UNA MARY JOSEPHINE SAUNDERS (1869–1953)

Una Mary Josephine Saunders was a member of the West End London Saunders family featured in chapter 11. Her younger sister was Grace Helena Saunders. Baptized on October 6, 1869, she was a member of the Church of England. Saunders attended Kensington High School. Then she was a student at Somerville College, Oxford University, between 1895 and 1896. Saunders studied Sanskrit for a year at Oxford University. Like other members of her family, she was extremely well traveled.

Saunders felt called to minister to "leisured women" like herself, encouraging them to serve others. She also believed that women should be independent individuals. Saunders disliked simplistic women and said she could not "abide by the calf love of some of these young women."[24]

Prior to her SCM ministries, Saunders served as mistress on staff at Kensington High School from 1893 to 1895. In 1896, she traveled to India to work in the Bombay Settlement for University Women, along with Clara Ruth Rouse and Agnes de Selincourt. She remained there until 1899, when she was forced to return home because of sickness.

After serving as a traveling secretary for the American SVMFM from 1905 to 1906, Saunders served as a traveling secretary for the British SCM from 1906 to 1910, assistant editor for the *International Review of Missions* from 1911 to 1912, WSCF executive committee member between 1900 and 1912 and again from 1920 to 1938 and vice president from 1930 to 1938. She was also national director for the Canadian YWCA from 1912 to 1920. In 1931, living in Geneva, Switzerland, Saunders was the vice president of the World's YWCA.

Saunders was a member of the Anglican Group for the Ordination of Women to the Historic Ministry of the Church. Lasting from 1930 to 1968, this advocacy group used research, education, publications, and memorials to encourage the Church of England and the Anglican Communion to ordain women as bishops, priests, and deacons. Its leaders were bishops, Anglican clergy, and some notable women.[25]

Saunders was the author of many articles and at least one book. She authored *Mary Dobson: Musician, Writer and Missionary.*[26]

---

24. Tissington Tatlow, *The Story of the Student Christian Movement of Great Britain and Ireland* (London: SCM Press, 1933), 494.

25. For more information, see Records of the Anglican Group for the Ordination of Women to the Historic Ministry of the Church, held at the Women's Library at the London School of Economics and Political Science, London, England.

26. Una M. Saunders, *Mary Dobson: Musician, Writer and Missionary* (London: A. and C. Black, 1926).

Una Mary Josephine Saunders
(Special Collections, Yale Divinity School)

Dobson had served in Bombay with Saunders. Saunders also gave many speeches.

She never married and at her death at eighty-three, she left an estate worth £21,524, which would have been £559,625 in 2016.

THE SPIRITUAL CAUSES
OF THE WOMAN'S MOVEMENT

Even though SCM pioneers such as Una Mary Josephine Saunders identified many reasons why the movement existed, they believed that it was *primarily spiritual in genesis*.[27] To demonstrate this fact, Saunders cited the role of prayer in the suffrage fight, one of the most important concerns of the women's movement:

---

27. Council of North American Student Movements, *The Social Needs of Today and the Colleges of North America: Conference on Social Needs Held under the Auspices of the Council of North American Student Movements, Garden City, April, 1914* (New York: International Committee of the YMCA, 1914), 18.

As we sum up the causes of this great change in public sentiment we must, I believe, add to those already mentioned—service, sacrifice and organization well-used—the unseen but potent factor of prayer. Few know how many groups met together for prayer in the days when some important suffrage petition was before Parliament, nor have all realized the church unions for suffrage, and the occasional services held, such as that at which the writer was present in Edinburgh under the auspices of the women of Scottish churches. Believing as we do in God, mighty in his righteousness, true and just in His dealings, it is our firm conviction that His over-ruling hand can be seen in the growth of the movements for woman's suffrage and in the miracle of the change in legislation now bringing fresh hope and joy to the earnest-minded among the women of Great Britain.[28]

Agreeing with the premise that the women's movement was *primarily spiritual in genesis*, Suzanne de Dietrich said that the emancipation of women was the result of the principles that Christ expounded centuries ago.[29] These principles were summarized in what was called Christ's "Law of Love" that was found in Matthew 19:19b, "You shall love your neighbor as yourself." Rouse contended that "Christ's teaching on the law of love is working out in the movement, unconsciously or consciously."[30] She also maintained that changes in women's lives were due in part to the presence of missionaries.

---

28. Una Saunders, "Britain and the Woman's Vote," *North American Student* 5 (October 1916–July 1917): 340.
29. Weber, *Courage to Live*, 31.
30. Rouse, "Ideal of Womanhood," 153.

15

The Benefits of the Women's Movement

Among the benefits of the women's movement that were examined and noted by women in the Student Christian Movement (SCM) were the following:

- The women's movement argued for the equality of women and men in personhood and role.
- It created the *unleashed woman*.
- It defended heterosexual marriage.
- It supported motherhood at home and in the community.
- It fostered altruism and settlement houses.

THE EQUALITY OF
WOMEN AND MEN IN PERSONHOOD AND ROLE

SCM women believed that one of the benefits of the women's movement was how it made the case for the equality of men and women in personhood and role. However, of all their benefits, this one was the weakest argument. A minority of the SCM's pioneers argued that men and women were equal in personhood and role. In her appeals for mixed leadership of men and women in all SCM groups, Ruth Rouse spoke of the day when men and women would be considered equal human beings working side by side for the cause of Christ.[1]

However, a majority of SCM women followed Zoe Fairfield's tentative, ambiguous approach found in *Some Aspects* (1915). On one hand, she believed that the Bible taught the spiritual equality of men and women in Galatians 3:28: "There is neither Jew nor Gentile, neither slave nor free, nor is there male or female, for you are all one in Christ

---

1. Wilmina M. Rowland, "The Contribution of Ruth Rouse to the World's Student Christian Federation" (MA thesis, Yale University, 1937), 185–96, 259–65; Ruth Franzén, *Ruth Rouse among Students: Global, Missiological, and Ecumenical Perspectives* (Uppsala: Swedish Institute of Mission Research, 2008), passim.

217

Jesus." Summarizing this text in her own words, Fairfield wrote, "In the fellowship of that body, there is complete spiritual equality, there is neither male nor female, bond nor free, Jew nor barbarian. The barriers of class, sex and nationality are done away with."[2] And Fairfield argued that some things may need to change: "What in our moral code is true and fundamental and calls for further application, what is conventional and temporary? Out of it all, a deeper and purer and fuller conception of the relation of men and women may and will come."[3]

However, in a footnote on the same page, Fairfield muddied the water: "Barriers, that is to say, not characteristics or special contributions or differing gifts. The thought of the Body is of that in which each several part is different but essential."[4] It is unclear what Fairfield is arguing. Perhaps for her, real changes were as yet unknown, and if those changes were to occur, they would have to be based on Christianity. Also these changes would take further thought and discussion.

Many who followed Fairfield's approach thought like Suzanne de Dietrich. She believed in the spiritual equality of men and women, yet she wanted each to blossom according to his or her specific nature and limits. De Dietrich believed that women who wanted the equality of men and women were "demagogues" who wanted to level all differences contrary to nature. This, she thought, would result in universal mediocrity.[5]

With hindsight, it was easy to see that the problem with Fairfield, de Dietrich, and others with similar views was their inability to define what was meant by differing contributions, gifts, characteristics, specific nature, and limits. Perhaps merely asking the question was important enough at this time. Later generations of SCM women would be left to contend with this issue.

THE UNLEASHED WOMAN

SCM feminists maintained that another gain of the women's movement was its fostering of a new brand of womanhood, the *unleashed* woman. They hoped that this woman would replace existing inferior types of womanhood. Although they did not use the term the *unleashed*

---

2. Zoe Barbara Fairfield, ed., *Some Aspects of the Woman's Movement* (London: SCM Press, 1915), 177–78.

3. Ibid., 172.

4. Ibid., 178.

5. Hans-Ruedi Weber, *The Courage to Live: A Biography of Suzanne de Dietrich* (Geneva: WCC Publications, 1995), 31.

woman, it best fitted their assumptions about this individual. Belle Harris Bennett, who was featured in chapter 13 for her ministry as a social gospel pioneer, used the term the *new woman* and summed up what this woman would be like:

> In this world-wide movement of women, for women and by women, the significant part is the *new* woman, *New,* because schoolroom and college doors have been thrown wide open to her. . . . *New,* because the law has made it possible for her to receive, obtain, and hold property. . . . *New,* because the world has been opened to her. . . . *New,* because, above all, a trained mind and the open word of God have made the *will* of God a real and personal thing to her. . . . She hears God's voice speaking to her.[6]

Here, Harris described a woman with education, legal rights, a global view, independence, and, most important, a deep spiritual life, which allowed the "new woman" to hear God's voice individually like any man. SCM women hoped that this type of woman would replace two other existing types.

THE UNTENABLE WOMAN

According to Fairfield, the first replaceable variety was the *untenable woman,* who suffered *arrested development.*[7] This type of woman's primary interests were her home and family. The untenable woman was sheltered from the storms of life by a man, who considered her his ornament or plaything. She had a finishing school education, which taught her how to act graciously in society. This middle- and upper-class untenable woman was rarely an independent thinker and usually ignored the problems of poor women. SCM pioneers believed that this model of womanhood could not survive, given turn-of-the-century conditions. It would cease to be a viable image of womanhood because in real life, women were no longer sheltered nor did they live on pedestals. They were in the middle of the struggles of life.

---

6. Mary De Bardeleben, *Lambuth-Bennett Book of Remembrance* (Nashville, TN: Lamar and Barton, 1922), 222.

7. Zoe Fairfield, "The Woman's Movement," *Student Movement* 15, no. 5 (February 1913): 94.

THE UNPLEASANT WOMAN

According to these pioneers, a second model that needed to be superseded was the *unpleasant woman*, an objectionable by-product of the women's movement.[8]

Rouse had many things to say about the unpleasant woman. She was typically portrayed as *religionslos*, or without religion. Rouse recalled one encounter where a woman said, "One student goes regularly to Mass; we can't conceive why: it can't be that she is really religious."[9] Rouse took this one step further and observed that many unpleasant women were also anti-Christian. These women were "a somewhat aggressive type of woman student—a sharp reaction against anything old and established, including the Christian religion . . . not seldom militantly anti-Christian."[10] Moreover, Rouse noted, "A curious feature of the free-thinking women students in Germany is their aggressive opposition to Christianity. They are more than indifferent, they are openly and aggressively antagonistic."[11]

Finally, Rouse had many things to say about the Russian version of unpleasant woman. This version was free-thinking, closely connected with male revolutionaries, outspoken, militant, mannish, aggressive, advanced on her views of women's questions, rude, and eccentric. They felt that everyone's hand was against them. The Russian version of the unpleasant woman smoked openly, protested in the streets, and wound up in jail or dead.

Commenting on Swiss unpleasant women, Elizabeth Clark wrote: "The Swiss students seem to me to be largely, though no means exclusively, composed of the more extreme (new woman) type, with many of them there is a certain carelessness about appearance, and an almost brusqueness of manner, that is not exactly attractive." When she made this comment, she also displayed, like Rouse, an Anglo-American smugness. Clark talked about how the "Anglo-American moral tone is almost invariably far above that of other nationalities."[12]

---

8. Ruth Rouse, "The Ideal of Womanhood," in "The Ideal of Womanhood as a Factor in Missionary Work," *International Review of Missions* 2 (1913): 152.

9. Ruth Rouse, *The World's Student Christian Federation: A History of the First Thirty Years* (London: SCM Press, 1948), 113.

10. Ibid., 111.

11. Ruth Rouse, *Woman Students in Germany* (November 1903), Archives of the WSCF, Record Group 46 (Box 44, Folder 359), 4, Special Collections, Yale Divinity School.

12. Elizabeth Clark, Report on Zurich (February–July 1907), 2, Archives of the WSCF, Record Group 46 (Box 49, Folder 393–95), Special Collections, Yale Divinity School.

ANNIE CAROLINE MACDONALD (1874–1931)

In a vein similar to that of Rouse and Clark, Annie Caroline Macdonald described the Japanese version as a certain aggressive type with the watchword, *jikaku*, or self-realization.[13]

A noted Canadian lay missionary, social reformer, and educator in Japan, Macdonald claimed she was a pioneer: "Being a pioneer myself, I am more interested in getting on with new things than bringing up the already done. I like to get ahead . . . and start a new fire burning."[14] Rouse said that Macdonald had "statesmanship, insight and undaunted faith."[15] She was noted for her sharp mind, willingness to work with all social classes, and her capacities for friendship and humor.

Macdonald was never a purely secular reformer. Once she wrote:

> Humanly speaking there is no way out of it all. If this nation does not come to know God soon, I do not know what the end will be. . . . A nation without God is a spectacle which one shudders really to think on. [Japan] is civilized and educated, but she's materialistic to the core. But God can penetrate into life here and He must.[16]

Macdonald started her ministry with an exclusive focus on personal conversion. But she became more and more critical of those missionaries who focused exclusively on personal conversion. Instead, while continuing to call for personal conversion, she became increasingly concerned with the social implications of the Gospel.

In 1874, Macdonald was born in Wingham, Ontario, to Peter (1835–1923) and Margaret Ross (?–?) Macdonald. Both parents had

---

13.   A. C. Macdonald, *Does Japan Need the Social Message?* (London: World's Young Women's Christian Association, 1912), 8. For more information on Macdonald, see John McNab, *The White Angel of Tokyo: Miss Caroline MacDonald, LL.D.* (Toronto: Centenary Committee of the Canadian Churches, n.d.); N. W. Rowell, "The Late Caroline Macdonald," *University of Toronto Monthly* 32, no. 1 (October 1931), supplement: 19–30; Sachiko Shiono, "Caroline MacDonald," in *Emma Kaufman and the Tokyo YWCA* (Tokyo: YWCA, 1963), ed. Matsuko Watanabe, 126–72; and Margaret Prang, *A Heart at Leisure from Itself: Caroline Macdonald of Japan* (Vancouver, BC: UBC Press, 1995). For the most part, her last name has been spelled Macdonald. There are a few exceptions; when it is spelled MacDonald, I will use Macdonald.

14.   Prang, *Heart*, 3.

15.   Rouse, *World's Student Christian Federation*, 123. For more information on Macdonald, see Prang, *Heart*.

16.   John P. Vaudry, "A. Caroline Macdonald of Japan," *Renewal Fellowship within the Presbyterian Church in Canada* (February 13, 2001), http://www.renewal-fellowship.ca.

Annie Caroline Macdonald
(University of Toronto Archives)

emigrated from Scotland. Peter Macdonald was a physician and was also elected to the Canadian Parliament. He eventually became Deputy Speaker of the House.

Both senior Macdonalds were deeply religious members of the Presbyterian Church of Canada. Their home emphasized church attendance, Bible study, theological discussion, and missions. Margaret Macdonald was one of the founders of the Women's Foreign Missionary Society at their local church as well as the organizer of the Happy Gleaners Mission Band that sought to encourage interest in overseas missions in the upcoming generation, including Macdonald.

In her childhood, Macdonald was a member of the Presbyterian Church of Canada and was active in Christian Endeavor. A 1901 honors graduate of the University of Toronto, Macdonald earned a BA in mathematics and physics. In her second year, she won a prize for her essay "Banking." That she won a prize in what was considered a male area of study shocked many. In 1925, she became the first women to be awarded an LLD from the same institution.

Macdonald was one of the first secretaries for the Canadian YMCA, president of the University of Toronto YWCA, and a Canadian

YWCA executive committee member. In 1901, Macdonald became general secretary of the Ottawa YWCA. Macdonald instituted an hour of prayer every Tuesday morning for the board. She also worked to improve the working lives of women office, domestic, and textile mills workers.

As traveling secretary for the Student Volunteer Movement for Foreign Missions (SVMFM), Macdonald traveled to colleges and universities. She served as an SVMFM executive committee member and city secretary for the Toronto YWCA. Macdonald also assisted in planning the 1902 SVMFM Quadrennial held in Toronto.

Although first drawn to missionary work in India, Macdonald eventually settled in Japan. Her choice came through an appeal of the World's Committee of the YWCA to launch an outreach among non-Christian women in Tokyo.

After sailing for Japan in 1904, Macdonald spent almost all of her professional life there, where she was given the nickname "the White Angel of Tokyo." Macdonald identified fully with the Japanese church and was ordained an elder in the Presbyterian Church of Japan. In the 1920s, Macdonald was probably the best-known foreign woman in Japan. In 1924, she was given the Sixth Order of Sacred Treasure by Emperor Taishō.

Macdonald helped establish the Japanese YWCA along with Michi Kawai and Ume Tsuda and was national secretary until 1915. Her ministry at this time included setting up a home for young women and teaching Bible classes for both men and women.

After a member of Macdonald's Sunday evening Bible class, Yamada Zen'ichi, murdered his wife and two sons, her ministry began to focus on men in prison. After spending a night in prayer over Zen'ichi, Macdonald went day after day to meet with him in prison, where they read the Bible together. Zen'ichi responded and returned to his faith in Christ.

Macdonald adopted an anti-capital punishment stance at this time and sought to have an anti-capital punishment law established in Japan. She argued that total repentance and a changed life were the goals of punishment. This, she argued, had been demonstrated in Zen'ichi's life, thanks to the grace of God.

During these years she was also a part-time English and Bible teacher at Tsuda College for Women. And she assisted in planning the 1907 World Student Christian Federation (WSCF) Conference in Tokyo. In 1910, Macdonald represented Japan at the World's YWCA Conference in Berlin and then attended the 1910 World Missionary Conference.

After the 1910 conference, Macdonald enrolled in theology at the United Free Church College in Aberdeen, Scotland, later known as Christ's College. There, she established a lifelong friendship and perhaps romantic interest in the recently widowed David S. Cairns (1862–1946), professor of systemic theology.

In 1915, Macdonald launched a freelance ministry, trusting in God to meet her financial needs. She received support from the Women's Missionary Society of the Presbyterian Church of Canada and the United Church even though she was not identified as an official missionary of either group.

Macdonald's typical round of ministry activities in this era included speeches to both secular and religious, pastoring prisoners and their wives and children, and hosting social activities. Macdonald went to New York City to meet with leaders in the field of criminology, social work, and prison reform. She also explored the social causes of crime, the most important of which she said was the neglect of children.

Macdonald established a settlement house for the wives and children of prisoners, ex-prisoners, juvenile delinquents, and factory workers. She helped organize schools for men and women and served as a mentor for the Japanese, especially in their labor movement and the Social Democratic Party. Macdonald spoke out during a major strike in Japan in 1927. In 1929, she went to Geneva, Switzerland, where she was an interpreter for the Japanese delegation at an international labor conference.

Macdonald's prison ministry included working with Ishii Tokichi, one of Japan's most infamous murderers. On New Year's Day, 1916, she and her fellow missionary Annie West gave him a New Testament. This resulted in his conversion. Macdonald continued to visit Tokichi and functioned as his pastor. She prepared an English translation of his autobiography, which included a discussion of his conversion.[17] Macdonald wrote several other articles on a variety of subjects.[18]

After developing lung cancer in 1931, Macdonald returned to Canada to die. On July 17, 1931, she died at fifty-six years of age. One of her

---

17. Ishii Tokichi, *A Gentleman in Prison, with the Confessions of Ishii Tokichi Written In Tokyo Prison*, trans. Caroline Macdonald (New York: George H. Doran, 1922).

18. A. Caroline Macdonald's writings include *Five Years in Japan* (New York: National Board of the YWCA, 1909); "The World of Japanese Women as It Appears to My Eyes," *Meiji No Joshi* 9, no. 6 (1912): 8–10; *Does Japan Need the Social Message?* (London: World's YWCA, 1912); "The Woman's Movement in Japan," *Joshi Seinem Kai* 15 (October 1918): 12–13; "Are Japanese Women Respected?" *Joshi Seinen Kai* 15 (October 1918): 12–13; "The Individual and the Social Problem," *Japanese Evangelist* (August–September 1929): 310–15; "Juvenile Delinquency in Japan," in *The Christian Movement in the Japanese Empire* (Tokyo: Conference on Federated Missions, 1919), 279–90; "The Environment of Our Work," *Japan Evangelist* (August–September 1929): 310–15; and "Problems in Japan and Their Solution," *Glad Tidings* (October 1931): 336–38.

colleagues in prison work noted on her death that Macdonald firmly believed that every human being was a child of God, and her "effortless" practice of that faith placed Macdonald "beyond every prejudice" of religion, race, and class. Macdonald was "a heart at leisure from itself."[19]

THE DEFENSE OF MARRIAGE

SCM pioneers argued that the women's movement defended heterosexual marriage. Ruth Rouse worked on this topic on several occasions. She cited experts, such as Helene Lange, a German educator and well-known feminist to make her point:

So long as the family continues to bear the responsibility, as it does today, for the highest moral and economic welfare of the next generation, so long is the women's movement bound to uphold and strengthen it. As the defender of the woman and child, our movement must vehemently protest any so-called members claiming the right in the name of personal satisfaction or enjoyment to deny the responsibilities that are bound up with marriage.[20]

In their support of marriage, Rouse said that the Finnish women's movement had brought about legal changes, such as the recognition of common law marriage, and the Swedish movement had persuaded its national legislature to pass a Married Woman's Property Act.

MOTHERHOOD IN THE HOME AND THE WORLD

According to SCM feminists, the women's movement supported motherhood in the home and in the world. That this was an extremely popular topic was proven by the extensive number of articles and speeches given about it.

M. GWEN SOUTHALL'S *A CHALLENGE TO GIRLS*

Evidence of this focus on motherhood is seen in M. Gwen Southall's popular SCM devotional, *A Challenge to Girls*.[21] This

---

19. See Prang, *Heart*, 274.

20. For more information on this subject, Rouse suggested Helene Lange (1848–1930), *Die Frauenbewegung in ihren modernen Problemen* (Leipzig: Verlag von Quelle und Meyer, 1914). See Rouse, "Ideal of Womanhood," 159.

21. M. Gwen Southall, ed., *A Challenge to Girls*, 3rd ed. (London: SCM Press, 1918).

devotional contained many different authors and topics, with essay titles ranging from "Vocation" to "A Call to Service for the Kingdom to Womanhood."

The ninth week of Southall's devotional focused on womanhood with the theme "women were created as mothers first and should live in that light in the home and the world." This theme was repeated over and over again in many different ways. For example, on Day One, titled, "God's Ideal Woman," Southall wrote that God had made the main function of women to be motherhood:

> Woman's part is that of bearing, cherishing, *mothering* the young life of the race. The carrying out of this part has developed her distinctive characteristics. Motherhood is the highest privilege of all girls and women as fatherhood is of men, but motherhood is not only fulfilled in marriage and the bearing of children: there is a spiritual motherhood which all women are called to exercise. It is their highest calling. For this they have special mental and spiritual gifts.[22]

The text then listed these gifts: insight, sympathy, intuition, tenderness, detail-orientation, tact (sense of touch), winsomeness, large-heartedness, a power to see the beautiful and good even in the unattractive, and unfailing longing to help and heal what is weak or ill. Southall added, "These gifts are implanted in all girls and women, often latent only, often much overlaid, but they are there as certainly as the powers of physical motherhood."[23]

THE CANADIAN STUDENT

Two articles published together in the *Canadian Student* in 1918 argue for women as mothers at home and in the world. In the first, "Experience of a Woman Pastor," this idea was present even though the article appears to ignore it. This piece detailed the ministry of a Presbyterian woman during World War I, who from all appearances was accepted like a male pastor.

The article gave information on her Sunday services and pastoral visits.[24] The main service was on Sunday afternoon so that it would

---

22. Ibid., 84.
23. Ibid.
24. "Experience of a Woman Pastor," *Canadian Student* 1, no. 4 (December 1918): 26–27.

not conflict with the Anglican service in the morning. This pastor felt that she was treated like a family member rather than a stranger during pastoral visits. Instead of staying only briefly, she was expected to remain all day.

To encourage other women to follow this pastor's lead, the article was followed immediately by a short piece by a pastoral observer, Peter Strong, the Canadian Presbyterian Home Missions Superintendent. He reported that after visiting several women pastors and their congregations during the summer of 1918 in rural, western Canada, he believed that his denomination could profit from continuing use of women pastors. He noted that all were successful, with well-attended services, good preaching, and well-organized Sunday schools.

However, even though these women ministered to men, women, and children, Strong identified only women and children as objects of these women's ministries.[25] He wrote that "the pastoral work they did cheered the women and children and proved a blessing to the homes." So in the end, Strong argued for the woman as mother theme.

LILY HARDY HAMMOND AND THE 1914 NEGRO CHRISTIAN STUDENT CONFERENCE

An example of the role of mothers in the home was Lily Hardy Hammond's talk titled "The Building of Homes" at the 1914 Negro Christian Student Conference.[26] This meeting was featured in chapter 13 as an example of how the SCM handled interracial issues but here for its inclusion of the role of motherhood for the improvement of the home. Society could be changed for the better, and a whole range of social problems of both men and women could be alleviated by focusing on motherhood, as noted in the conference report. Those in attendance assumed that the stability of human civilization and the advancement of the black race came only with improved home life, by which they meant the improvement of family life, the stimulation of family ideals, the honor of man, the protection of women, and the safeguarding of children.

---

25. Peter Strong, D. D., "How Did They Succeed?" *Canadian Student* 1, no. 4 (December 1918): 27.

26. Lily Hardy Hammond, "The Building of Homes," in the section titled "Family Ideals among Southern Negroes," in A. W. Trawick, ed., *The New Voice in Race Adjustments: Addresses and Reports Presented at the Negro Christian Student Conference, Atlanta, Georgia, May 14–18, 1914* (New York: SVMFM, 1914), 69–74. The 1914 Negro Christian Student Conference was featured in chapter 13.

LILY HARDY HAMMOND (1859–1925)

The fact that Hammond was a resident of the same town as this book's author made her appropriate to include in this story of SCM women leaders.[27] But her life and accomplishments make her even more appropriate to feature.[28] Christian author and social activist, Hammond was born in Newark, New Jersey, to parents who were southerners who had moved north. Because of some issues with documentation of her family background, Hammond's parents may have been Henry C. and Huldah Dozier Hardy, whose birth and death dates are unknown. Even though her original name might have been Lydia White Lamb Hardy, she used the name Lily Hardy Hammond.

She was a white woman who received an early education in private schools in Norfolk, Virginia, and then at the Packer Institute, Brooklyn, New York. Founded in 1845, the Packer Institute was primarily a girls' school for grades kindergarten up through junior college.

On September 10, 1879, she married John Dennis Hammond (1850–?). A southerner, he had come north on a scholarship to study at Drew Theological Seminary in New Jersey. As his wife, she served alongside him as he became a minister, bishop, college president, and bureaucrat in the Methodist Episcopal Church, South. The Hammonds had two daughters and one son.

Accompanying her husband, Hammond served in Methodist churches in Georgia and Missouri. She was a college president's wife at Central College, Fayette, Missouri, from 1888 to 1896; Wesleyan College, Macon, Georgia, from 1897 to 1898; and Paine College (Colored), Augusta, Georgia, from 1911–1915. The couple lived in the Nashville area from 1898 to 1911, while he was the Secretary of Education for the Methodist Episcopal Church, South.

Hammond became one of the leading figures in Southern Methodism's social activism, whether the cause be improving interracial relationships, the African American community, or women's place in society. She began the social services department for women's work in her denomination. She was a member of the Interracial Committee of Georgia and the Southern Commission on Interracial Cooperation. Hammond became a very productive Southern writer on these subjects.[29]

---

27. Franklin, Tennessee, is a suburb of Nashville.

28. For more information on Hammond, see Lily Hardy Hammond, *In Black and White: An Interpretation of the South* (New York: Fleming H. Revell, 1914).

29. Lily Hardy Hammond wrote for Southern Methodist publications such as *Our Home and Missionary* as well as such secular publications as *Harper's* and *South Atlantic Quarterly*. Hammond also wrote books, including *In Black and White*; *In the Garden of Delight* (New York: Thomas Y. Crowell, 1916); *Southern Women and Racial Adjust-*

In her speech to the 1914 Negro Student Christian Conference, Hammond spoke about the significance of well-ordered homes, which provided the foundation for a Christian, and hence moral, society.[30] Although this home building was the responsibility of both men and women, Hammond felt that it was mostly the work of women.

To emphasize this point, she used examples of two women who had sacrificed for their families: the homemaker who "doesn't fight things down, she loves them down," and her own mother who sacrificed for her eight children during the Civil War and postwar poverty and yet never had a frown or was impatient.[31] Hammond concluded by saying that all work began in homes and that homes must have the standard set by Jesus Christ. This standard assumed that motherhood was the primary role for women.

CHOOSING ALTRUISTIC CAREERS

According to SCM feminists, a final gain from the women's movement was that it encouraged women to enter altruistic careers, such as medicine and social work, in particular settlement house ministries. As Rouse explained, "Nothing strikes the observant student more forcibly than the way in which the note of self-expression is rapidly transcended by the note of service."[32]

SETTLEMENT HOUSES

Set up in the slums of major cities, settlement houses served as alternative communities for local residents and social workers who studied and sought solutions for local problems. The movement was involved in working to alleviate alcoholism, working conditions, prostitution, and juvenile crime.

Bertha Condé worked at Christadora House, which was established in 1897 for immigrants in the slums of New York's Lower East Side. Originally called the Young Women's Settlement, this institution was founded by Christina Isobel MacColl and Sarah Libby Carson, both with links to the YWCA.

---

ment (Lynchburg, VA: J. P. Bell, 1917); *In the Vanguard of a Race* (New York: Council of Women for Home Missions and Missionary Education Movement of the United States and Canada, 1922); and et al., *The Path of Labor*; *Theme: Christianity and the World's Workers* (New York: Council of Women for Home Missions, 1918).

30. See Hammond, "The Building of Homes," 69–74.

31. Ibid., 71.

32. Rouse, "Ideal of Womanhood," 155.

The SCM endorsed Jane Addams's Hull House located in the near west side neighborhood of Chicago. This neighborhood was where Mrs. O'Leary's cow supposedly started the Great Fire of Chicago in 1871. Hull House was founded by Addams and Ellen Gates Starr in 1889, and it served recently arrived European immigrants. About her ministry there, Addams said, "The Settlement . . . is an experimental effort to aid in the solution of the social and industrial problems which are engendered by the modern conditions of life in a great city. It insists that these problems are not confined to any one portion of the city. It is an attempt to relieve, at the same time, the over accumulation at one end of society and the destitution at the other."[33]

By 1911, Hull House had grown to thirteen buildings, and in 1912, it added a summer camp, the Bowen Country Club. Its educational, artistic, and social programs became the standard for settlement houses throughout the United States. Hull House closed in 2012 due to financial difficulties. But the University of Illinois at Chicago's Addams Hull House Museum remained open.

JANE ADDAMS (1860–1935)

Jane Addams, whose public persona was large, was interested in settlement work, social work, particularly child labor laws, world peace, philosophy, and women's issues, including suffrage and religion. Part of this visibility included many articles and books she authored.[34]

Born in Cedarville, Illinois, to John (1822–1881) and Sarah Weber (1817–1863) Addams, Jane was the youngest of nine children in a prosperous family. John Addams was a founding member of the Illinois Republican Party, an Illinois State Senator from 1855 to 1870 and a supporter of Abraham Lincoln. Lincoln visited the Addams home on several occasions. John Addams was a mill operator, a banker, and the president of two railroads. In 1881, her father died suddenly, and Addams inherited $50,000 which would equal $1,108,829.51 in 2016.

Addams graduated from Rockford Female Seminary (now Rockford University) in Rockford, Illinois, in 1881 with a college certificate and membership in Phi Beta Kappa. Addams then completed one year's study

---

33. Jane Addams, *Twenty Years at Hull House with Autobiographical Notes* (New York: Macmillan, 1910), 125–26.

34. Jane Addams, "The College Woman and the Family Claim," *Commons* 3 (September 1898): 3–7; *Democracy and Social Ethics* (New York: Macmillan, 1902); *Twenty Years at Hull House*; *A New Conscience and an Ancient Evil* (New York: Macmillan, 1912); and *The Spirit of Youth and the City Streets* (New York: Macmillan, 1923).

at the Woman's Medical College of Pennsylvania. She had to leave because of a spinal operation and a nervous breakdown. She had suffered with spinal issues since a childhood bout of tuberculosis of the spine, which caused her to limp and have curvature of the spine. In 1910, Addams received the first honorary degree given to a woman by Yale University.

Jane Addams participated in an almost endless list of groups. A few of her leadership roles include an appointment to the Chicago Board of Education (1905), the first woman president of the National Conference of Charities and Corrections (1909), first vice president of the National American Women Suffrage Association (1911), and first president of the Women's International League for Peace and Freedom (1919). Addams co-founded the American Civil Liberties Union (1920), and she was the first American woman to be awarded the Nobel Peace Prize (1931). She was considered the founder of the social work profession in the United States.

Addams died from a suddenly discovered cancer in 1935. She was buried among family members in Cedarville Cemetery, Cedarville, Illinois.

Despite some attempts to secularize Addams, she was a Christian on her own terms.[35] Addams was a Presbyterian and had a deeply religious childhood in church and Sunday school, with Bible reading and Bible memorization. She was baptized in the Cedarville Presbyterian Church in 1889. Later in life, while still a Presbyterian, Addams attended a Unitarian church and was associated with the Ethical Culture Society.

Addams believed that Christianity should be deeply involved in the world and its issues. Because of this, her religious faith was central in the founding of Hull House. She sought converts and held a highly successful weekly time of prayer for residents and staff. Still, her main focus was on social service. Addams said that the life and actions of Jesus provided a role model for her.

Her extensive SCM connections appeared in many ways. In one example in 1902, under "Association Notes," the Students' Christian Association at the University of Michigan, excitedly announced that she would speak.[36]

Addams participated in the Men and Religious Forward Movement, whose purpose was to re-masculinize North American Protestantism. This movement was sponsored by almost every leading religious and

---

35. Although I do not normally recommend Wikipedia, their brief discussion on this issue is good. For more information on the religious experiences of Addams, see Kacy J. Taylor, *Teaching the Progressive Era through the Life and Accomplishments of Jane Addams* (MA thesis, Louisiana State University, December 2005), http://etd.lsu.edu.

36. "Jane Addams," *Weekly Bulletin* (Ann Arbor, MI: Students' Christian Association) 24, no. 18 (March 14, 1902): 1, 5.

men's society in existence and was intended to dissolve after a real push between September 1911 and April 1912. Addams joined many famous Protestants, such as Walter Rauschenbusch, Washington Gladden, and William Jennings Bryan, in giving over 9,000 speeches to 1.5 million men. The movement culminated in the 1912 Christian Conservation Congress. The SVMFM was represented by John R. Mott, Robert Speer, and Addams, who was the only female speaker at this meeting. She challenged men in the churches to stamp out the social evil of prostitution.

Addams was used as an example to follow in an SCM editorial.[37] In 1916, she hosted an SVMFM medical conference at Hull House on the progress of medicine in Asia.[38] Addams's name appeared in British SCM files on stationery used by the British section of the Women's International Committee for Permanent Peace, when it attempted to recruit Tissington Tatlow or "some leading light in the student movement as a speaker."[39] Finally, she served on the WSCF's advisory committee for the Student Friendship Fund.[40]

---

37. "The Snare of Preparation," in Editorial Notes, *North American Student* 5, no. 1 (October 1916): 25.

38. "The Medical Conference at Hull House," *North America Student* 5, no. 8 (May 1917): 357.

39. See A. Maude Royden to Tissington Tatlow, October, 19, 1916, SCM General Correspondence, 1919–1920 (SCM/A66, Records of the Student Christian Movement), Cadbury Research Library, Special Collections, University of Birmingham.

40. See Student Friendship Fund Letter, October 2, 1921, Archives of the WSCF, Record Group 46 (Box 13, Folder 103), Special Collections, Yale Divinity School.

Conclusion

Final Thoughts

When I was working on a concluding chapter for this book, I was startled to discover that many books containing a collection of stories about men and women usually just end without any concluding chapter. In these, each chapter features one individual and then after the last chapter is concluded, the book simply ends. That seemed somehow incomplete. As a result, I am adding my final thoughts on the stories of these Student Christian Movement (SCM) women leaders who worked with men and in mixed groups of men and women.

I began this project over thirty-five years ago. In 1981, I walked into a small Christian bookstore in Fairfax, Virginia, and purchased C. Howard Hopkins's definitive and lengthy book, *John R. Mott, 1865–1955, A Biography*.[1] From that point on, I was hooked on the history of the SCM. As I learned more and more about the SCM, I was increasingly touched by its Christian ministry to students, challenged by its complex network of organizations, and inspired by the life-changing influence these women and men leaders had on so many people.

As time passed, I focused more and more on the women leaders of this movement. These individuals played significant roles as committee members and officers, secretaries and pioneers. I started with an interest in Clara Ruth Rouse, but was challenged by Dr. Dale Johnson, the former dean of Vanderbilt Divinity School and former president of the American Society of Church History, to see if there were any other women like her. What I found was that although Rouse was unique in many ways, she was not alone in serving as a leader in SCM circles. There was a whole untouched category of women leaders.

My focus on these women was featured in my 1989 article, "Can the Story be Told without Them? The Role of Women in the Student Volunteer Movement." This appeared after I presented this material at

---

1. C. Howard Hopkins, *John R. Mott, 1865–1955, A Biography* (Grand Rapids, MI: Eerdmans, 1980).

the 1987 annual meeting of the American Society of Missiology.[2] It was the subject of my 1999 PhD dissertation at Vanderbilt University titled, "Women Leaders in the Student Christian Movement and the Rise of the New Woman, 1880–1920."

In my research, I was able to examine the archives of the Student Volunteer Movement for Foreign Missions and the World's Student Federation at Yale University. Because of a Vanderbilt Dissertation Enhancement Award, I was able to travel to England to tap into the rich resources of the Girton College Archives, Cambridge, and British Student Christian Movement Archives, then at Selly Oak Colleges, Birmingham. This meant that I could include the stories of many women from the United Kingdom. And because these depositories had records of women from outside the United States and the United Kingdom, I was able to add individuals from Japan, Persia, Africa, and India.

A few scholars encountered my research. Noted SCM women's scholar, Dr. Johanna Selles, recently said, "Yours was one of the first articles I found."

What have I learned while writing this book?

First, I had the privilege of meeting an amazing group of women. Most of these women came from similar middle- and upper-class backgrounds and had college degrees at a time when that was rare. This gave them the skills to succeed in anything they did, and they had the wherewithal to do so.

I also learned that these women for the most part had a set of even more amazing parents who had the wisdom to encourage their daughters to do these things. Many of the stories of these parents have remained untold.

Moreover, these women were firmly committed Christians. Their stories are full of how they believed God had led them to their SCM ministries and how God worked through them in what they did. This gave these women the courage to face dangers, rejection, and even death because they firmly believed they were doing what God wanted them to do.

To be honest, I have also learned that some of these women had what we would now call "attitude problems," a smug Anglo-American superiority or a smug modernist mind-set that put down others, particularly the fundamentalists. As a result, I also see much more clearly now the devastating effects of the fundamentalist-modernist split on

---

2. Thomas A. Russell, "Can the Story be Told without Them? The Role of Women in the Student Volunteer Movement," *Missiology: An International Journal* 17 (April 1989): 159–75.

friends, colleagues, and Christian groups. And to the question I have been asked on several occasions—Have your opinions about particular women changed?—I can say yes. I have grown to appreciate some more and some less. As to which women I am talking about here, it is left to conversations in other contexts.

Reading these women's stories affirmed my belief that religion is an underlying change agent. On several occasions, my secular friends have argued that religion has nothing to do improving society. They maintain that real social transformation occurs when human beings are political activists without any religious inspiration. The lives and ministries of these women demonstrate that this is simply not true. Their significant influence shows how religion serves as a catalyst for change. To miss this is to miss the story of human history.

Also, I learned that if these women existed, then others did as well. They were not alone but were part of a larger group of yet to be discovered women who made a difference in their time and place.

Because of these women's ministries, I have learned that the idea that women did not have religious leadership authority with men in the Victorian Era is false. Although it true that they faced limitations to their work, such as the lack of ordination (with the exception of one), they overcame these difficulties to serve as pastors, mentors, evangelists, and inspirational speakers for men and women.

The existence of these women suggests that a group of women leaders exists today that could be just as influential. They are Hamlet's "undiscovered country." If you are a woman leader in a religious community, these women role models challenge you to be faithful in your ministry. If you are a man in a religious community with women leaders, these women encourage you to respect them and encourage their leadership. If you are part of a religious community that has no women leaders with men, these women challenge you to accept the fact that these faithful women existed and served Christ successfully in a way different from your way.

To all my friends whose story I have been honored to tell, thank you for your ministries. After spending decades with you, I feel I can call you my friends. If the Christian church is truly made up of those who have gone on before, those who are alive today, and those who will come in the future, then we are friends on a similar journey who will meet up one day in heaven. So thanks. The Victorian world was a better place because of your work, and the world today is as well.

Bibliography

MANUSCRIPT COLLECTIONS AND ARCHIVES

England

Archives, Newnham College, Cambridge
Archives (Professional Services), Queen Mary University of London (For Westfield College), London
British SCM Archives, Cadbury Research Library: Special Collections, University of Birmingham
Church Missionary Society Archives, Cadbury Research Library: Special Collections, University of Birmingham
Girton College Archives, Cambridge
London Missionary Society, Archives & Special Collections and Library and Information Services (LIS), School of Oriental and African Studies (SOAS), University of London
Somerville College Archives, Oxford

United States

Archives and Special Collections and Digital Assets and Preservation Services, Library Information and Technology Services, Mount Holyoke College, South Hadley, Massachusetts.
Archivist and Head of Special Collections and Archives, Gould Library, Carleton College, Northfield, Minnesota.
Charles K. Ober Papers, Kautz Family YMCA Archives, University of Minnesota
Hillsdale College Archives, Hillsdale, Michigan
Historical Medical Library, The College of Physicians of Philadelphia Yale Divinity School Legacy Center: Archives & Special Collections, College of Medicine Drexel University, Philadelphia, Pennsylvania Library Special Collections
Record Group 42 (RG 42): Student Volunteer Movement for Foreign Missions
Record Group 45 (RG45): John R. Mott
Record Group 46 (RG 46): World Student Christian Federation
Reference Staff, Sophia Smith Collection, Smith College, Northampton, Massachusetts
YWCA Archives

Turkey

The American Research Institute, Ewing Memorial Library, Istanbul

Pakistan

Forman Christian College, Lahore, Pakistan

PERSONAL PAPERS

Michele Guinness, Geraldine Guinness Taylor Papers
Timothy Garlow and C. R. White, Reverend Barbara Groenendyke Papers

PERIODICALS

Association Monthly
Canadian Student
Intercollegian
International Bulletin of Missionary Research
Oakland Tribune
Protestant Standard
North American Student
Student Movement
Student World

BOOKS, ARTICLES, AND PAMPHLETS

Addams, Jane. "The College Woman and the Family Claim." *Commons* 3 (September 1898): 3–7.
———. *Democracy and Social Ethics*. Citizen's Library of Economics, Politics, and Sociology. New York: Macmillan, 1902.
———. *A New Conscience and an Ancient Evil*. New York: Macmillan, 1912.
———. *The Spirit of Youth and the City Streets*. New York: Macmillan, 1923.
———. *Twenty Years at Hull House with Autobiographical Notes*. New York: Macmillan, 1910.
"Agnes de Selincourt." *Girton Review* (Michaelmas Term 1917): 7–9.
Anderson, Dame Adelaide. *Humanity and Labour in China: An Industrial Visit and Its Sequel, 1923–1928*. London: SCM, 1928.
———. *Women in the Factory: An Administrative Adventure, 1893–1921*. London: Murray, 1922.
Antler, Joyce. "After College, What?: New Graduates and the Family Claim." *American Quarterly* 32 (Fall 1980): 409–34.
———. "The Educated Woman and Professionalization: The Struggle for a New Feminine Identity, 1890–1920." PhD diss., State University of New York, 1977.

Armstrong, Agnes Wrong. "There's Too Much Waiting to Be Done." *Food for Thought* 16 (March 1956): 258–63.

Art Students and the Christian Movement in British Colleges: Being Some Account of a Meeting of Students from the London Schools of Art, Held at the Invitation of Blanche, Countess of Rosilyn, at 8, Seamore Place, Park Lane, on Saturday, the 27th of November, 1897. Also of the ASCU Formed March, 1898, as an Outcome of the Meeting. London: BCCU, 1902.

August, Kari. *Reaching Rocky Mountain Jim: A Novel Based on the True Life Stories of James Nugent and Isabella Bird.* Denver: Mountain Track Publishing, 2014.

Baker, William K. *John T. Dorland.* Edited by Anne W. Richardson. London: Headley, 1898.

Bardeleben, Mary. *Lambuth-Bennett Book of Remembrance.* Nashville, TN: Lamar and Barton, 1922.

Barr, Patricia. *To China with Love: The Lives and Times of Protestant Missionaries in China, 1860–1900.* London: Secker and Warburg, 1972.

Barton, James L. "American Colleges in Turkey." *Student World* 11 (1918): 5–11.

Bates, Eula. "The Importance of the Secretaryship." *1889 Report of the Second National Convention of the YWCAs Held at Bloomington, Illinois, April 11–14, 1889:* 35–38.

Beach, Harlan P. "The Atlanta Negro Student Christian Conference." *Student World* 7, no. 2 (April 1914): 109–14.

Beahm, William M. "Factors in the Development of the SVMFM." PhD diss., University of Chicago, 1941.

Belmonte, Kevin. *D. L. Moody, A Life: Innovator, Evangelist, World Changer.* Chicago: Moody Press, 2014.

Bennett, Joseph E. "The Prince of Dakota Sioux." *Northern Light: A Window for Free Masonry,* 30, no. 2 (May 1999): 6.

Berger, Rev. Daniel. *History of the Church of the United Brethren in Christ.* Dayton, OH: United Brethren Publishing House, 1897.

Bevan, Edwyn. *A Memoir of Leslie Johnson.* London: SCM Press, 1921.

Bidgrain, Suzanne. *Cantate Domino: World's Student Christian Federation Hymnal.* Geneva: World's Student Christian Federation, 1924.

———. "Ruth Rouse (1872–1956)." *The Student World* 50 (1st Quarter 1957): 73–77.

Bird, Isabella (Bishop). *Among the Tibetans.* London: Religious Tract Society, 1904.

———. *The Englishwoman in America.* London: John Murray, 1856.

———. *The Golden Chersonese and the Way Thither.* New York: G. P. Putnam, 1883.

———. *The Hawaiian Archipelago: Six Months among the Palm Groves, Coral Reefs and Volcanoes of the Sandwich Islands.* London: John Murray, 1875.

———. *Journeys in Persia and Kurdistan, including a Summer in the Upper Karun Region and a Visit to the Nestorian Rayahs.* 2 vols. London: John Murray, 1891.

————. *Korea and Her Neighbors: A Narrative of Travel with an Account of the Recent Vicissitudes and the Present Position of the Country.* New York: Fleming H. Revell, 1898.

————. *A Lady's Life in the Rocky Mountains.* New York: G. P. Putnam, 1879–80.

————. *Unbeaten Tracks in Japan: An Account of the Travels on Horseback on the Interior including Visits to the Aborigines of Yezo and the Shrines of Nikko and Ise.* New York: G. P. Putnam, 1881.

————. *The Yangtze Valley and Beyond: An Account of Journeys in China, Chiefly in the Province of Sze Chuan and among the Man-tse of Somo Territory.* New York: G. P. Putnam, 1900.

A Book of Prayer for Students. London: SCM Press, 1915.

Boyd, Nancy. *Emissaries: The Overseas Work of the American YWCA, 1895–1970.* New York: Woman's Press, 1986.

Boyd, Robin. "The Witness of the Student Christian Movement." *International Bulletin of Missionary Research* 31, no. 1 (January 2007): 4.

Braisted, Ruth Evelyn Wilder. *In This Generation: The Story of Robert P. Wilder.* New York: Friendship Press, 1941.

Brittain, Vera. *The Rebel Passion: A Short History of Some Pioneer Peacemakers.* Nyack, NY: Fellowship Publishers, 1964.

Brouwer, Ruth Compton. "Margaret Wrong and the Gendering of African Writing, 1929–1963." *International Journal of African Historical Studies* 31, no. 1 (1998): 53–71.

————. "Margaret Wrong's Literacy Work and the 'Remaking of Woman' in Africa, 1929–1948." *Journal of Imperial and Commonwealth History* 23, no. 3 (September 1995): 427–52.

————. *Modern Women Modernizing Men: The Changing Missions of Three Professional Women in Asia and Africa, 1902–69.* Vancouver, BC: UBC Press, 2002.

Brown, Arthur Judson. *The Foreign Missionary: An Incarnation of a World Movement.* New York: Fleming H. Revell, 1907.

Bruce, Steve. "The Student Christian Movement and the Inter-Varsity Fellowship: A Sociological Study of Two Student Movements." PhD diss., University of Stirling, 1980.

Burton, Margaret E. *Comrades in Service.* Nashville, TN: Smith and Lamar, 1915.

The Call, Qualifications and Preparation of Missionary Candidates: Papers by Missionaries and Other Authorities. New York: SVMFM, 1906.

Campbell, Barbara Kuhn. *The Liberated Woman of 1914; Prominent Women of the Progressive Era.* Ann Arbor, MI: UMI Research Press, 1979.

Capitani, Diane. "Imaging God in Our Ways: The Journals of Frances E. Willard." *Feminist Theology: The Journal of the Britain and Ireland School of Feminist Theology* 12, no. 1 (2003): 57–88.

Chandler, Douglas R. "Bennett, Belle Harris." In *Notable American Women, 1607–1950.* Edited by Edward T. James. Cambridge, MA: Belknap Press of Harvard University Press, 1971.

"A Christian Conservation Congress, April 19–24." *Intercollegian* 34, no. 7 (July 1911): 37.

Christlieb, Marie Luise (Louise). *If I Lived in India*. Edinburgh: Edinburgh House Press, 1930.

———. *Indian Neighbours*. London: Student, 1930.

———. *Lalappa: An Indian Story*. London: London Missionary Society, 1928.

———. *An Uphill Road in India*. London: George Allen and Unwin, 1927.

———. *The Way of Christ in the Mission Field*. Madras: CLS, 1924.

Christlieb, Marie Luise (Louise), and Edyth Hinkley. *A Struggle for a Soul, and Other Stories of Life and Work in South India*. Philadelphia: Union Press, 1907.

Clark, Nettie Dunn. *Report of Deaths of American Citizens Abroad, 1835–1974*. NARA Inventory 15, Entry 205, 1910–1962, Box 1700: 1945–1949.

Clarke Elizabeth. "At a Swiss University." *Association Monthly* 4, no. 8 (September 1910): 314–17.

Clifford, Joan. *The Cambridge Seven: For Christ and China*. London: Marshall Pickering, 1990.

Coe, George Albert. *The Psychology of Religion*. Chicago: University of Chicago Press, 1916.

Coggan, F. D., ed. *Christ and the Colleges: A History of the Inter-Varsity Fellowship of Evangelical Unions*. London: IVFEU, 1934.

Collet, Clara. *Educated Working Women: Essays on the Economic Position of Women Workers in the Middle Classes*. London: P. S. King and Son, 1902.

Condé, Bertha. *The Business of Being a Friend*. Boston: Houghton Mifflin, 1916.

———. "Hopeful Signs." *Fisk University News* 6 (February 1919): 30.

———. *The Human Element in the Making of a Christian: Studies in Personal Evangelism*. New York: Charles Scribner's Sons, 1917.

———. "Ideals Essential to Radiant Living, GFS Told." *Syracuse Herald*, February 4, 1930, 3.

———. *Spiritual Adventures in Social Relations*. Nashville, TN: Cokesbury Press, 1931.

———. *Spiritual Adventuring, Studies in Jesus' Way of Life*. Nashville, TN: Cokesbury, 1926.

———. *The Way to Peace, Health and Power, Studies in the Inner Life*. New York: Scribner, 1930.

———. "What's Life All About? Bertha Condé Answers," *Oakland Tribune*, July 6, 1930, 10-S.

———. *What's Life All About? A Key for Those Who Ask the Question*. New York: Scribner, 1930.

Coston, Herbert Reece, Jr. "The World's Student Christian Federation as an Ecumenical Training Ground." PhD diss., Northwestern University, 1963.

Council of North American Student Movements. *The Social Needs of Today and the Colleges of North America: Conference on Social Needs Held under the Auspices of the Council of North American Student Movements, Garden City, April 1914*. New York: International Committee of the YMCA, 1914.

Counsel to New Missionaries from Older Missionaries of the Presbyterian Church. New York: Board of Foreign Missions of the Presbyterian Church, 1905.

Covell, Ralph R. "Taylor, James Hudson." In *Biographical Dictionary of Christian Missions*, ed. Gerald H. Anderson (New York: Macmillan Reference, 1998), 657–58.

Day, George M. "The Russian Student Movement." *Student World* 10 (July 1917): 241–49.

Dayton, Donald W. "Evangelical Roots of Feminism." *Covenant Quarterly* (November 1976): 41–56

Dean, Joanna. *Religious Experience and the New Woman: The Life of Lily Dougall*. Bloomington: Indiana University Press, 2007.

"Death of a Woman's Board Leader." *Intercollegian* 25, no. 3 (December 1902): 69.

Deaths: "Bertha Condé." *Living Church* 109, no. 10 (September 3, 1944): 21.

DeBerg, Betty A. *UnGodly Women: Gender and the First Wave of American Fundamentalism*. Macon, GA: Mercer University Press, 2000.

Deloria, Ella Cara. *Dakota Texts*. New York: G. E. Stechert, 1932.

———. *Speaking of Indians*. New York: Friendship Press, 1944.

———. *Waterlily*. Lincoln: University of Nebraska, 1988.

Deloria, Ella Cara, and Franz Boas. *Dakota Grammar*. Washington, DC: United States Government Printing Office, 1941.

DeSmither, Carol Marie. "From Calling to Career: Work and Professional Identity among American Women Missionaries to China, 1900–1950." PhD diss., University of Oregon, 1987.

Dietrich, Suzanne de. *Dessien de Dieu: God's Unfolding Purpose: A Guide to the Study of the Bible*. Translated by Robert McAfee Brown. Philadelphia: Westminster Press, 1960.

———. *Fifty Years of History: The WSCF, 1895–1945*. Geneva: WSCF, 1993.

———. *Free Men*. Philadelphia: Westminster Press, 1961.

———. *God's Word in Today's World*. Valley Forge, PA: Judson Press, 1967.

———. *Heure l'élévation: And He Is Lifted Up: Meditations on the Gospel of John*. Translated by Dennis Pardee. Philadelphia: Westminster Press, 1969.

———. *Rediscovering the Bible*. Geneva: WSCF, 1942.

———. *This We Know: A Study of the Letters of John*. Richmond, VA: John Knox Press, 1963.

———. *Toward Fullness of Life: Studies in the Letter of Paul to the Philippians*. Philadelphia: Westminster, 1966.

———. *The Witnessing Community: The Biblical Record of God's Purpose*. Philadelphia: Westminster Press, 1958.

———. *The Word and His People: A Bible Study Guide*. Greenwich, CT: Seabury Press, 1958.

———. *The Word with Power*. New York: Friendship Press, 1965.

Dobkin, Marjoram Houspian, ed., *The Making of a Feminist: Early Journals and Letters of M. Carey Thomas*. Kent, OH: Kent State University Press, 1979.

Dodge, Grace Hoadley. *A Bundle of Letters to Busy Girls on Practical Matters.* New York: Funk and Wagnall's, 1887.

Dodge, Grace Hoadley, with Thomas Hunter et al. *What Women Can Earn: Occupations of Women and Their Compensation.* New York: F. A. Stokes, 1889.

Dorsett, Lyle W. *A Passion for Souls: The Life of D. L. Moody.* Chicago: Moody, 2003.

Dougall, Lily. *Beggars All, Lovereen: A Canadian Novel under a Male Pseudonym.* New York: Longmans, Green, 1891.

———. *Concerning Prayer: Its Nature, Its Difficulties and Its Face Value.* New York: Macmillan, 1917.

———. *God's Way with Man: An Exploration of the Method of Divine Working Suggested by the Facts of History and Science.* London: SCM, 1924.

———. *Immortality: An Essay in Discovery.* New York: Macmillan, 1917.

———. *Pro Christo et Ecclesia.* London: Macmillan, 1900.

———. *The Spirit: God and His Relation to Man Considered from the Standpoint of Philosophy, Psychology and Art.* London: Macmillan, 1920.

Eddy, Sherwood. *Pathfinders of the World Missionary Crusade.* New York/Nashville: Abingdon-Cokesbury Press, 1945.

"Editorial." *Student Movement* 5, no. 3 (December 1902): 58.

Elliot, Elisabeth. *Through Gates of Splendor*, 1st ed. New York: Harper and Brothers, 1957.

"Experience of a Woman Pastor." *Canadian Student* 1, no. 4 (December 1918): 26–27.

Fairfield, Zoe. "Nicholas Zernov." *Sobornost*, n.s. 2, no. 10 (June 1937): 38.

———. "Some Aspects of the Woman's Movement." *North American Student* 3, no. 1 (October 1914): 59–64.

———, ed. *Some Aspects of the Woman's Movement.* London: SCM, 1915.

———. "The Woman's Movement." *Student Movement* 15, nos. 4, 5, 7 (January, February, and April 1913): 78–80, 92–95, 128, 138–31; reprint ed., London: SCM Press, 1913.

Fenn, Eric. *Learning Together.* London: SCM Press, 1939.

Ferguson, John. "Stevenson, Lilian Sinclair." In *Biographical Dictionary of Modern Peace Leaders.* Edited by Harold Josephson. Westport, CT: Greenwood Press, 1985.

Filene, Peter Gabriel. *Him/Her/Self: Sex Roles in Modern America.* New York: Harcourt Brace Jovanovich, 1974.

Findlay, J. F. *Dwight L. Moody: American Evangelist, 1837–1899.* Grand Rapids, MI: Baker Books, 1973.

Fletcher, Sheila. *Maude Royden: A Life.* London: Basil Blackwell, 1989.

Forrey, Carolyn. "The New Woman Revisited." *Women Studies* 2, no. 1 (1974): 37–56.

Francis-Dehqani, Gulnar. "Medical Missions and the History of Feminism: Emmeline Stuart of the CMS Persia Mission, 1897–1934." *Currents in World Christianity Position Paper* 103: 15, 1999.

———. "Religious Feminism in an Age of Empire: CMS Women Missionaries in Iran, 1869–1934." PhD diss., University of Bristol, 1999.

Franzén, Ruth. "The Legacy of Ruth Rouse." *International Bulletin of Missionary Research* 17, no. 4 (October 1993): 154–58.

———. "Ruth Rouse." In *Mission Legacies: Biographical Studies of Leaders of the Modern Missionary Movement*, edited by Gerald H. Anderson et al., 93–101. Maryknoll, NY: Orbis Books, 1994.

———. *Ruth Rouse among Students: Global, Missiological, and Ecumenical Perspectives*. Uppsala: Swedish Institute of Mission Research, 2008.

———. *Student Ecumenism and Revivalism: The Student Christian Movement of Finland at the International Crossroads, 1924–1950*. Helsingfors: Finska Kyrkohistoriksa Samfundet, 1987.

Fraser, Agnes R. *Donald Eraser of Livingstonia*. London: Hodder and Stoughton, 1934.

Freeman, Douglas Southall. *R. E. Lee: A Biography* 4. New York: Charles Scribner's Sons, 1934.

Fries, Karl. *Mina Minnen* [My reminiscences]. Stockholm: Triangelförlaget, 1939.

Furuki, Yoshiko. *The White Plum: A Biography of Ume Tsuda: Pioneer in the Higher Education of Japanese Women*. New York: Weatherhill, 1991.

Gage, Frances, to Mrs. John Bell, October 6, 1896, Minnesota State Historical Society Library.

Giddings, Paula. *When and Where I Enter: The Impact of Black Women on Race and Sex in America*. New York: W. Morrow, 1984.

Girton College Review (May 1904).

"Go Ye and Preach the Gospel—Five Devout Americans in Remote Ecuador Follow This Precept and Are Killed." *Life Magazine* 40, no. 6 (January 30, 1956): 10–19.

Graham, Abbie. *Grace H. Dodge: Merchant of Dreams*. New York: Woman's Press, 1926.

Groenendyke, Rev. Ellen. "Medical Work among Women." In *Students and the Modern Missionary Crusade: Addresses of the SVMFM, Nashville, Tennessee, February 28–March 4, 1896*. New York: SVMFM, 1906.

Guinness, Fanny Emma Fitzgerald. *Congo Recollections: Edited from Notes and Conversations of Missionaries*. London: Hodder and Stoughton, 1890.

———. *The New World of Central Africa: With a History of the First Christian Mission on the Congo*. London: Hodder and Stoughton, 1890.

———. "She Spake of Him." In *Being Recollections of the Loving Labors and Early Death of the Late Mrs. Geraldine Dening, an Essay by Fanny E. Guinness (1872)*. In Michele Guinness, *Genius of Guinness: The Enduring Legacy of an Irish Dynasty*. Greenville, SC, and Belfast: Ambassador International, 2005.

Guinness, Joy. *Mrs. Howard Taylor: Her Web of Time*. London: SCM Press, 1949.

Guinness, Lucy. *In the Far East: Letters from Geraldine Guinness in China*. London: CIM, 1894.

Guinness, Michele. *Genius of Guinness: The Enduring Legacy of an Irish Dynasty*. Belfast: Ambassador International, 2005.

———. *The Guinness Legend: The Changing Fortunes of a Great Dynasty.* London: Hodder and Stoughton, 1989.

Hamilton, Mrs. J. Simpson. *The Story of the Alabama Woman's Christian Temperance Union* (1959).

Hammack, Mary L. "Lilian Sinclair Stevenson." In *A Dictionary of Women in Church History*, 139. Chicago: Moody Press, 1984.

Hammond, Lily Hardy. "The Building of Homes." In *The New Voice in Race Adjustments: Addresses and Reports Presented at the Negro Christian Student Conference, Atlanta, Georgia, May 14–18, 1914*, edited by Arcadius McSwain, 69–74. New York: SVMFM, n.d.

———. *In Black and White: An Interpretation of Southern Life.* New York: Fleming H. Revell, 1914.

———. *In the Garden of Delight.* New York: Thomas Y. Crowell, 1916.

———. *In the Vanguard of a Race.* New York: Council of Women for Home Missions and Missionary Education Movement of the United States and Canada, 1922.

———. *Southern Women and Racial Adjustment.* Lynchburg, VA: J. P. Bell, 1917.

Hammond, Lily Hardy, et al. *The Path of Labor; Theme: Christianity and the World's Workers.* New York: Council of Women for Home Missions, 1918.

Harder, Ben. "The Student Volunteer Movement for Foreign Missions and Its Contribution to 20th-Century Mission." *Missiology: An International Review* 8, no. 2 (April 1980): 141–54.

Harris, Barbara J. *Beyond Her Sphere: Women and the Professions in American History.* Westport, CT: Greenwood Press, 1978.

Hastings, Adrian. *A History of English Christianity, 1920–1990.* 3rd ed. London: SCM Press, 1991.

A History of the Woman's Missionary Association of the United Brethren in Christ. Dayton, OH: United Brethren Publishing House, 1894.

Hogg, William Richey. *Ecumenical Foundations; A History of the International Missionary Council and Its Nineteenth-Century Background.* New York: Harper and Brothers, 1952.

Hopkins, C. Howard. *History of YMCA in North America.* New York: Association Press, 1951.

———. *John R. Mott, 1865–1955.* Grand Rapids, MI: William B. Eerdmans, 1980.

———. "The Legacy of John R. Mott." *International Bulletin of Missionary Research* 5, no. 2 (April 1981): 71.

———. *The Social Gospel: Religion and Reform in Changing America.* Philadelphia: Temple University Press, 1976.

Horne, Herman H. *Psychological Principles of Education.* New York: Macmillan, 1906.

Horowitz, Helen Lefkowitz. *The Power and Passion of M. Carey Thomas.* New York: Alfred A. Knopf, 1994.

Hugh Crichton-Miller, 1877–1959: A Personal Memoir by His Friends and Family. Dorchester: Longmans, 1961.

Hunton, Addie Waites. "Negro Womanhood Defended." *Voice of the Negro* (July 1914): 280–82.

———. *William Alphaeus Hunton: A Pioneer Prophet of Young Men.* New York: Association Press, 1938.

Hunton, Addie Waites. and Kathryn M. Johnson. *Two Colored Women with the American Expeditionary Forces.* Brooklyn: Brooklyn Eagle Press, 1920.

Hutson, Jean Blackwell. "Addie Hunton." In *Notable American Women, 1607–1950: A Biographical Dictionary,* edited by Edward T. James, 240–41. Cambridge, MA: Belknap Press of Harvard University Press, 1971.

In Memoriam Abbie B. Child, April 8, 1840–November 9, 1902. Boston: Woman's Board of Missions, 1902.

"In Memory of Grace Dodge." *Association Monthly* (May 1918): 63–115.

International Survey of the YMCA and YWCA's: An Independent Study of the Foreign Worker of the Christian Associations of the United States and Canada. New York: International Survey Committee, 1932.

Inter-Varsity Christian Fellowship. *A Brief History of the Inter-Varsity Fellowship.* London: IVFEU, 1929.

Jackson, Eleanor M. *Red Tape and the Gospel; A Study of the Significance of the Ecumenical Missionary Struggle of William Paton, 1886–1943.* Birmingham: Phlogiston Pub. in association with Selly Oak Colleges, 1980.

———. "William Paton." In *Mission Legacies: Biographical Studies of the Leaders of the Modern Missionary Movement,* edited by Gerald H. Anderson et al., 581–90. Maryknoll, NY: Orbis Books, 1994.

James, William. *Talks to Teachers on Psychology and to Students on Some of Life's Ideals.* New York: H. Holt, 1914.

———. *The Varieties of Religious Experience.* New York: Longmans Green, 1902.

"Jane Addams." *Weekly Bulletin* 24, no. 18 (Ann Arbor, MI: Students' Christian Association, March 14, 1902): 1, 5.

Johnson, Douglas. *Contending for the Faith: A History of the Evangelical Movement in the Universities and Colleges.* London: Inter-Varsity Press, 1979.

Jones, Elizabeth Vaughan. *One Hundred Years of the Girls' Friendly Society, 1875–1975.* Bristol, England: Girls' Friendly Society, 1975.

Kawai, Michi. *My Lantern.* Tokyo: Kyo Bun Kwan, 1939.

———. *Sliding Doors.* Tokyo: Kasai, 1950.

King, Colonel Edwin J. *The Knights of St John in the British Empire: Being the Official History of the British Order of the Hospital of St. John of Jerusalem.* London: St. John's Gate, 1934.

Lange, Helene. *Die Frauenbewegung in ihren modernen Probleme.* Leipzig: Verlag von Quelle und Meyer, 1914.

Langenskjold, Greta. *Baron Paul Nicolay: Christian Statesman and Student Leader in Northern and Slavic Europe.* New York: George H. Doran, 1924.

Latourette, Kenneth Scott. *World Service: A History of the Foreign Work and World Service of the Young Men's Christian Association of the United States and Canada.* New York: Association Press, 1957.

Leavitt, Almira. *Italian Student Federation for Religious Culture, Branch of the WSCF: The Salotto.* Naples: privately printed, 1909.

Lehtonen, Risto. *Story of a Storm: The Ecumenical Student Movement in the Turmoil of Revolution, 1968–1973.* Grand Rapids, MI: William B. Eerdmans, 1998.

Leonard, John William, ed. "Elizabeth Morris Clarke." In *Woman's Who's Who of America: A Biographical Dictionary of Contemporary Women of the United States and Canada, 1914–1915,* 180. New York: American Commonwealth Company, 1915.

"The Life of Isabella Bird." *Spectator* (London, January 1907): 6.

A Litany of Intercession for Women. The Representative Council of Girls' Associations.

"Lives Her Own Doctrine after Dream during Childhood Spent in Auburn, World Traveler." *Syracuse Herald,* February 9, 1930, sections 3, 4, and 5.

Logan, Rayford W. "Addie Hunton." In *Dictionary of American Negro Biography,* edited by Rayford W. Logan and Michael R. Watson, 33–38. New York: Norton, 1982.

London Missionary Society. "The Qualifications Needed for a Woman Missionary." In *The Call, Qualifications and Preparation of Candidates for Foreign Missionary Service: Papers by Missionaries and Other Authorities,* 167–78. New York: SVMFM, 1906.

Long, Kathryn Teresa. *The Revival of 1857–1858: Interpreting an American Religious Awakening.* 1st ed. Religion in America Series. New York: Oxford University Press, 1998.

Lubove, Roy. *The Professional Altruist: The Emergence of Social Work as a Career, 1880–1930.* Cambridge, MA: Harvard University Press, 1965.

Lundy, Darryl. *The Peerage* (October 16, 2016): Person Page, 14,070.

———. *The Peerage* (October 31, 2016: Person Page, 29,967.

Luzzi, Giovanni. *The Struggle for Christian Truth in Italy.* New York: Fleming H. Revell, 1913.

———. *The Waldensian Church: Her Work, Her Difficulties, Her Hopes.* New York: Dodd, Mead, 1914.

Macdonald, Annie Caroline. "Are Japanese Women Respected?" *Joshi Seinem Kai* 15 (October 1918): 12–13.

———. *Does Japan Need the Social Message?* London: World's YWCA, 1912.

———. "The Environment of Our Work." *Japan Evangelist* (August–September 1929): 310–15.

———. *Five Years in Japan.* New York: National Board of the YWCA, 1909.

———, trans. *A Gentleman in Prison, with the Confessions of Ishii Tokichi Written in Tokyo Prison.* New York: George H. Doran, 1922.

———. "The Individual and the Social Problem." *Japanese Evangelist* (August–September 1929): 310–15.

———. "Juvenile Delinquency in Japan." In *The Christian Movement in the Japanese Empire,* 279–90. Tokyo: Conference on Federated Missions, 1919.

———. "Problems in Japan and Their Solution." *Glad Tidings* (October 1931): 336–38.

———. "The Woman's Movement in Japan." *Joshi Seinem Kai* 15 (October 1918): 12–13.

―――. "The Woman's Movement in Japan." In *The Christian Movement in the Japanese Empire* (Tokyo: Conference on Federated Missions, 1919), 266–78.

―――. "The World of Japanese Women as It Appears to My Eyes." *Meiji No Joshi* 9, no. 6 (1912): 8–10.

MacDonell, R. W. *Belle Harris Bennett: Her Life Work*. Nashville, TN: Cokesbury Press, 1928.

MacLachlan, Gretchen E. "Addie W. Hunton." In *Black Women in America: An Historical Encyclopedia*, edited by Darlene Clark Hine, 596–97. Brooklyn: Carlson, 1993.

Make Jesus King: Report of the International Students' Missionary Conference, Liverpool, January 1–5, 1896. New York: F. H. Revell, 1896.

Mansfield, Stephen. *The Search for God and Guinness: A Biography of the Beer That Changed the World*. Nashville, TN: Thomas Nelson, 2014.

The Marquis of Ruvigny and Raineval, Melville Henry Massue. *The Plantagenet Roll of the Blood Royal Being A Complete Table of All the Descendants Now Living of Edward III, King of England*. London: T. C.& E. C. Jack, 1905–11.

Marsden, George. "Fundamentalism as an American Phenomenon: A Comparison with English Evangelicalism." *Church History* 46 (June 1977): 215–33.

"Massacre at Marsovan." *Los Angeles Herald* 45, no. 58 (December 8, 1895): 2.

Matthews, May L. "The Story of Mount Holyoke Missionary Association." *Missionary Review of the World* 57 (December 1934): 565.

McCaughey, J. Davis. *Christian Obedience in the University: Studies in the Life of the SCM of Great Britain and Ireland, 1930–1950*. London: SCM Press, 1958.

McComb, Samuel. *The Power of Self-Suggestion*. New York: Moffat, Yard, 1909.

McDougall, Eleanor. "The Influence of Christianity on the Position of Women." *International Review of Missions* 1 (1912): 435–51.

McMillen, Sally. *Seneca Falls and the Origin of the Women's Rights Movement*. Oxford: Oxford University Press, 2009.

McNab, John. *The White Angel of Tokyo: Miss Caroline MacDonald, LL.D.* Toronto: Centenary Committee of the Canadian Churches, privately published, n.d.

"The Medical Conference at Hull House." *North American Student* 5, no. 8 (May 1917): 357.

Medicine, Bea. *Reminiscences of Ella Deloria: Standing Rock Sioux Tribe of South Dakota*. Sanford: Microfilming Corp. of America, 1979.

Merriam, Ruth Levy. *A History of the Deanery, Bryn Mawr College*. Bryn Mawr: Bryn Mawr College, 1965.

The Michigan Christian Advocate (March 10, 1894): 4.

Miller, Mary Marshall. "The SVMFM: A Study of a Social Institution." MA thesis, University of Missouri, 1936.

Mills, Reverend Job Smith. *Mission Work in Sierra Leone, West Africa*. Dayton, OH: United Brethren Publishing House, 1898.

Mission Studies 36, no. 1 (January 1, 1918): 27–28.

"The Missionary Campaign of Dr. and Mrs. Howard Taylor." *Intercollegian* 23, no. 8 (May 1901): 180–82.

Moorhead, Max Wood, ed. *The Student Missionary Enterprise: Addresses and Discussions of the Second International Convention of the SVMFM Held at Detroit, Michigan, February 28 and March 1, 2, 3, and 4, 1894.* Boston: T. O. Metcalf, 1894.

Morley, Bertha B. *Marsovan 1915: The Diaries of Bertha Morley.* Armenian Genocide Documentation Series 3, 2nd ed. Ann Arbor, MI, and Princeton, NJ: Gomidas Institute; and Reading, Eng.: Taderon Press, 2000.

Morley, Edith, ed. *Women Workers in Seven Professions: A Survey of Their Economic Conditions and Prospects.* London: G. Routledge and Sons, 1914.

Morse, Rebecca. *Young Women: A History of the American Committee of the YWCA.* Chicago: American Committee of the YWCA, 1901.

Morse, Richard Clay. *History of the North American YMCAs.* New York: Association Press, 1913.

Mott, John R. *Achievements of the SVMFM during the First Generation of Its History, Report of the Executive Committee, 1920.* New York: SVM, 1920.

———. *Addresses and Papers of John R. Mott.* 6 vols. New York: Association Press, 1946–47.

———. *The Evangelization of the World in This Generation.* New York: SVMFM, 1905.

———. *History of the Student Volunteer Movement for Foreign Missions.* Student Volunteer Series 1. Chicago: SVMFM, 1892.

———. *The Present-Day Summons to the World Mission of Christianity.* Nashville, TN: Cokesbury Press, 1931.

———. *Strategic Points in the World's Conquest.* New York: Fleming H. Revell, 1897.

———. *The World's Student Christian Federation; Origin, Achievements, and Forecast.* New York: WSCF, 1920.

Munsterberg, Hugo. *Psychotherapy.* New York: Moffat, Yard, 1909.

Nimura, Janice P. *Daughters of the Samurai: A Journey from East to West and Back.* New York: W. W. Norton, 2015.

Noll, Mark, David Bebbington, and George A. Rawlyk, eds. *Evangelicalism: Comparative Studies of Popular Protestantism in North America, the British Isles, and Beyond, 1700–1900.* New York: Oxford University Press, 1994.

Ober, Charles K. *Luther D. Wishard: Projector of World Movements.* New York: Association Press, 1927.

Oldham, Henry Wingate. *Old Paths in Perilous Times: An Account of the Cambridge Intercollegiate Christian Union.* London: Inter-Varsity Press, 1932.

———. *The Student Christian Movement of Great Britain and Ireland: Its Origin, Development, and Present Position.* London: British College Christian Union, 1899.

O'Neill, Frederick William Scott. *The Quest for God in China*. London: George Allen & Unwin, 1925.

Origin, Doctrine, Constitution, and Discipline of the United Brethren in Christ. Dayton: United Brethren Publishing House, 1889.

Orr, James Edwin. *The Fervent Prayer: The Worldwide Impact of the Great Awakening of 1858*. Chicago: Moody Press, 1974.

Paddock, A. Estelle. *Overtaking the Centuries: Modern Women of Five Nations*. New York: National Board of the YWCA, 1915.

Padwick, Constance. *Temple Gairdner of Cairo*. London: SCM Press, 1941.

Parker, Michael. *The Kingdom of Character: The Student Volunteer Movement for Foreign Missions, 1886–1926*. Lanham, MD: American Society of Missiology and University Press of America, 1998.

Paton, William. "Zoe Fairfield." *Student Movement* 3, no. 1 (1933): 205–6.

The Patriarch of Constantinople to the Rev. C. H. Demetry, D. D., in *Report of the Tenth Conference of the World's Student Christian Federation, Lake Mohonk, New York, June 2–8, 1913*, p. 464. New York: World's Student Christian Federation, 1913.

Patterson, James A. "The Legacy of Robert P. Wilder." *International Bulletin of Missionary Research* 15, no. 1 (January 1991): 26.

———. "Speer, Robert Elliott." In *Biographical Dictionary of Christian Missions*, ed. Gerald H. Anderson, 633. New York: Macmillan, 1998.

Peabody, Francis Greenwood. *Jesus Christ and the Social Question; An Examination of the Teaching of Jesus in Its Relation to Some of the Problems of Modern Social Life*. New York: Macmillan, 1900.

Phipps, Pauline. *Constance Maynard's Passions: Religion, Sexuality, and an English Educational Pioneer, 1849–1935*. Toronto: University of Toronto Press, 2015.

Pollock, John Charles. *The Cambridge Movement*. London: John Murray, 1953.

———. *The Cambridge Seven: The True Story of Ordinary Men Used in No Ordinary Way*. Basingstoke, Hants: Marshalls, 1985.

———. *The Keswick Story: An Authorized History of the Keswick Convention*. Chicago: Moody Press, 1964.

Potter, Beatrix. *The Tale of Peter Rabbit*. London: Frederick Warne, 1902.

Potter, Philip, and Thomas Wieser. *Seeking and Serving the Truth: The First Hundred Years of the World Student Christian Federation*. Geneva: WCC Publications, 1997.

Prang, Margaret. *A Heart at Leisure from Itself: Caroline MacDonald of Japan*. Vancouver, BC: UBC Press, 1995.

Presbyterian Church in the U.S.A. Board of Foreign Missions. *Counsel to New Missionaries from Older Missionaries of the Presbyterian Church*. New York: Board of Foreign Missions of the Presbyterian Church, 1905.

Pym, Dora Ivens. *Outlines for Teaching Greek Reading*. London: J. Murray, 1946.

———. *Readings from the Literature of Ancient Greece in English Translations*. New York: Harcourt, Brace, 1924.

———. *Readings from the Literature of Ancient Rome from English Translations*. New York: Harcourt, Brace, 1923.

———. *Tom Pym: A Portrait*. Cambridge: Heffer, 1952.

Rauschenbusch, Walter. *Christianity and the Social Crises*. New York: Macmillan, 1907.

———. *Christianizing the Social Order*. New York: Macmillan, 1912.

———. *For God and His People: Prayers of the Social Awakening*. Boston: Pilgrim Press, 1910.

———. *The Social Principles of Jesus*. New York: Association Press, 1918.

———. *A Theology for the Social Gospel*. Nashville, TN: Abingdon Press, 1917.

Rawlyk, George A., and Mark A. Noll. *Amazing Grace: Evangelicalism in Austria, Britain, Canada and the United States*. Grand Rapids, MI: Baker Books, 1993.

"Report of the National Board of the YWCA of the USA to the Sixth National Convention at Cleveland, Ohio," April 13–20, 1920.

Rice, Anna. *A History of the World's YWCA*. New York: Woman's Press, 1947.

Rice, Julian. *Deer Women and Elk Men*. Albuquerque: University of New Mexico Press, 1992.

———. *Ella Deloria's The Buffalo People*. Albuquerque: University of New Mexico Press, 1993.

———. *Ella Deloria's Iron Hawk*. Albuquerque: University of New Mexico Press, 1993.

Richardson, Anne W. *Lectures on Moderate Drinking, etc.* N.p., 1893.

———. *The Nation and Alcohol*. London: SCM Press, 1920.

———. *The Practical Side of Scientific Temperance: A Paper Read at the Autumnal Conference of British Women's Temperance Association, Held at York, October, 1892*. London: British Women's Temperance Association, 1892.

———. *The Quaker View of War*. London: Headley Brothers, 1900.

———. Review of *Jesus Christ and the Social Question: An Examination of the Teaching of Jesus in Its Relation to Some of the Problems of Modern Social Life*, by Francis Greenwood Peabody, *Student Movement* 5, no. 5 (February 1903): 113–16.

———. *The Spiritual Application of Quakerism*. London: Privately printed, 1929.

Robinson, Marion O. *Eight Women of the YWCA*. New York: National Board of the YWCA, 1966.

"Root, Mary Pauline." In *Woman's Who's Who of America: A Biographical Dictionary of Contemporary Women of the United States and Canada, 1914–1915*, 701. New York: American Commonwealth, 1914; reprint ed. Detroit: Gale Research, 1976.

Rosenberg, Rosalind. *Beyond Separate Spheres: Intellectual Roots of Modern Feminism*. New Haven, CT: Yale University Press, 1982.

Rosenthal, Lee. "Christian Statesmanship in the First Missionary Ecumenical Generation." PhD diss., University of Chicago, 1989.

Rothman, Sheila. *Woman's Proper Place: A History of Changing Ideas and Practices, 1870 to the Present*. New York: Basic Books, 1978.

Rougemont, Fritz de. "The Work among Foreign Students in Switzerland." *Student World* (July 1914): 81–92.

Rouse, Jacqueline Anne. *Lugenia Burns Hope: Black Southern Reformer.* Athens: University of Georgia Press, 1992.

Rouse, C. Ruth. "The Blessedness of Purpose." In *The Student Missionary Appeal: Addresses at the International Convention of the SVMFM, Cleveland, Ohio, February 23–27,* 268–70. New York: SVMFM, 1898.

———. *The Commonwealth of Man.* London: SCM Press, 1939.

———. "Extracts from Report on Women's Work under the WSCF, Presented at the Women's Section of the Conference at Driebergen, Holland, May 5, 1905." *Report of the Conference of the WSCF Held at Zeist, Holland, May 3–5, 1905,* 121–33. New York: WSCF, 1905.

———. *The Federation in the World War 1914–1918.* Geneva: WSCF, 1940.

———. "The Ideal of Womanhood as a Factor in Missionary Work." *International Review of Missions* 2 (1913): 148–64.

———. "International Conferences: Their Place in Federation History." *Student World* (1923): 3–9.

———. "The Meaning of Vocation." In *God Speaks to This Generation: Being Some of the Addresses Delivered at a Conference on International and Missionary Questions, Birmingham, 1st to 7th January, 1937,* edited by Hugh Martin, 107–9. London: SCM Press, 1937.

———. "The Missionary Settlement for University Women." In *Make Jesus King: Report of the International Students' Missionary Conference, Liverpool, January 1–5, 1896,* 242–43. London: SVMU, 1896.

———. *Rebuilding Europe: The Student Chapter in Post-War Reconstruction.* London: SCM Press, 1925.

———. "The Training of Students for World Leadership." *The Fourth Biennial Convention, Richmond, Virginia, April 9–15, 1913,* 113–17. New York: National Board of the YWCA of the USA.

———. *The World's Student Christian Federation: A History of the First Thirty Years.* London: SCM Press, 1948.

Rouse, C. Ruth, and H. Crichton Miller. *Christian Experience and Psychological Processes with Special Reference to the Phenomenon of Auto-Suggestion.* London: SCM, 1918.

Rouse, C. Ruth, and Stephen Neill, eds. *A History of the Ecumenical Movement, 1517–1948.* London: SPCK, 1954.

Rowell, N. W. "The Late Caroline MacDonald." *University of Toronto Monthly* 32, no. 1 Supplement (October 1931): 19–30.

Rowland, Wilmina M. "The Contribution of Ruth Rouse to the World's Student Christian Federation." MA thesis, Yale Divinity School, 1937.

Royden, Maude. *Beauty in Religion.* New York: G. P. Putnam's Sons, 1923.

———. *Christ Triumphant.* New York: G. P. Putnam's Sons, 1924.

———. *Equality in the Spiritual World.* London: League of the Church Militant (Anglican), n.d.

———. *The Making of Women.* London: G. Allen and Unwin, 1917.

———. *The Ministry of Women.* London: League of the Church Militant (Anglican), n.d.

———. *The Threefold Cord.* New York: Macmillan, 1947.

———. *"Votes and Wages": How Women's Suffrage Will Improve the Economic Position of Women*. London: National Union of Women's Suffrage Societies, 1912.

———. *Women and the Sovereign State*. New York: Stokes, 1916.

———. *Women at the World's Crossroads*. New York: Woman's Press, 1923.

Russell, Thomas A. "Can the Story Be Told without Them? The Role of Women in the Student Volunteer Movement." *Missiology: An International Review* 17, no. 2 (April 1989): 159–75.

Saunders, Grace. "Red Cross Work in the Balkans." *North American Student* 2, no. 1 (October 1913): 16–19.

Saunders, Una. "Britain and the Woman's Vote." *North American Student* 5 (October 1916–July 1917): 340.

———. *Mary Dobson, Musician, Writer and Missionary*. London: A. and C. Black, 1926.

———. "Why Men Should Support Women's Suffrage." *North American Student* 5 (October 1916–July 1917): 149.

———. "Women in the WSCF." *Evangel* 18, no. 179 (1906): 13.

Schneller, B. E. "Isabella Bird Bishop." In *Dictionary of British Women Writers*, edited by Jan Todd, 64–66. London: Routledge, 1989.

Scudder, Julia Vida Dutton. *The Christian Attitude toward Private Property*. Milwaukee: Morehouse, 1934.

———. *On Journey*. London: J. M. Dent and Sons, 1937.

———. *Socialism and Character*. Boston: Houghton Mifflin, 1912.

———. *Socialism and Spiritual Progress: A Speculation*. Boston: Church Social Union, 1896.

Selincourt, Agnes de. "The Place of Women in the Modern National Movements of the East." *International Review of Missions* 1 (1912): 98–107.

Selles, Johanna. "Women's Role in the History of the World Student Christian Federation, 1895–1945: An Essay Commissioned to Commemorate the Centennial of the Founding of the WSCF." *Yale Divinity School Library Occasional Publication* no. 6. New Haven, CT: Yale Divinity School Library, 1995.

———. *The World Student Christian Federation, 1895–1925: Motives, Methods, and Influential Women*. Eugene, OR: Pickwick, 2011.

Shedd, Clarence Prouty. *A History of the World's Alliance of the YMCAs*. London: SPCK, 1955.

———. *Two Centuries of Student Christian Movements: Their Origin and Intercollegiate Life*. New York: Association Press, 1934.

Shenk, Wilbert R. *Write the Vision: The Church Renewed*. Eugene, OR: Wipf and Stock, 1995.

Shepherd, R. H. W. *Lovedale, South Africa, 1824–1955*. Cape Town: Lovedale Press, 1955.

Shiono, Sachiko. "Caroline MacDonald." In *Emma Kaufman and the Tokyo YWCA*, Matsuko Watanabe, ed., 126–72. Tokyo: YWCA, 1963.

Showalter, Nathan D. *The End of a Crusade: The Student Volunteer Movement for Foreign Missions and the Great War*. Lanham, MD: Scarecrow Press, 1998.

Sinclair, Margaret. *William Paton*. London: SCM Press, 1949.

Skeel, Caroline A. J. "Agnes de Selincourt, Born September 4, 1872, Died August 31, 1917." *Girtonian Review* (Michaelmas Term 1917): 7–9.

Smith, Jessie Carey, "Addie Waites Hunton." In *Notable Black Women*, 536–39. Detroit: Gale Research, 1992.

Smith-Rosenberg, Carroll. *Disorderly Conduct: Visions of Gender in Victorian America*. New York: Knopf, 1985.

"The Snare of Preparation." In Editorial Notes. *North American Student* 5, no. 1 (October 1916): 24–25.

"Social Problems." *North American Student* 2, no. 9 (June 1914): 411–12.

"Some Women." *Woman Citizen: The Woman's National Political Weekly* 3, no. 23 (November 2, 1918): 474.

Sondheimer, Janet. *Castle Adament in Hampstead: A History of Westfield College, 1882–1982*. London: Westfield College, 1983.

Southall, M. Gwen. *A Challenge to Girls*. 3rd ed. London: SCM, 1918.

Speer, Mrs. Robert. "She Remembers His Commandments to Do Them." *North American Student* 3, no. 5 (February 1915): 189–93.

Stanley, Brian. *The World Missionary Conference: Edinburgh 1910*. Grand Rapids, MI: William B. Eerdmans, 2009.

Steven, George. *The Psychology of the Christian Soul*. London: Hodder and Stoughton, 1911.

Stevenson, Lilian. *Amore Vincit Omnia: Thoughts on the War, Together with Notes on What to Read and Helps to Intercession*. London: SCM Press, 1917.

———. *A Child's Bookshelf: Suggestions on Children's Reading with an Annotated List of Books on Heroism, Service, Patriotism, Friendliness, Joy, and Beauty*. London: SCM Press, 1917.

———. *Towards a Christian International: The Story of the International Fellowship of Reconciliation*. Paris: International Fellowship of Reconciliation, 1936.

Strong, Peter, D. D. "How Did They Succeed?" *Canadian Student* 1, no. 4 (December 1918): 27.

Stuart, Dr. Emmeline Marie. "The Social Conditions of Women in Muslim Lands." *Church Missionary Review* (London: CMS, August 1909): 458–64.

———. "The Woman's Hospital Isfahan." In *Mercy and Truth* (London: CMS, 1906), 368–70.

The Student Missionary Appeal: Address at the 3rd International Convention of the SVMFM Held at Cleveland, Ohio, Feb. 23–27, 1898. New York: SVMFM, 1898.

Students and the Modern Missionary Crusade: Addresses Delivered before the Fifth International Convention of the SVMFM, Nashville, Tennessee, February 28 to March 4, 1906. New York: SVMFM, 1906.

Students and the Present Missionary Crisis: Addresses Delivered before the Sixth International Convention of the SVMFM, Rochester, New York, December 29, 1909 to January 2, 1910. New York: SVMFM, 1910.

"The Study of the Bible." *Student Movement* 5, no. 1 (October 10, 1902): 6–32.

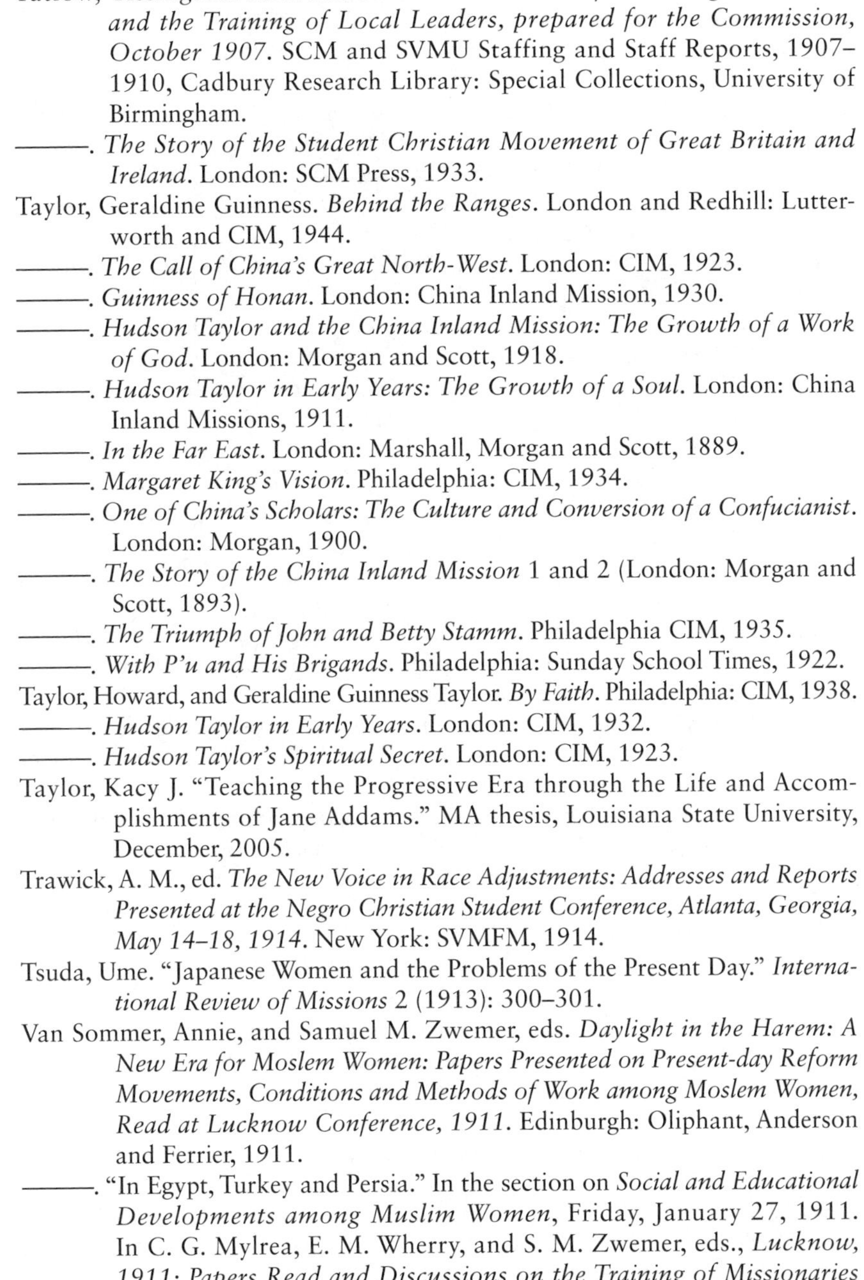

Tatlow, Tissington. *Memorandum on the Work of Traveling Secretaries and the Training of Local Leaders, prepared for the Commission, October 1907.* SCM and SVMU Staffing and Staff Reports, 1907–1910, Cadbury Research Library: Special Collections, University of Birmingham.

———. *The Story of the Student Christian Movement of Great Britain and Ireland.* London: SCM Press, 1933.

Taylor, Geraldine Guinness. *Behind the Ranges.* London and Redhill: Lutterworth and CIM, 1944.

———. *The Call of China's Great North-West.* London: CIM, 1923.

———. *Guinness of Honan.* London: China Inland Mission, 1930.

———. *Hudson Taylor and the China Inland Mission: The Growth of a Work of God.* London: Morgan and Scott, 1918.

———. *Hudson Taylor in Early Years: The Growth of a Soul.* London: China Inland Missions, 1911.

———. *In the Far East.* London: Marshall, Morgan and Scott, 1889.

———. *Margaret King's Vision.* Philadelphia: CIM, 1934.

———. *One of China's Scholars: The Culture and Conversion of a Confucianist.* London: Morgan, 1900.

———. *The Story of the China Inland Mission* 1 and 2 (London: Morgan and Scott, 1893).

———. *The Triumph of John and Betty Stamm.* Philadelphia CIM, 1935.

———. *With P'u and His Brigands.* Philadelphia: Sunday School Times, 1922.

Taylor, Howard, and Geraldine Guinness Taylor. *By Faith.* Philadelphia: CIM, 1938.

———. *Hudson Taylor in Early Years.* London: CIM, 1932.

———. *Hudson Taylor's Spiritual Secret.* London: CIM, 1923.

Taylor, Kacy J. "Teaching the Progressive Era through the Life and Accomplishments of Jane Addams." MA thesis, Louisiana State University, December, 2005.

Trawick, A. M., ed. *The New Voice in Race Adjustments: Addresses and Reports Presented at the Negro Christian Student Conference, Atlanta, Georgia, May 14–18, 1914.* New York: SVMFM, 1914.

Tsuda, Ume. "Japanese Women and the Problems of the Present Day." *International Review of Missions* 2 (1913): 300–301.

Van Sommer, Annie, and Samuel M. Zwemer, eds. *Daylight in the Harem: A New Era for Moslem Women: Papers Presented on Present-day Reform Movements, Conditions and Methods of Work among Moslem Women, Read at Lucknow Conference, 1911.* Edinburgh: Oliphant, Anderson and Ferrier, 1911.

———. "In Egypt, Turkey and Persia." In the section on *Social and Educational Developments among Muslim Women,* Friday, January 27, 1911. In C. G. Mylrea, E. M. Wherry, and S. M. Zwemer, eds., *Lucknow, 1911: Papers Read and Discussions on the Training of Missionaries and Literature for Muslims at the General Conference on Missions to Muslims, Held at Lucknow, January 23–28, 1911.* London, Madras, and Columbo: Christian Literature Society for India, 1911.

———. *Our Moslem Sisters: A Cry for Need from Lands of Darkness Interpreted by Those Who Heard It.* New York: Fleming H. Revell, 1907.

"The Visit of a Traveling Secretary." New York: National Board of the YWCA, n.d.

Wallstrom, Timothy C. *The Creation of a Student Movement to Evangelize the World: A History and Analysis of the Early Stages of the SVMFM.* Pasadena, CA: William Carey International University, 1980.

Walsh, Mary Roth. *Doctors Wanted: No Woman Need Apply.* New Haven, CT: Yale University Press, 1977.

Weber, Hans-Ruedi. *Asia and the Ecumenical Movement, 1895–1961.* London: SCM Press, 1966.

———. *The Courage to Live: A Biography of Suzanne de Dietrich.* Geneva: WCC Publications, 1995.

Weisberg, D. Kelley. "Barred from the Bar: Women and Legal Education in the United States, 1870–1890." *Journal of Legal Education* 38 (1977): 485–507.

Wellman, Judith. *The Road to Seneca Falls: Elizabeth Cady Stanton and the First Woman's Rights Convention.* Urbana: University of Illinois Press, 2004.

"What's Life All About: Bertha Condé Answers." *Oakland Tribune* (July 6, 1930): 10–S.

Wilder, Robert Parmelee. *The Great Commission: The Missionary Response of the Student Volunteer Movements of North America and Europe.* London: Oliphants, 1937.

———. *The Student Volunteer Movement for Foreign Missions: Some Personal Reminiscences of Its Origin and Early History.* New York: Student Volunteer Movement, 1935.

Wilson, Elizabeth. *Fifty Years of Association Work amongst Young Women, 1866–1916: A History of the Young Women's Christian Association in the United States of America.* New York: YWCA, 1916.

———. *The Road Ahead: Experiences in the Life of Frances C. Gage.* New York: Woman's Press, 1918.

———. *The Story of Fifty Years of the YWCA in India, Burma, and Ceylon.* Calcutta: Association Press, 1923.

World-Wide Evangelization—The Urgent Business of the Church: Addresses Delivered before the Fourth International Convention of the SVMFM, Toronto, Canada, February 26–March 2, 1902. New York: SVMFM, 1902.

White, James Terry. *The National Cyclopedia of American Biography* 37. New York: J. T. White, 1951.

Woloch, Nancy. *Women and the American Experience.* New York: Knopf, 1984.

"The World of Japanese Women as It Appears to My Eyes," *Meiji No Joshi* 9, no. 6 (1912): 8–10.

Wrong, Margaret. *Africa and the Making of Books.* London: International Committee on Christian Literature for Africa, 1934.

———. *Five Points of Africa.* London: Edinburgh House Press, 1942.

———. *For a Literature West Africa.* New York: Friendship Press, 1946.

———. *Ideals and Realities in Europe*. London: SCM, 1925.

———. *The Land and Life of Africa*. London: Edinburgh House Press, 1935.

———. "The Value of Bible Study II." *Canadian Student* 1, no. 2 (October 1918): 16–17.

———. *West African Journey, in the Interests of Literacy and Christian Literature, 1944–45*. London: Livingstone Press, 1946.

Wrong, Margaret, Jackson Davis, and Thomas M. Campbell. *African Advancing: A Study of Rural Education in West Africa and the Belgian Congo*. London: Friendship Press, 1945.

Zernov, Nicholas, and James Pain, eds. *Sergius Bulgakov: A Bulgakov Anthology by Sergius Bulgakov*. Eugene, OR: Wipf and Stock, 2012.

WEBSITES

Amerikan Bord Heyeti (American Board), Istanbul, "Memorial records for Edith Hazlett Wiley," American Research Institute in Turkey, Istanbul Center Library, online in Digital Library for International Research Archive, Item #17490, http://www.dlir.org/archive/items/show/17490.

Eisenberg, Bonnie and Mary Ruthsdotter. "Living the Legacy: The Women's Rights Movement 1848–1998." History of the Women's Rights Movement (Santa Rosa, CA: National Women's History Project, 1998), n.p. See http://www.nwhp.org/resources/womens-rights-movement/history-of-the-womens-rights-movement.

"Ella Deloria: A Biographical Sketch." Chamberlain, SD: Dakota Indian Foundation, n.d.). http://zia.aisri.indiana.edu/deloria_archive/about.php?topic=ella.

"FC College: a Pandora's Box." archives.dawn.com (June 1, 2003). Pakistan Herald Publication (Pvt.), Karachi, Pakistan.

Fraser, Anne Beatrice Glass. CMS/ACC915. http://calmview.bham.ac.uk/Record.aspx?src=Catalog&id=XCMSACC/915.

"The History of Mission: Grace Wilder," The Traveling Team, http://www.thetravelingteam.org/articles/grace-wilder

List of Rail Accidents. https://en.wikipedia.org/wiki/List_of_rail_accidents.

Morley, Stephen. *Historical UK Inflation Rates and Calculator*. http://inflation.stephenmorley.org.

Ritchie, Marlene. "Michi Kawai: An Inspiring Woman with a Mission." *New Directions*. Tokyo, Child Research Net, May 21, 2010, n.p. http://www.childresearch.net/papers/new/2010_02.html.

Smith, Olivia. "Visit to the Burial Ground at the Friend Meeting House," January 30, 2014, http://derrymoreestate.blogspot.com/2014_01_01_archive.html.

Spellen, Suzanne (aka Montrose Morris), Building of the Day: 532 Clinton Avenue, *Brownstoner*, Brooklyn, NY, March 19, 2012, http://www.brownstoner.com/architecture/building-of-the-day-532-clinton-avenue.

"Spotlight on the United Methodist Church in Sierra Leone." *Standard Times Press* (February 13, 2009): n.p. http://www.standardtimespress.org/artman/publish/article_3768.shtml.

St. John Parish Magazine, June 1916 (D/P172/28A/24), https://berkshirevoiceswwi. wordpress.com/2016/04/28/missionaries-told-not-a-hair-on-your-head-shall-be-injured.

Vaudry, John P. "A. Caroline Macdonald of Japan." *Renewal Fellowship within the Presbyterian Church of Canada* (February 13, 2001), http://www. renewal- fellowship.ca/93.

Weitbrecht, Mary. *A Memoir of the Reverend John James Weitbrecht, Late Missionary of the Church Missionary Society at Brudwan, in Bengal: Comphrending a History of the Burdwan Mission.* London: James Nisbet, 1854.

Welch, Ian. "Women's Work for Women: Women Missionaries in 19th-Century China." A paper presented to the Eighth Women in Asia Conference 9/26–9/28/2005. Women's Caucus of the Asian Studies Association of Australia & the University of Technology. Reproduced on Project Canterbury, 2005: 1–30, see http://anglicanhistory.org.

Wilder, Grace Evelyn. "The Secret of God's Will." http://www.findagrave.com/ cgi-bin/fg.cgi?page=gr&GRid=144577662.

Winship, Kihm. "Michi Kawai at Silver Bay, May, 1902." *Silver Bay Blog* (May 13, 2013), n.p. https://kihm4.wordpress.com/2013/05/13/michi-kawai-at-silver-bay-1902.

Zernov, Nicolas and Militza. *The History of the Fellowship of St. Alban & St. Sergius: A Historical Memoir (1979).* http://www.sobornost.org/ Zernov_History-of-the-Fellowship.pdf.

Acknowledgments

Ecclesiastes 12:12 says, "Be warned: The writing of many books is endless and excessive devotion to books is wearying to the body" (NASB). Without the helpful support of many individuals and institutions, this statement would apply to me. But instead, my book writing journey has been a pleasant experience.

I thank descendants of some of the women found in this book for their enthusiastic support and much-needed information. They have given me a much greater personal understanding of two women in the Student Christian Movement (SCM). Michele Guinness, the "Keeper of the Guinness Flame," has given me a glimpse into the life of Mary Geraldine Guinness Taylor through email and books. Timothy Garlow's fervent interest in his ancestor, the Reverend Barbara Ellen Groenendyke, has helped me learn about her. I would have never connected with him if not for the hard work of C. R. White, who has worked with Groenendyke's *Find-A-Grave* website.

I am thankful for Dr. Johanna M. Selles, Professor Emeritus of Emmanuel College of Victoria University at the University of Toronto, for gracious words about the influence of my work on women on her later projects.

The list of archives and archivists around the world who have helped with this book is itself almost endless. I am grateful and express a big thanks to this huge group. From outside North America, help came from the Middle East, India, and the United Kingdom. Thank you to Brian Johnson from the American Research Institute, Istanbul, Turkey; Dr. Anthony Greenwood, who connected me with Mr. Johnson; archivists at the Ewing Memorial Library, Forman Christian College, Lahore, Pakistan; Naomi Sturges, Archives Assistant, Archives, Girton College, Cambridge; Vicky Chub and Martin Killeen from the Cadbury Research Library, Special Collections, the University of Birmingham; Lorraine Screene, College Archivist, Archives (Professional Services), Queen Mary University of London (for Westfield College), London; Joanne Ichimura, Archivist, Archives & Special Collections and Library and Information Services (LIS), School of Oriental and African Studies (SOAS), University of London, London; Anne Thomson, College Archivist, Newnham College, Cambridge, England.

From inside North America, I am grateful for the assistance of Linda Moore, Public Services Librarian, Hillsdale College, Hillsdale, Michigan; Thomas A. Lamb III, College Archivist and Head of Special Collections and Archives, Gould Library, Carleton College, Northfield, Minnesota; Deborah Richards, Special Collections Archivist, Samantha Snodgrass, Archives and Special Collections Assistant, and James Gehrt, Digital Projects Lead, Digital Assets and Preservation Services, all from Library Information and Technology Services, Mount Holyoke College, South Hadley, Massachusetts; Beth Lander, MLS, College Librarian, Historical Medical Library, The College of Physicians of Philadelphia, who connected me with Matt Herbison, Archivist, Legacy Center: Archives & Special Collections, College of Medicine Drexel University, Philadelphia, Pennsylvania; Amy Hague, Reference Staff, Sophia Smith Collection, Smith College, Northampton, Massachusetts; and Martha Smalley, Special Collections Consultant, Yale Divinity School, New Haven, Connecticut. Finally, I especially thank Paige Carter, Interlibrary Loan Specialist at Belmont University, Nashville, Tennessee. Her efforts to locate and acquire materials for this book went above and beyond the call of duty.

I am thankful for the existence of calculators, which can suggest what amounts of money from a different era are worth in 2016 pounds or dollars. This is a tricky business. But I found the *Historical UK Inflation Rates and Calculator* to make these calculations for pounds.[1] Another website did the same for dollars.[2]

My appreciation extends to the website ancestry.com for providing a wealth of information on the women featured in this book.

I am deeply grateful to the American Society of Missiology Series Committee for approving this book for publication. This group includes Robert Hunt, Paul Hertig, Robert Gallagher, Kristopher W. Seaman, Hendrick Pieterse, Brian Froehle, Peter Vethanyagamony, Francis Adeney, and Lisa White. I am thankful for the assistance of James T. Keane, editor for the American Society of Missiology Series for Orbis Books.

Most of all, I am very thankful to my wife, Anne Elizabeth Holmes Russell, who has put up with my endless hours of writing and rewriting and with my repeated request, "Can you read another chapter and tell me what you think?"

---

1   See http://inflation.stephenmorley.org.
2   See http://www.in2013dollars.com.

Previously Published in
The American Society of Missiology Series

1. *Protestant Pioneers in Korea*, Everett Nichols Hunt Jr.
2. *Catholic Politics in China and Korea*, Eric O. Hanson
3. *From the Rising of the Sun: Christians and Society in Contempory Japan*, James M. Phillips
4. *Meaning across Cultures*, Eugene A. Nida and William D. Reyburn
5. *The Island Churches of the Pacific*, Charles W. Forman
6. *Henry Venn: Missionary Statesman*, Wilbert R. Shenk
7. *No Other Name? Christianity and Other World Religions*, Paul F. Knitter
8. *Toward a New Age in Christian Theology*, Richard Henry Drummond
9. *The Expectation of the Poor: Latin American Base Ecclesial Communities in Protest*, Guillermo Cook
10. *Eastern Orthodox Mission Theology Today*, James J. Stamoolis
11. *Confucius, the Buddha, and Christ: A History of the Gospel in China*, Ralph R. Covell
12. *The Church and Cultures: New Perspectives in Missiological Anthropology*, Louis J. Luzbetak, SVD
13. *Translating the Message: The Missionary Impact on Culture*, Lamin Sanneh
14. *An African Tree of Life*, Thomas G. Christensen
15. *Missions and Money: Affluence as a Western Missionary Problem . . . Revisited* (Second Edition), Jonathan J. Bonk
16. *Transforming Mission: Paradigm Shifts in Theology of Mission*, David J. Bosch
17. *Bread for the Journey: The Mission and Transformation of Mission*, Anthony J. Gittins, C.S.Sp.
18. *New Face of the Church in Latin America: Between Tradition and Change*, edited by Guillermo Cook
19. *Mission Legacies: Biographical Studies of Leaders of the Modern Missionary Movement*, edited by Gerald H. Anderson, Robert T. Coote, Norman A. Horner, and James M. Phillips
20. *Classic Texts in Mission and World Christianity*, edited by Norman E. Thomas
21. *Christian Mission: A Case Study Approach*, Alan Neely
22. *Understanding Spiritual Power: A Forgotten Dimension of Cross-Cultural Mission and Ministry*, Marguerite G. Kraft
23. *Missiological Education for the 21st Century: The Book, the Circle, and the Sandals*, edited by J. Dudley Woodberry, Charles Van Engen, and Edgar J. Elliston
24. *Dictionary of Mission: Theology, History, Perspectives*, edited by Karl Müller, SVD, Theo Sundermeier, Stephen B. Bevans, SVD, and Richard H. Bliese
25. *Earthen Vessels and Transcendent Power: American Presbyterians in China, 1837–1952*, G. Thompson Brown
26. *The Missionary Movement in American Catholic History*, Angelyn Dries, OSF
27. *Mission in the New Testament: An Evangelical Approach*, edited by William J. Larkin Jr. and Joel W. Williams